D1599189

TRANSATLANTIC HISTORY

NUMBER THIRTY-SEVEN:
The Walter Prescott Webb
Memorial Lectures

EDITED BY STEVEN G.
REINHARDT AND
DENNIS REINHARTZ

Transatlantic History

Contributions by

WILLIAM H. MCNEILL

CARLA RAHN PHILLIPS

DENNIS REINHARTZ

DAVID BUISSERET

STANLEY H. PALMER

ALUSINE JALLOH

Published for the University of Texas at Arlington
by Texas A&M University Press
College Station

Copyright © 2006 by the University of Texas at Arlington
Manufactured in the United States of America
All rights reserved
First edition
The paper used in this book meets the minimum requirements
of the American National Standard for Permanence
of Paper for Printed Library Materials, Z39.48–1984.
Binding materials have been chosen for durability.
♾

Library of Congress Cataloging-in-Publication Data
Transatlantic history / edited by Steven G. Reinhardt and Dennis
    Reinhartz ; contributions by William H. McNeill . . . [et al.]. —
    1st ed.
        p. cm. — (The Walter Prescott Webb memorial lectures ; 37)
        ISBN 1-58544-486-3 (cloth : alk. paper)
        ISBN-13 978-1-58544-486-1 (cloth : alk. paper)
        1. History, Modern. 2. Civilization, Modern. 3. International
    relations. I. Reinhardt, Steven G., 1949– II. Reinhartz, Dennis.
    III. McNeill, William Hardy, 1917– IV. Series
    D210.T73 2006
    909′.09821—dc22
                                                    2005027360

To R. R. Palmer, Transatlantic Historian
1909–2002

Contents

Preface

THE THIRTY-SIXTH ANNUAL Walter Prescott Webb Memorial Lectures were designed to celebrate the recent creation of the Department of History's doctoral program in transatlantic history at the University of Texas–Arlington (UTA). With much enthusiasm, we invited noted scholars to participate in the lectures held on campus on March 15, 2001. They were asked to address various aspects of this exciting new field of historical study that focuses on the complex, continuing process of exchange and adaptation that began when Africans, Amerindians, and Europeans came into contact. While the authors may vary in their approaches and, in some respects, their conclusions, they essentially agree that the field of transatlantic history is of crucial importance to understanding the origins of the modern global community in which we live.

Transatlantic history is a field of study defined primarily by its conceptual approach, which focuses on the interconnectedness of human experience over the centuries in the Atlantic Basin. Like the new, more precisely defined field of world history, it is problem oriented and dedicated to analyzing the dynamic process of encounter and interchange among the peoples on all sides of the Atlantic Ocean. Moreover, transatlantic history is inherently interdisciplinary, transnational, and comparative in approach. It embraces whatever geographical, social, or cultural field is appropriate to scholarly inquiry, transcends conventionally defined academic disciplines, and moves beyond the boundaries imposed by the concept of the nation-state. Transatlantic history is therefore for the imaginative—those willing to rethink, reconceptualize, and recast their approach to both new and familiar material.

In order to situate this newly emergent field in relation to the already established field of world history, we turned to the doyen of world historical studies, William H. Mc Neill, history professor emeritus at the University of Chicago, whose most recent book (coauthored with J. R. McNeill) is *The Human Web: A Bird's-eye View of World History* (2003). McNeill views transatlantic history as a subset of world history, that is, an extension of a far longer history of overseas contacts and encounters that began much earlier in the monsoon seas. We also sought the participation of noted scholar Carla Rahn Phillips, professor of history at the University of Minnesota and an expert on Spanish maritime history. She is the author (along with William D. Phillips) of *Spain's Golden Fleece: Wool Production and the Wool Trade from the Middle Ages to the Nineteenth Century* (1997), which won the Leo Gershoy Prize for 1998. Her chapter explores the developing dynamic of economic and social life in the early modern Iberian Atlantic.

We called on four of our own faculty members to guide us in further explorations of the transatlantic world from the earliest days of contact up to the twenty-first century: Dennis Reinhartz is professor of history at the University of Texas–Arlington, past president of the Society for the History of Discoveries and the Texas Map Society, and consultant to the U.S. Holocaust Museum in Washington, D.C. He is the author of *The Cartographer and the Literati: Herman Moll and His Intellectual Circle* (1997) and coauthor (with Gerald Saxon) of *The Mapping of the Entradas into the Greater Southwest* (1998).

David Buisseret began his career as a historian of ancien régime France and then migrated to the Department of History at the University of the West Indies (1964–1980). He is former director of the Smith Center for the History of Cartography at the Newberry Library in Chicago and is currently the Jenkins and Virginia Garrett Endowed Chair in Greater Southwestern Studies and the History of Cartography at the University of Texas–Arlington. Buisseret edits *Terrae Incognitae,* the journal of the Society for the History of Discoveries and, in 2003, published *The Mapmakers' Quest: Depicting New Worlds in Renaissance Europe.*

Stanley Palmer, professor of history, served as graduate advisor (1997–2002) at a time that was critical for the establishment and growth of UTA's doctoral program in transatlantic history. He is the author of a comparative volume titled *Police and Protest in England and Ireland, 1780–1850* (1988) and is currently researching comparative frontiers in three parts of the world that came under British influence.

Alusine Jalloh, associate professor of history and founding director of the Africa Program at UTA, is the author of *African Entrepreneurship: Muslim Fula Merchants in Sierra Leone* (1999) and coeditor of *The African Diaspora* (1996) (with Stephen E. Maizlish), *Islam and Trade in Sierra Leone* (1997) (with David E. Skinner), and *Black Business and Economic Power* (2002) (with Toyin Falola). His current work on modern-day West Africans who have migrated to the United States reminds us that transatlantic encounters continue to the present.

On behalf of UTA's Department of History, the editors wish to acknowledge several benefactors and friends of the Walter Prescott Webb Memorial Lecture Series. The lectures were inaugurated in 1965 by Will Holmes, Harold Hollingsworth, and department chair E. C. Barksdale. In recent decades—under the successive leadership of Richard G. Miller, Stanley H. Palmer, Ken Philp, and Don Kyle—the lecture series and publications have grown in stature and gained a national reputation. The lectures are published by means of a generous endowment from C. B. Smith Sr. of Austin, a graduate of UTA and a former student of Walter Prescott Webb at the University of Texas–Austin. Additional funding is now provided by a generous grant from the Rudolf Hermanns Endowment for the Liberal Arts. Thanks also go to Jenkins Garrett and Virginia Garrett of Fort Worth, who have long shown both loyalty and generosity to UTA's Special Collections and to the History Department. Finally, it is our pleasure to acknowledge the support provided by UTA's president, James Spaniolo.

TRANSATLANTIC HISTORY

WILLIAM H. MCNEILL

Transatlantic History in World Perspective

WHEN HUMAN BEINGS first learned how to sail and steer rafts, canoes, and eventually ships, the seas and oceans that had once been barriers to human movement reversed their roles for humankind by becoming especially conducive to long-distance encounters among coastal populations. For a long time, historians remained insensitive to this dimension of the past because they concentrated their attention on politics and state—or nation—building and regarded shorelines as natural boundaries, which in fact they were for rulers whose power rested on rents and taxes collected from an agricultural peasantry. Even when towns and trade attained critical importance for politics and war, connections across open water remained marginal and foreign for most historians. With the rise of social history in the aftermath of World War II, historians began to open their eyes to the reality of complementary and sometimes contrary developments among peoples living apart from one another, yet connected rather than separated by navigable bodies of water.

Fernand Braudel's *The Mediterranean and the Mediterranean World in the Age of Philip II* (1949) is deservedly famous as the pioneering exemplar of how to write sea-centered history, searching out some of the exchanges and rivalries that united North Africa and the Levant with Mediterranean Europe in the sixteenth century. Almost simultaneously, Philip Curtin began investigating "the Atlantic plantation complex" as part of his study of comparative tropical history, and, I believe, it was from his pioneering work that transatlantic history has proliferated in the United States.

What can a "world perspective" bring to that enterprise? An irritating and irrelevant distraction is perhaps the most obvious answer for those who are already struggling to understand how African, European, and American societies intersected and combined to create the transatlantic world we have inherited. Yet some people think differently, and, when challenged to think about it, I soon persuaded myself that there are useful comparisons to be made and parallel studies that might profitably be undertaken—most of which, I confess, are yet to be successfully carried out.

THE MOST OBVIOUS world perspective that comes to mind is the recognition that transatlantic history is part of a much larger phenomenon, inasmuch as other bodies of navigable water also transmitted powerful and transformative influences to the peoples along their shores and have done so from early prehistoric times.

We know most about the Mediterranean, where sailing across open water apparently dates back to about 5000 B.C.E. Archaeologists have found the first signs of human habitation of islands such as Crete or Cyprus from about that time. Two and a half millennia later, shipping became capable of intensifying long-range encounters and skill transfers in eastern Mediterranean coastlands, as demonstrated by the rise of Minoan civilization in Crete. That civilization was stimulated by seaborne contact with Egypt and other parts of the Levant and was sustained by the exchange of olive oil (and a few other luxuries) from Crete for metals and other raw materials from remoter parts of the Mediterranean shoreline. The subsequent radiation of Cretan influences into the Aegean islands and coastlands and then of Phoenician and Greek influences in the central and western Mediterranean as well as northward into the Black Sea is the stuff and substance of classical history. This was followed by the eventual formation of the Roman empire, uniting all the shores of the Mediterranean into a single state. And as the Roman conquest of Britain attested, even fair-weather shipping of the sort available to ancient Mediterranean mariners sufficed to carry Roman armies across the English Channel.

The central role of waterborne contacts in ancient Greek and Roman history was always obvious but scarcely noticed until recently. Except for a few passages, such as the account of St. Paul's shipwreck in the Book of Acts (chapters 27–28), ancient texts say little about seafaring or the economic exchanges that shipping sustained; historians regarded the cultural transformations that followed in the wake of the critically important seaborne contacts as self-evident, self-propelled processes of Hellenization, Romanization, or the spread of mystery religions and then of Christianity. After World War II, however, new techniques of underwater archaeology enabled divers to investigate ancient shipwrecks. Their findings yielded detailed knowledge of ancient shipbuilding techniques and an analysis of scores of cargoes. Classical historians thus became more conscious of the maritime undergirding of Greek and Roman history, and several authors have drawn on underwater archaeology to write about trade, shipping, timber supply, and related aspects of the ancient Mediterranean maritime economy. Through an independent path of development, sophisticated studies of the main result of waterborne transport (i.e., two-way cultural—especially religious—encounters and mingling among the diverse peoples of the Mediterranean coastlands) have become the chief area of growth for classical history.

Less is known about Mediterranean seafaring in early medieval centuries, when Byzantine and Arab fleets and traders dominated the scene, but with the revival of Italian shipping after 1000 C.E., written records proliferate, and a rich tradition of scholarship has exploited them, climaxing in Braudel's masterpiece, which shows how Mediterranean seafaring was eventually eclipsed by cheaper and more seaworthy Dutch and English ships beginning abruptly in 1590.

These ships came from the other seaway that is comparatively well known to historians. It abuts upon western Europe and comprises the strip of the North Atlantic lying between Iberia and the Canary Islands, together with the Bay of Biscay, the Irish and English Channels, the North Sea, Norwegian coastal waters, and the Baltic. Seafaring in this area appears in the archaeological record with megalith builders who sailed along these coasts in the third millennium B.C.E. and left behind distinctive stone monuments to their vanished religion all the way from Morocco to southern Sweden. They were followed by a few venturesome Phoenicians, perhaps seeking the tin of Cornwall and who may or may not have circumnavigated Africa about 600 B.C.E., as Herodotus suggests.

Nonetheless, early navigation on the stormy, tide-beset Atlantic shores of Europe and North Africa remained risky and sporadic. Throughout classical times, Greek and Roman sailors found Mediterranean storms too dangerous to risk winter voyages. Even in summer, the North Atlantic and its adjacent seas were too hazardous for them to traverse confidently. Nonetheless, about 350 B.C.E., an explorer name Pythias of Massilia ventured northward along the Atlantic face of Europe, reaching what he called Ultima Thule, somewhere close to the Arctic circle. This remained the northernmost landfall known to ancient classical geographers.

Then, in the Middle Ages, Anglo-Saxon pirates and settlers, Irish saints, Viking raiders, Portuguese, Basque, and Dutch fisherman, and, after 1300, merchants in stoutly constructed vessels continued to brave the storms and tides of the North Atlantic and its adjacent seas and did so with increasing success and frequency. Vikings crossed the Atlantic long before Columbus and established settlements in Iceland (875–900), Greenland (982–985), and Newfoundland (1000). However, Eskimo hunters and climatic hardship brought on by the Little Ice Age (ca. 1320–1550) extinguished the Greenland settlement in the fifteenth century, and the handful of Viking settlers who set themselves up in Newfoundland remained there only a few decades.

In general, the long, slow conquest of the northern seas is a complicated and imperfectly recorded story, and I am not aware that anyone has yet tried to put it all together. Separate parts are familiar enough, and the overall trend is apparent. What began with the initial human occupancy of Ireland and the Hebrides (ca. 6000 B.C.E.)—thanks, presumably, to sporadic and precarious voyaging in tiny coracles made of animal skins—developed some 7,500 years later (by 1450 C.E.) into a capacious network of all-weather navigation throughout the waters abutting western Europe, despite the fact that they are among the stormiest on earth.

This required a swarm of light fishing smacks to ride atop the waves and a smaller number of stout oaken vessels weighing many tons that cut through the waves instead of riding on top of them, as coracles and fishing boats could do. Gradual technical improvement in naval architecture came about by dint of largely unrecorded accumulation of specialized skills and knowledge. Vessels constructed of overlapping wooden planks, using oars to supplement a single sail and capable of carrying a crew of as many as fifty men, were a start. Viking ships were of this design. Larger ships needed a stronger framework to withstand the waves, and, beginning about 1000 C.E., European shipbuilders hit upon a rib-and-keel design, featuring a skeleton of heavy timbers to which they nailed oaken planks both inside and out. They then caulked the crevices between the planks to make the hull watertight and further strengthened it by constructing one or more waterproof decks across the top. (Interestingly, if one turns such a hull upside down and translates it into stone, a Gothic cathedral arises by replicating the principle of framing a load-bearing structure, this time with a skeleton of piers and ribs. Whether there is any connection between these two architectural triumphs I cannot say.)

Sternpost rudders, multiple masts and sails, not to mention block and tackle, ingeniously constructed wooden barrels (standardized as tuns, which in turn became the measure of a ship's capacity), together with an ample supply of long hempen rope, seagoing missile weapons (first crossbows, then cannon and other firearms), as well as compasses, sextants, astrolabes, portolan charts, and astronomic tables for the calculation of latitude were further essentials for long-distance navigation. They all came onstream very rapidly between 1300 and 1450. However, what made the burst of transoceanic exploration after 1492 so amazingly sudden was the decipherment of the prevailing wind and current patterns of the North Atlantic. Portuguese sailors, stimulated by Prince Henry the Navigator's systematic efforts (1418–1460) to venture southward along the African coast, were the principal decipherers. At first their knowledge remained oral and at least semisecret.

Nevertheless, it is obvious from his actions that Columbus knew ahead of time that, by going south to the latitude of the Canaries, he would find northeast trade winds to carry his ships westward. He also knew that he must sail northward into the zone of prevailing westerlies for the return voyage. Once European sailors understood how to take advantage of this natural windmill, transatlantic navigation became routine. Successful searches for similar patterns on other oceans thus swiftly followed, allowing European sailors to inaugurate a worldwide, transoceanic, rapid-transit system that ultimately affected nearly all of the earth's inhabited coastlines within a single generation (1492–1519).

Our planet still reverberates from the changes inaugurated by this amazingly rapid alteration in the pattern of global encounters. As I said, however, I am unaware that anyone has yet integrated the background story of Atlantic Europe's navigation, shipbuilding, and resulting raid, trade, migration, and cultural exchanges into a single whole. Separate national records still dominate most historians' range of inquiry. There is also an opposite embarrassment, for efforts to understand the background of Columbus, Vasco da Gama, Magellan, and their successors have shown that Atlantic European advances in shipbuilding and navigation were not independent of Mediterranean developments. Mediterranean seamen were, in turn, at least sporadically in touch with what was happening in the Indian Ocean and even the South China Sea, where Chinese shipbuilding and navigation underwent a parallel advance toward stout, seaworthy, and capacious all-weather shipping simultaneously with, or a little in advance of, European achievements.

In other words, a properly balanced and complete account of how transoceanic shipping and navigation came into being in Atlantic Europe between 1000 and 1500 must include Chinese, Japanese, Southeast Asian, and Indian Ocean seafaring and trace transfers and contrasts between separate shipbuilding traditions and navigational methods in each of these areas. Not strictly a world historical perspective but a pan-Eurasian perspective is required, for it was within an interconnected circle of Eurasian seafarers that technical means for all-weather, transoceanic voyaging was worked out. And the fact that stormy and tidal seas prevailed along not only the Atlantic face of Europe but also the coasts of Japan and part of China does much to explain why technical improvements in seafaring between 1000 and 1500 concentrated in these separate and only slenderly connected locations.

Throughout the process, Europeans were mostly borrowers. The compass, lateen sails, sternpost rudders, and gunpowder weaponry, for example, all came from China and/or the Indian Ocean. Because they featured watertight compartments and adjustable centerboard keels, the flat-bottomed Chinese junks were fundamentally different from the European vessels with rib-and-keel construction. The strength and rigidity of European decked-over hulls were probably superior to anything the Chinese built. At any rate, European ships easily withstood the recoil of the heavier cannon that the Chinese put on board their far larger vessels—an advantage of critical importance for European ships when first they intruded into Asian waters after 1499.

The fact is that seafaring in the Eurasian African world was like a communicable disease. Any improvement that really worked was infectious and tended to spread rapidly regardless of point of origin as sailors met one another in distant ports and warily, but inevitably, exchanged information. Obstacles sometimes inhibited borrowing, as when shipbuilders of the Indian Ocean adhered to their tradition of using vegetable fibers to tie the planks of their dhows together long after Chinese and then European intruders exposed them to ways of making far stronger vessels. But iron nails were expensive, whereas vegetable fiber was cheap, and for most purposes the comparatively calm waters of the Indian Ocean made stronger hulls and heavier construction a wasteful extravagance.

The biggest gap and by far the most significant world-historical parallel to transatlantic history has to do with the transoceanic history of Southeast Asia and adjacent waters in the Indian Ocean and Southwest Pacific. This awkward label covers a vast area of navigable water whose history is still largely unknown. Archaeology is scant, speculation rampant, and facts remain distressingly scarce. Nonetheless, this was almost surely where seafaring started and where sporadic improvements in navigation inaugurated a series of revolutionary long-range contacts extending across many millennia before 1500, when transatlantic history abruptly took precedence. Indeed, transatlantic history may best be conceived of as a climactic postlude to a process that had been going on in Southeast Asian, Southwest Pacific, and Indian Ocean waters since about 40,000 B.C.E., or whenever human beings first conveyed themselves across the open water separating Australia from the Asian mainland.

Human settlement of Australia is, in fact, the earliest certain evidence that humankind had learned how to sail, or perhaps merely to float and paddle, across comparatively long distances. Exactly how much open water the migrants had to cross is unclear because shorelines in Southeast Asia and throughout the world changed radically when sea levels rose as the glaciers melted away from North America and northern Eurasia beginning about 14,000 B.C.E. But the famous "Wallace line" dividing Australian from Asian fauna and flora attests to the impenetrability of a sea barrier between the two continents for most forms of life throughout geologic time. Moreover, the initial human crossing did not result in sustained linkages across the Wallace line, even though from time to time subsequent landings brought novelties into Australia, most notably dingoes (a distinctive kind of dog) and a new style of microlith, both dating from about 5000 B.C.E.

Most likely sea travel started so very early in Southeast Asia because the monsoon winds that blow across the Indian Ocean and the Southwest Pacific were peculiarly conducive to long-distance sailing. Driven by the seasonal heating and cooling of the atmosphere over Central Asia, the monsoons blow for about half the year from one direction and then reverse themselves in the following six months. Severe seasonal storms—typhoons, the equivalent of Atlantic hurricanes—sometimes occur, but most of the time the monsoon winds blow almost as steadily and gently as do those global conveyor belts for sailors, the trade winds. Sailing with the monsoon downwind for weeks and months at a time and then sailing back when the monsoon reversed itself was comparatively easy. Such long-distance navigation required no more than a mast and sail attached to a raft, dugout canoe, or some other sort of vessel small enough to be steered by the combined effect of sail, keel, and paddles or oars, allowing sailors to proceed in any desired direction within something approaching 90 degrees of directly downwind.

However, such elementary vessels leave little or no archaeological trace, and as long as technological and other cultural differences among the coastal populations of the monsoon seas remained modest, there is little hope of reconstructing the range or cultural significance that small-boat long-distance navigation may have had. Furthermore, the fact that early coastal settlements were inundated by rising sea levels when the glaciers melted also defeats archaeological investigation of early seafaring in and around Southeast Asia. We are therefore left to wonder and can only imagine what may have happened along the monsoon coastlines.

Yet there are some hints—derived from sites often situated on inland lakes or rivers—that a combination of fishing and tropical gardening supported settled communities in Southeast Asia from very early times. The emergence of agricultural settlements of grain farmers in Western Asia, beginning about 8000 B.C.E., has been carefully studied by archaeologists because it was these farmers who eventually provided the rural basis for the emergence of civilization in the land of Sumer (modern Iraq) between 4000 and 3000 B.C.E. Moreover, their style of grain agriculture still undergirds the civilizations of much (though not all) of the modern world. Nonetheless, sessile tropical gardening may well be more ancient and, when combined with fishing, was probably capable of sustaining relatively dense populations. The discovery of surprisingly populous farming communities in upland New Guinea as recently as the 1930s, when aviators first noticed clearings in the island's forests, showed that tropical gardeners could indeed support dense human populations on favorable soils even without additional resources from the sea, as early Southeast Asian coastal populations surely did.

However, a fundamental feature of tropical gardening inhibits the rise of monumental buildings, extensive states, and other familiar markers of early civilizations, all of which depended on the management of comparatively vast resources by some kind of central authority. In the tropics, plants grow year-round. At almost any season of the year, gardeners can therefore harvest their crops, which vary with local rainfall patterns and depend only on human ability, through vegetative reproduction, to keep a suitable number of edible plants perpetually ready for harvest. All that was needed to ensure an almost steady food supply was to replant the top of a harvested root at the time it was taken from the soil and then make certain of its regrowth with whatever weeding or fertilizing turned out to be worth the effort.

Having no need to store foodstuffs between harvest seasons, tropical gardeners have little or nothing that outsiders—rulers and landowners, who live on taxes and rents—can collect from their gardens and use for their own purposes. In contrast, grain farmers had to store their harvest for months on end. Such stores were a standing invitation for outsiders, first by threat and force and eventually by immemorial custom, to preempt all or part of the harvest. Cities and cultures, priests and temples, armies and states, walled cities and all the other traces that ancient civilizations leave for archaeologists to discover thus became possible wherever grain farmers labored in the fields. In the absence of a seasonal glut requiring large-scale storage of foodstuffs, nothing of the kind was possible where tropical gardening prevailed.

Nonetheless, archaeologists have recently begun to detect faint traces left by ancient villages in Southeast Asia and southern China, and time horizons for root and rice cultivation in that part of the world have suddenly been pushed back to equal, or more probably exceed, the time horizon for grain cultivation in western Asia. They theorize that in those early coastal sites settled gardening almost certainly began as soon as fishermen learned how to sail and steer whatever rafts or boats they may have had and, by returning regularly to a convenient landing place, established permanent settlements. Sessile living, in turn, then allowed fishermen's wives to improve on age-old gathering techniques by concentrating useful plants nearby in what thus became permanent gardens. In all probability, therefore, early seafaring and tropical gardening existed in and around the shores of Southeast Asia for quite some time.

Although the drowning of early coastal sites deprives archaeologists of physical evidence, linguistic evidence suffices to show that human encounters extended across long sea distances in monsoon waters from comparatively early times and persisted for millennia. In particular, what is called the

Austronesian dispersal spread a family of related languages across a multitude of islands in the Southwest Pacific, extending as far from the mainland as the Soloman Islands sometime between 3500 and 2000 B.C.E. This migration was eventually followed by the even more remarkable Polynesian dispersal across the enormous expanses of the rest of the Pacific, reaching as far as Hawaii, Easter Island, and New Zealand. Polynesian oral traditions refer to an ancestral place that has been plausibly identified as the island of Samoa, and experts agree that their migration started about 500 C.E. and was completed about five hundred years later with the occupation of New Zealand.

Parallel migrations westward across the Indian Ocean had similarly far-ranging results, most notably the settlement of Madagascar off the African coast by Malay speakers, who arrived there about 700 C.E. and apparently came from Borneo, where their closest linguistic relatives are still to be found. These settlers probably did not cross the Indian Ocean directly but instead reached Madagascar by coasting along East Africa after skirting the northern shores of the Indian Ocean. They certainly traveled in small vessels and presumably put ashore from time to time for rest and resupply.

Such coastal voyaging was already very old by the time the Malays settled on the previously uninhabited island of Madagascar. From the time when small vessels began to move to and fro along the coasts of the Indian Ocean, they must have provoked sporadic biological and cultural exchanges wherever they put ashore. Local consequences were sometimes important. For example, anthropologists have long realized that yams, native to Southeast Asia, were a staple food for many African communities, even, or especially, in West Africa, but just when this crop reached Africa and how it got to West Africa remain unrecorded. Perhaps rice reached the Ganges basin of India via the same water route, if it is true that this crop originated in flood-prone lake shores of south China, where traces of rice cultivation have recently been discovered and dated as early as 8200 B.C.E.

Even more interesting is the fact that the Sumerians, who constructed the earliest known cities and pioneered the Southwest Asian style of civilization, left written records of an oral tradition to the effect that their ancestors had come to the land of Sumer by sea from the south. If so, one can argue that the breakthrough to urbanity and civilization in ancient Sumer took place where a network of sea communication along the shores of the Indian Ocean intersected with a newer overland network of donkey caravans, arising only subsequently to the initial domestication of that animal, which occurred about 5000 B.C.E. Where shipping and caravans converged at the head of the Persian Gulf, it is easy to suppose that Sumerian-speaking intruders from the sea found themselves in an optimal position to pick and choose among ideas and techniques accessible to them from diverse and far-flung hinterlands. Thus, they were able for the first time to bring together and then elaborate on all of the specialized skills needed to create and sustain urban life and civilization.

Little or nothing is known about early shipbuilding and navigation in the monsoon seas. We can assume that the dugout canoes of the Southwest Pacific had a long and successful career since Polynesians were still using them when Europeans eventually arrived on the scene. Perhaps the extraordinary feats of navigation that carried Polynesians so far depended on the invention of outriggers to stabilize their sailing canoes against big ocean waves, but in fact no one knows for sure when outriggers were invented. Nearer to the Asian mainland, built-up ships displaced canoes, at least for long-distance navigation, at some unknown time. The horizon for our knowledge of the existence of this sort of shipping stands at about 3000 B.C.E., when rock carvings in Egypt near the Red Sea coast portray Sumerian ships as built-up vessels, carrying a single mast, but that is about all that can be deciphered from the crude and weathered remains. There is no reason to think that such ships were not older—perhaps much older. Again, however, no one can say for certain.

Still, we do know that ships connected Sumer with India since distinctive Sumerian seals used to record ownership of packaged cargo have been discovered at Harappa and Mohenjo-daro, the two capital cities of the Indus civilization. Since it is always easier to borrow and adapt than it is to invent de novo, such contacts presumably helped to provoke the emergence of the Indus civilization itself. The same was true for Egypt, for Sumerian-style ships also visited the shores of the Red Sea in predynastic times, whence caravans reached the Nile valley by traversing the Wadi Hammamat, where rock carvings can still be seen. Resulting encounters with Sumerian skills and knowledge gave the Egyptians models for the construction of their earliest monumental architecture and may have stimulated them to invent hieroglyphic writing, which used the same principles as Sumerian cuneiform writing but relied on entirely different symbols. The skills of civilization, in short, were contagious. The fact that independent centers of urban-based civilized society, complete with organized religion, imperial states, monumental architecture, and writing, arose in the Yellow River valley of China (c. 2200 B.C.E.) and eventually also in the Ganges valley of India (c. 1000 B.C.E.) suggests that monsoon navigation carried an ever-increasing freight of cultural baggage.

Full-blown civilization required grain farming. In south China, Japan, Java, and various river valleys of Southeast Asia, rice took the place of wheat, barley, and millet, which were staples of West Asian and earliest Chinese agriculture. Rice paddy cultivation was fundamentally different from other kinds of grain farming, depending as it did on elaborate water management and on transplanting seedlings from special seedbeds into waterlogged fields by stoop labor. The burdensome toil such farming required was matched by spectacularly higher yields, with seed-to-harvest ratios of as much as 100 to 1, compared with a mere 6 to 1 for medieval European wheat farmers. Far denser human occupancy of cultivated landscapes was one consequence, as well as fewer domesticated animals. All the same, rice, like other grains, had to be harvested and stored and was therefore eminently suited to maintain rulers, landlords, and all their urban dependents that together sustained and continually elaborated rice-based East Asian styles of civilization.

Two obstacles hindered the spread of rice paddies. One was the back-breaking effort they required. This meant that rice paddies could spread only where populations were already dense and land was short so that hard-pressed farmers had no option but to shift to the intensified labor that rice cultivation required. However, crowded populations also increased infections, making heavy labor all but unsustainable. For many centuries this undoubtedly held back the spread of rice paddies. South China, for example, was notoriously unhealthy in Han times (303 B.C.E. to 221 C.E.) and remained a thinly occupied frontier region and place of exile where death from disease routinely struck down newcomers from the north. Only in T'ang times (608–907 C.E.), as tea drinking became commonplace in China, did the south begin to thrive, perhaps because boiling water to make tea killed off bacteria in the drinking water, thus making other health hazards—malaria above all—tolerable even for the closely-packed human settlements that contiguous rice paddies sustained.

As the case of Sumer already suggests, the dawn of civilization and the enriched archaeological and written evidence it left behind make the role of monsoon seafaring more obvious. As rice paddy farming came slowly onstream (between about 8000 B.C.E. and 1000 C.E.) in south China, eastern India, Japan, Java, and the principal river valleys of Southeast Asia, sea traffic linked the emerging civilizations of each of these regions together. But for a long time rice paddies and the local civilizations that rice-harvesting sustained remained exceptional because they were embedded in a landscape inhabited by diverse "forest peoples," among whom tropical gardening continued to prevail. Indeed, remnants of such peoples still exist in innumerable hilly districts of Southeast Asia, as American soldiers discovered in Vietnam.

Among the emerging temple states of Southeast Asia, Indian styles of religion and government initially proved most attractive, as the spread of Hindu and Buddhist religions attests. After about 700 C.E., Moslem sailors tended to displace Indian merchants and missionaries and eventually established outposts of their faith in Malaya and Indonesia and as far afield as Mindanao in the Philippines. China, however, had its own zone of cultural and commercial influence in Japan, Korea, and Vietnam. Then, after about 1000 C.E., the expansiveness of Chinese civilization and the attractiveness of Chinese technology attained a new level of primacy within the monsoon seas and indeed throughout the entire Eurasian African world.

The upsurge of Chinese influence depended on the commercial exploitation of a cheap, reliable, internal transport network operating along China's internal waterways. Merchants took advantage of an extensive canal system that was built mostly for irrigation and secondarily for carrying in-kind taxes from south to north via the Grand Canal, which connected the Yangtze with the Yellow River valley after 605 C.E. When a multitude of canal boats and small-scale merchants mastered the art and rules of bazaar trading, they created a vast domestic market that had the effect of rewarding efficient producers of goods of common consumption as well as of the luxury and military commodities that had previously been the staples of most long-distance commerce. Skillfully managed paper currency fueled the emerging Chinese market, agricultural and craft specialization rapidly intensified, and competing specialists made innumerable inventions, thus raising Chinese skills far above those found in the rest of the world.

From many points of view, China's internal commercialization, extending down the social scale to embrace millions of ordinary peasants, and the subsequent radiation of Chinese skills across the southern seas and along the caravan routes of Central Asia, mark the beginning of modern times. The familiar landmark of 1500 might better be viewed as inaugurating a second chapter (i.e., Western) of modernity largely on the strength of the well-known transatlantic interactions.

As far as monsoon seafaring is concerned, China's emerging primacy was demonstrated soon after 1000, when increasingly seaworthy Chinese junks began to sail all the way around the Malay peninsula instead of off-loading and portaging goods across the Kra peninsula as before. Archaeological evidence of China's new presence in the Indian Ocean turns up in the form of thousands of precisely datable porcelain shards that have been discovered on numerous beaches of India and Africa. Readers are probably already familiar with the amazing story of Zheng-he's seven imperial voyages into the Indian Ocean between 1403 and 1433, during which he visited the Indian and African coasts, penetrated the Persian Gulf and Red Sea, and even collected tribute from Mecca. Vast armadas of Chinese ships easily overawed local potentates wherever they showed up and persuaded them to acknowledge Chinese superiority by engaging in the ritualized gift giving, or "tribute" exchanges. Nevertheless, such tribute trade never came close to covering the cost of building and supplying Zheng-he's fleets, which were instead met by the Chinese government at the command of the reigning emperor. Thus, it is not really surprising that when the emperor who ordered these extraordinary expeditions died, his successor (or rather a circle of mandarins around him) withheld funds, allowed the imperial fleet to rot away, and forbade further construction of large, seaworthy, and costly junks.

This deliberate abdication of overseas empire proved to be a major turning point in world history, for if a Chinese fleet remotely comparable to the one that Zheng-he commanded had been operating in the Indian Ocean when Vasco da Gama showed up at Calicut in 1499, the Portuguese could never have established their always precarious Asian empire. Indeed, it is easy to imagine how roles might have been reversed if a Chinese fleet had rounded Africa and discovered Europe about the same time that another fleet began colonizing California, around 1450. Assuredly Chinese ships and seamen were technically capable of such feats by the midfifteenth century. What inhibited them was their dependence on a distant imperial court whose officials decided (very wisely in the short run) that guarding against ever-present dangers from steppe horsemen was far more important than continued expenditures on overseas ventures.

As things turned out, therefore, the expansion of Chinese skills and knowledge between 1000 and 1500 prefigured and contributed to the subsequent expansion of Europe, just as the expansion of Islam and of West and Central Asian styles of civilization generally between 300 and 1000 C.E. had previously prefigured and contributed to the expansion of China. For China borrowed the practices of bazaar trading from Western and Central Asia along with Buddhism and a multitude of other practical techniques before 1000, just as Western Europe and other civilized peoples of Eurasia borrowed gunpowder weaponry, printing, and the compass from China before 1500.

If one compares the era of transatlantic primacy after 1500 with the era of monsoon Asian primacy before that time, significant contrasts come to mind. First and foremost, the decay of the Amerindian population under the scourge of infectious diseases imported from Europe and Africa was far more drastic than any disease disaster attending navigation across the monsoon seas of which we have evidence. It took millennia for civilized populations of Eurasia to build up resistances to infections, and innumerable local disasters certainly occurred along the way whenever a new malady invaded what epidemiologists refer to as a "virgin population." I have already mentioned the difficulty the Chinese from the north had in making the Yangtze valley habitable for dense populations. Similarly difficult adjustments between humans and disease organisms surely cropped up elsewhere—not least in the Mediterranean, where the spread of new forms of malaria (perhaps out of Africa), assisted perhaps by local violence, turned many fertile plains into deserted wastes in early medieval times. However, all such disasters, recorded and un-recorded, pale beside the die-off that took place in the Americas after 1500 and the scale of population transfer from Africa and Europe that ensued.

On the other hand, the ecological invasion of America by Eurasian flora and fauna that followed in the wake of European shipping had numerous parallels within the circle of monsoon navigation. Polynesians arriving in New Zealand, like Malays arriving in Madagascar, brought with them a swarm of new organisms that collaborated with human intruders in killing off many indigenous species. Likewise, the diffusion of American food crops across much of Eurasia and Africa, whose impact on human life around the globe rivaled the swifter diffusion of disease, had many analogues in the history of monsoon navigation. I have already mentioned the importance of yams from Southeast Asia for African agriculture. Sugar cane, citrus fruit, rice, and several less important crops also arrived in Western Asia and Mediterranean Europe from across the monsoon seas in medieval times. Of equal significance was the further transfer of sugar to the Atlantic islands and then to the Caribbean and mainland South America that followed.

Finally, there is the issue of slavery. Within the ambit of monsoon naviga-tion, there is nothing comparable to the destruction of indigenous popula-tions in the Americas after 1500 that provoked compulsory migration and slave labor. The transatlantic slave trade, it seems to me, was unique in scale and significance because of the enormity of the decline in population that re-sulted from the huge disease gap between Europe and Africa, on the one hand, and Amerindian peoples, on the other. The only parallel to Atlantic slavery was nineteenth-century indentured labor, during which millions of Indian and Chinese coolies were delivered to tea gardens in Assam, as well as various Pacific islands, and parts of the Americas wherever native popula-tions were too scant or too difficult to coerce to work on plantations and in mines. It is ironic to realize that it was exactly when African slavery was abol-ished throughout the British Empire by act of parliament in 1833 that massive resort to Chinese and Indian indentured labor began. In fact, it was legally permissible in India as late as 1920.

Despite basic similarities, therefore, the perturbations to global, ecologi-cal, demographic, economic, and cultural balances provoked by transatlantic navigation differed from those arising from the far older navigation of the monsoon seas in being more sudden, drastic, and massive. Indeed the world's ecosystem and humankind at large are still in the process of accommodating the upheavals that European ships and sailors precipitated after 1492. Realiz-ing that present-day transatlantic history is a continuation and climax of a far longer history of overseas contacts and encounters, centered mainly in the monsoon seas, will provide us an appropriate world historical perspective.

SUGGESTED READINGS

Abu-Lughod, Janet. *Before European Hegemony: The World System, 1250–1350 AD* (New York: Oxford University Press, 1989).

Algaze, G. *The Uruk World System: The Dynamics of Expansion of Early Mesopotamian Civilization* (Chicago: University of Chicago Press, 1993).

Bass, George F., ed. *A History of Seafaring Based on Underwater Archaeology* (London: Thames and Hudson, 1972).

Begley, Vimila, and Richard D. DePuma, eds. *Rome and India: The Ancient Sea Trade* (Madison: University of Wisconsin Press, 1991).

Bellwood, Peter S. *Man's Conquest of the Pacific: The Prehistory of Southeast Asia and Oceania* (New York: Oxford University Press, 1979).

Braudel, Fernand. *The Mediterranean and the Mediterranean World in the Age of Philip II*, trans. Siân Reynolds (New York: Harper and Row, 1972).

Bray, Francesca. *The Rice Economies: Technology and Development in Asian Societies* (Oxford, UK, and New York: Blackwell, 1986).

Casson, Lionel. *Ships and Seamanship in the Ancient World*, rev. ed. (Princeton, N.J.: Princeton University Press, 1971).

Chaudhuri, K. N. *Trade and Civilisation in the Indian Ocean: An Economic History from the Rise of Islam to 1750* (Cambridge and New York: Cambridge University Press, 1985).

———. *Asia before Europe: Economy and Civilization of the Indian Ocean from the Rise of Islam to 1750* (Cambridge and New York: Cambridge University Press, 1990).

Crosby, Alfred W. *Ecological Imperialism: The Biological Expansion of Europe, 900–1900* (Cambridge: Cambridge University Press, 1996).

Curtin, Philip. *Rise and Fall of the Plantation Complex* (Cambridge and New York: Cambridge University Press, 1990).

Diamond, Jared. *Guns, Germs, and Steel: The Fates of Human Societies* (New York: W. W. Norton, 1997).

Hourani, George F. *Arab Seafaring in the Indian Ocean in Ancient and Early Medieval Times* (Princeton, N.J.: Princeton University Press, 1951).

Levathes, Louise. *When China Ruled the Seas: The Treasure Fleet of the Dragon Throne 1405–1433* (New York : Simon and Schuster, 1994).

Lewis, Archibald, and Timothy J. Runyan. *European Naval and Maritime History 300–1500* (Bloomington: Indiana University Press, 1985).

McNeill, William H. *Plagues and Peoples* (Garden City, N.Y.: Anchor Press, 1976).

Needham, Joseph. *Science and Civilization in China*, vol. 3, part 3, "Nautics" (Cambridge: Cambridge University Press, 1971).

Oppenheimer, Stephen. *Eden in the East: The Drowned Continent of Southeast Asia* (London: Phoenix, 1999).

Parry, John H. *The Discovery of the Sea* (New York: Dial Press, 1974).

Pryor, John H. *Geography, Technology, and War: Studies in the Maritime History of the Mediterranean, 649–1571* (Cambridge and New York: Cambridge University Press, 1988).

Reader, John. *Africa: A Biography of the Continent*, 1st Amer. ed. (New York: Knopf, 1998).

Smith, R. B., and W. Watson, eds. *Colloquy on Early South East Asia: Essays in Archaeology, History, and Historical Geography* (New York: Oxford University Press, 1979).

Watson, Andrew M. *Agricultural Innovation in the Early Islamic World: The Diffusion of Crops and Farming Techniques, 700–1100* (Cambridge and New York: Cambridge University Press, 1983).

Wink, André. *Al-Hind: The Making of the Indo-Islamic World,* vol. 1, *Early Medieval India and the Expansion of Islam, 7th–11th Centuries,* 2d ed. (Leiden, the Netherlands, and New York : E. J. Brill, 1991).

Yü, Ying-shih. *Trade and Expansion in Han China: A Study of Sino-barbarian Economic Relations* (Berkeley: University of California Press, 1967).

Economy and Society in the Iberian Atlantic

CARLA RAHN PHILLIPS

THE SEVENTEENTH-CENTURY CRISIS

TRANSATLANTIC HISTORY POSES an interesting dilemma because of its simultaneous demands for breadth and depth. How can scholars understand enough of the transatlantic context to make sense of their own research? Until very recently, historians were usually trained to specialize in a well-defined place and time. When I was in graduate school, we were told that a broad context, while necessary for teaching survey courses and for contextualizing one's research, was not appropriate for serious research itself. I tend to agree, in part because that was the way I was trained, but also because I think that well-focused research into primary documents and material culture is the only way to develop a critical sense of what constitutes valid or at least plausible interpretations. Nevertheless, to grasp the complexities of huge conceptual frameworks such as transatlantic history, we are forced to rely not only on our own research but also on the work of others, most of all when we venture beyond our own discipline. I contend that, without a critical sense grounded in one of the traditional academic disciplines, it is nearly impossible to range beyond the boundaries of place, time, and discipline and say anything worthwhile.

One incident in particular drove that point home to me. In 1992, there was an extended commemoration of Columbus's 1492 voyage across the Atlantic Ocean—the beginning of transatlantic history. At one of the many conferences I attended, someone was presenting a very articulate paper and using charts, graphs, maps, documents, and slides to support his argument. I knew nothing about his discipline or topic, but I could think of serious questions and objections regarding every point he made. In short, though the presentation was well received by the audience, it seemed to me absolute nonsense. But what did I know? I leaned over to the person sitting next to me, a respected professional in a nonacademic field who also knew nothing about the speaker's topic, and I said, "Do you believe any of this?" And he replied, "Not a word." In short, both of us came to the same conclusion about the presentation, based not on our own certain knowledge of the topic but on the standards of proof in our own disciplines. I believe that means something.

Assuming that we have somehow developed a critical sense, how do we define a topic of research in transatlantic history? The process is the same as in more traditional history, but the scope is necessarily much broader:

1. Select a time frame.
2. Select a theme that can be usefully examined in a transatlantic context.
3. Select a problem within that theme.
4. Select places on both sides of the Atlantic in which to investigate the theme.
5. Define a set of questions to ask, a working hypothesis to test, or a theoretical framework in which to examine the problem.
6. Find out what evidence exists that you can examine within your area of expertise.
7. Find out what other scholars have done that might inform your research or provide useful comparisons.
8. Test your hypothesis with evidence from your own research and that of others.
9. Decide what conclusions you can draw about the problem in the context of transatlantic history.

The time frame that I find most intriguing is the early modern period—roughly from the mid-fourteenth to the mid-eighteenth century, and my preferred theme is economy and society. Within those parameters, one interesting problem has occupied scholars of Europe off and on for the better part of a century—the so-called seventeenth-century crisis.[1] For the purpose of this chapter, it is worthwhile to ask whether the notion of a seventeenth-century crisis makes sense in a transatlantic context. To narrow the inquiry somewhat, I focus only on the Iberian Atlantic world. I am grounded in the history of early modern Europe with a specialization in Spain. To examine the seventeenth-century crisis in the Iberian Atlantic as a whole, I rely on the work of others regarding Portugal, West Africa, and Latin America.

In the *Random House Dictionary of the English Language,* two pertinent meanings of "crisis" are "a stage in a sequence of events at which the trend of all future events, esp. for better or for worse, is determined; a turning point" and "a condition of instability, as in social, economic, political, or international affairs, leading to a decisive change." Scholars generally use the term *crisis* to mean a turning point, but not one so decisive that it is irreversible.

Few events or changes in history would meet the latter criterion in the Iberian Atlantic or anywhere else. In keeping with traditional historiography, I use the word *crisis* in the discussion that follows, but I also use a broader range of concepts to describe what happened in the Iberian Atlantic.

The consensus is that Europe experienced widespread instability and upheaval in the seventeenth century, compared to relatively more stable times in the sixteenth and eighteenth centuries.[2] There are several major strands of interpretation that treat the causes of this "crisis." To oversimplify, the Marxian interpretation holds that feudal social structures bred economic recession; the political explanation focuses on growing tensions in the relations between governments and the governed; non-Marxian economic interpretations emphasize crises in population, agriculture, or trade; the cultural approach highlights an intellectual malaise; and the relatively new environmental emphasis concentrates on the consequences of farming marginal lands in the sixteenth century. This range of views has come to define rival approaches to the problem, with authors tending to join one camp or another. The most obvious split usually separates the Marxian interpretation from everything else.[3] Adherents to the various non-Marxian branches of economic causality can diverge from one another as much as from Marx. Yet the whole notion of a seventeenth-century crisis is so broad that it should preclude any attempts to reduce it to a single branch of causality, let alone a single twig on that branch.

Where, if at all, did the Atlantic world fit into this picture? One of the most important pieces of scholarship on the crisis—the Marxian interpretation of Eric Hobsbawm in an article published in 1954—defines a key role for the transatlantic context.[4] Hobsbawm argues that profits from trade with colonies in the Americas allowed certain parts of Europe, which was suffering from a crisis of production under the feudal system, to emerge strengthened and ready to industrialize. In other words, viewing the very long term from about 1580 to 1720, he maintains that the seventeenth-century crisis triggered the growth of capitalism, leading to the Industrial Revolution in England. Very few others have dared to take so broad a view, and it is hardly surprising that Hobsbawm's article has generated lively debate ever since. His most trenchant critics reject not only his Marxian framework but also any explanation of the seventeenth-century crisis based on economic analysis. That stance seems to me unfortunate and self-defeating, for reasons that I hope will become clear in the course of this chapter.

Hobsbawm grappled with understanding the role that Atlantic colonies and trade played in resolving Europe's seventeenth-century crisis. As broadly as he cast his inquiry, comparative transatlantic history compels us to phrase our questions even more broadly: Is the concept of a seventeenth-century crisis valid for the Atlantic world as a whole—Europe, Africa, and the Americas? If so, how did the crisis primarily manifest itself: in economic matters? in politics? in society or culture? And, most important, can transatlantic connections and chains of causality help us to understand the incidence and timing of the crisis?

The notion of transatlantic history is particularly relevant to the Iberian world. Despite the travels of Leif Erickson around the year 1000, transatlantic history began with the forays of Portuguese and Spanish mariners into the Atlantic and down the African coast in the fifteenth century and became a reality with the voyages of Columbus. Trade was the primary goal of those and later voyages, even before Iberian mariners knew exactly where they were going. (Portuguese mariners at first had no idea how large Africa was, and Columbus and his early contemporaries believed they were trading with islands off the coast of Asia.) Nonetheless, they engaged in trade every step of the way. The House of Trade in Seville was established in 1503 to oversee and regulate navigation, trade, and migration to the new lands. Spain also began to organize the colonial economies for production and commerce while the initial conquests were still under way. Yet it was not until decades later that Spaniards had a clear idea of the dimensions and relative location of the lands they had claimed as colonies and sources of productive labor and wealth.

By the late sixteenth century, ships from England, the Netherlands, and France were making regular voyages into the Iberian Atlantic world, challenging the control claimed by Spain and Portugal over trade with Africa and the Americas. The Netherlands profited greatly from taking over trade routes in Africa and the Americas that had been pioneered by the Iberian powers. In part because of that trade, the Netherlands enjoyed its "golden age" from 1590 to about 1660, when much of the rest of Europe, including Iberia, was enduring the seventeenth-century crisis. The Netherlands' own crisis began when its European neighbors recovered. Even then, however, Dutch merchants of the West India Company continued to pursue clandestine, contraband, and occasionally sanctioned trade in the Iberian Atlantic world. The same applied to English and (to a much lesser extent) French merchants. Though these cases are beyond the scope of this chapter, we should keep in mind that virtually every European power buying and selling in the Atlantic had some connection to the Iberian Atlantic world.[5]

Spain, Portugal, and their trading connections and colonies in Africa and America covered about 13 million square miles of land and included perhaps 25–30 million people at the start of the seventeenth century.[6] Given that vastness, scholars have usually chosen to focus on smaller units of study: for example, Spain and Portugal; West Africa; or one of the traditional divisions of Latin America. Broader approaches sometimes examine Spain with Spanish

America and Portugal with Brazil. A limited focus makes sense when scholars study localized themes—for example, the development of colonial society in Mexico. For a topic such as the seventeenth-century crisis, we are unavoidably drawn into the Iberian Atlantic as a whole. Any generalizations made over so large an area and involving so many diverse peoples and cultures is bound to be wrong somewhere. Many generalizations are also certain to be right somewhere. Everything depends on where, what, and when we are examining. The most useful generalizations about the seventeenth-century crisis are those that apply as widely as possible, even if they do not apply everywhere at once and in equal measure.

Historians have looked at many topics that relate to the seventeenth-century crisis in the Iberian Atlantic, and the published literature is vast. Themes as diverse as demography, agriculture, manufacturing, and trade fit under the headings of economy and society, but so do rebellions, piracy, warfare, the witch craze, and a number of other less obvious topics. Clio's web is seamless. I do not pretend to have seen all of the published work, much less to have read it all. In trying to arrive at a useful set of generalizations, I merely survey some of the evidence on Spain, Portugal, West Africa, and Latin America and consider ways in which their seventeenth-century histories can be usefully compared.

For Spain, the overwhelming majority of authors agree that there was some sort of economic crisis in the first half of the seventeenth century. Precisely when it began, how severe it was, and how long it lasted vary from place to place. For example, the dry-farming regions of the Castilian interior seem to have been hit earlier, harder, and longer than coastal areas. The cause of the crisis continues to be a matter of debate. In 1956, Pierre Vilar published an analysis that has been as influential in Spanish history and literature as Eric Hobsbawm's article has been in the broader historiography. Vilar argued that Spain's social structure and the feudal mentality of the governing classes made it impossible for Spaniards to change the way they did business—in other words, to break free of the feudal mode of production and move into the capitalist mode.[7]

Although his analysis was brilliant for its time, Vilar relied more on Marxist theory and traditional generalizations about "the Spanish character" than on detailed research into the economy. For that reason, many historians have found his conclusions wanting. Some of the best Spanish scholars during the authoritarian regime of Francisco Franco (1939–1975) worked on the economy and society of the early modern period—partly because such work could avoid the political risks of doing nineteenth- and twentieth-century history. Their research led the way for other scholars inside and outside Spain in the 1970s and 1980s (myself included) to examine the early modern Spanish economy. The fruit of those labors was an emerging consensus that I summarized in an article in 1987.[8] Later investigations have added more case studies to the literature, but I maintain that the basic outline of the story remains valid.

To sum up that story, the Spanish population rose from about six million to more than eight million people during the sixteenth century, in part because of favorable weather and an absence of serious epidemics.[9] By the late sixteenth century a crisis of subsistence had developed in the agrarian economy as the growing population outran the land's productive capacity, despite the stream of emigration toward America. Over the course of several decades, shock waves from the agrarian crisis spread to urban markets, the manufacturing sector, finance, and international trade.[10] The population also fell, due to epidemics, migration, and a lower birthrate. The worst phase of the crisis occurred from about 1620 to 1640, exacerbated by the strains of the Thirty Years' War.

Ironically, the depths of the crisis also held the seeds of its resolution because the declining population reduced the pressure on resources. Once the worst had passed, the Spanish economy showed unmistakable signs of recovery, perhaps as early as the 1650s and definitely before 1680.[11] In other words, the sharp but temporary economic downturn in seventeenth-century Spain was not a crisis in the rigorous sense—that is, an irreversible turning point—but rather a recession or contraction in a series of economic ups and downs over the centuries. Such ups and downs form the backbone of what used to be called "serial history"—the study of long-term fluctuations in prices, population, agricultural production, trade, and so on.[12]

Agricultural production was intimately linked to climate and weather patterns. Very slight changes in the average global temperature can have major effects on the environment in which human beings live. However, though broad climate changes affect the earth as a whole, their timing and effects differ from place to place. One scholarly debate related to the seventeenth-century crisis concerns the existence and effects of what has been dubbed the Little Ice Age. In the 1970s, available evidence suggested that the European climate began to cool from about 1540–1560 to about 1600. Thereafter, with minor fluctuations, the climate stayed cooler until about 1850 and especially from 1550 to about 1700.[13]

Over the last several decades climatologists have been subjecting the evidence for historical changes in the world's climate to rigorous analysis. The current scientific consensus suggests that there was considerable variation in the timing and incidence of global cooling.[14] Nonetheless, the evidence for a Little Ice Age remains quite strong for many parts of Europe. In the long term, European farmers presumably adapted to the changed climate; in the short term, the change arguably caught them unawares, reducing harvests and making it harder to feed populations that had grown during better times. Difficulties in agriculture presumably contributed to the end of sixteenth-century economic growth and the beginning of the seventeenth-century crisis. The scant climatological evidence for Spain does not support the idea that the climate cooled as it did in northern Europe.[15] Nonetheless, the possibility remains that climatic conditions changed in some other way that hampered agricultural production in the late sixteenth century.

I am an unapologetic neo-Malthusian in seeing both the genesis and the resolution of the Spanish crisis in the agrarian economy—in other words, in the relationship between population and resources, though I would never claim that was the only meaningful relationship in the Spanish economy. Some scholars place most of the blame for the economic downturn in Spain on government policies—especially taxation and monetary policies—and there is no question that taxes rose in the late sixteenth century and continued to be high well into the seventeenth century. The government also tinkered with the money supply to increase state revenues and then tried to put a lid on prices to protect consumers from inflation, which discouraged economic innovation. I would argue, however, that those policies made the crisis worse rather than initiating it.

Other scholars blame the Spanish nobility or the governing classes in general for the crisis because most of them invested in land or credit instruments rather than manufacturing or other activities that could have transformed the economy. There is some merit in those arguments. The nobility, individually and collectively, tried to maximize their income and maintain and enhance their political and social status. So did merchants and bureaucrats. They invested in whatever they thought would yield the highest returns in money, status, or power. Land was an attractive investment for many social groups, both in the rising economy of the sixteenth century and in the downturn of the seventeenth century, though for different reasons. Land investment was not inherently irrational or retrograde in the sixteenth and seventeenth centuries, any more than it is today. Moreover, although the governing classes did not manage their investments in a way that would transform the economy, that was not their aim. One could argue that in the long run their traditional outlook held Spain back in the process that led to industrialization.

It is more difficult to decide what their outlook meant in terms of the seventeenth-century crisis. Both government and the elite pursued very similar strategies before, during, and after the crisis, while the economic situation shifted from one mode to another around them. Sometimes the actions of the government and the elite worsened the situation, and sometimes they ameliorated it, but I am not convinced that either of them can be blamed for the onset of the crisis. And, to my knowledge, no one has attempted to credit either the government or the elite with bringing about the economic recovery of the late seventeenth century. From my point of view, a Malthusian mechanism defined by the relationship between population and resources has the greatest power to explain both the onset and the resolution of the seventeenth-century crisis in Spain; it also allows ample room to include the effects of government policies, the attitudes of the elite, and various other factors.

Within the political sphere, seventeenth-century Spain certainly had its ups and downs. There were several serious rebellions in areas ruled by the Spanish Habsburgs—in the Netherlands, Catalonia, the Kingdom of Naples, and Portugal—plus a few minor upheavals elsewhere. Overall, however, the Spanish Habsburgs faced far fewer troubles than, for example, the French Bourbons or the English Stuarts. France experienced hundreds of revolts and rebellions in the early seventeenth century, and England suffered a calamitous civil war and the execution of a king. By contrast, the Spanish monarchy enjoyed remarkable stability. Even when the "major" Habsburgs of the sixteenth century were succeeded by the "minor" Habsburgs of the seventeenth century, there was no civil war or major rebellion in the heart of the monarchy in Castile, and one could argue that the monarchy's status and bureaucratic apparatus emerged stronger for its trials during the seventeenth century, despite political and economic turmoil. That is not to say that the Habsburgs were absolute monarchs in any rigorous sense. Perhaps even more than their counterparts elsewhere, they ruled largely by negotiation and consensus with elites at both the national and local levels.[16]

The Portuguese case is less documented and less studied, but demographic trends suggest that Portugal followed a trajectory similar to Spain's during the sixteenth century. The Portuguese population rose from about 1 million in 1500 to about 2 million in 1600, but it is likely that emigration relieved potential population pressure before it reached a Malthusian ceiling. A generation ago, scholars put very high figures on total Portuguese migration overseas, but more recent work estimates that about 100,000 Portuguese emigrated across the Atlantic from about 1500 to about 1700, nearly all of them to Brazil after 1600.[17] The most densely settled regions of northern Portugal produced a disproportionate share of those migrants.[18] The Portuguese economy may also have resisted the seventeenth-century crisis through the resale of tobacco and other exotic products from Brazil because such luxuries tended to hold up well in the declining international market. Moreover, the discovery of gold and diamonds in Brazil in 1695 spurred growth not only in Brazil and Portugal but also in the Atlantic economy as a whole.[19]

Politically, Portugal shared the Habsburg kings who ruled Spain between 1580 and 1640, but they staged a successful war of independence against Habsburg rule beginning in 1640. Overall, therefore, the notion of a crisis in the seventeenth century has a very different meaning and timing in Portugal than it does elsewhere in Europe. Some have argued that Portugal experienced a brief economic crisis in the early seventeenth century that helped to spur its rebellion against the Habsburgs. During and after the rebellion, however, Portugal's growing dependence on England arguably led to economic decline and English control over the profits from Brazil.[20]

And what about Africa? There is no question that West Africa was increasingly integrated into the Atlantic world, especially the areas subjected to the transatlantic slave trade. Attempts to analyze the volume and impact of that commerce have occupied generations of scholars, and studies of the slave trade continue to be one of the most active areas of transatlantic research.[21] Overall, estimates of the forced migration of Africans to the Americas range from about 5 million to 10 million or more in the period before 1800, the vast majority of them in the eighteenth century.[22] Some brilliant work has been done by modern scholars to estimate the population of West Africa affected by the slave trade. Though written sources are limited or nonexistent for most regions before the nineteenth century, credible estimates have been crafted in part by making projections based on the carrying capacity of the land in various regions.[23] Did some areas experience a large rise in population in the sixteenth century, similar to the ones in Iberia and elsewhere in Europe? There is some evidence that they did. Between about 1500 and 1600, a period of regular and abundant rainfall altered the basic conditions for farming in west central Africa, leading to better and more predictable crop yields and notable population increases.[24]

Did some areas in West Africa experience agricultural difficulties in the late sixteenth and early seventeenth centuries, akin to what has been documented for Spain? Here again, there is some evidence that they did, and there are also some hints that the problems might have related to a worsening climate. Several historians have noted localized droughts and epidemics in the late sixteenth and early seventeenth centuries in various parts of West Africa.[25] In 1982, Joseph C. Miller assembled information about droughts, epidemics, and famines in west central Africa from the sixteenth to the early nineteenth centuries, which shows an increase in unfavorable conditions from the late sixteenth century on.[26] George E. Brooks argues that drier conditions returned to West Africa as a whole from about 1630 to about 1860, bringing a renewal of the periodic droughts, locust plagues, and famines that beset farmers in the region.[27] Fertile areas that had sustained a rising population in times of adequate rainfall were especially vulnerable to these worsening conditions. Although it is possible that the region became even drier in the nineteenth and twentieth centuries,[28] the end of relatively more humid conditions by the 1630s arguably had a serious short-term effect on local agriculture. The available evidence about climate thus suggests that West Africa experienced at least some aspects of the seventeenth-century crisis.

How was the crisis resolved? Trading connections between Iberia and West Africa provided commodities that African rulers wanted, but trade also stimulated the market for slaves in Europe and America. The difficult conditions for agriculture in West Africa presumably worsened tensions among rival ethnic groups in the area. Those rivalries, which were exacerbated by the external market for slaves, channeled increasing numbers of people into the involuntary migration of Africans across the Atlantic. How did population changes, including the drain from the slave trade, affect individual communities, and how might the slave trade relate to the notion of a seventeenth-century crisis? Viewed purely from a numerical standpoint, the involuntary migration from West Africa across the Atlantic presumably reduced population pressure in communities whose numbers were approaching the limits of their resources. On the other hand, if slavers took workers from communities that were short of labor to begin with, the losses may have crippled their economic capacities. In the long term, the population of West Africa proved to be remarkably resilient, as farmers adapted to the return of drier conditions. Aided by the introduction of American crops such as manioc and maize, they were also able to plant on previously inhospitable land and support populations that continued to rise through the seventeenth century and beyond, despite the slave trade.

The most complicated debates about the seventeenth-century crisis in the Atlantic world have concerned Latin America—the largest part of that world. Scholars who have entered the debate generally focus on one theme or geographical area—for example, either New Spain or Peru, though a few have taken on the area as a whole.[29] Most of the vast region included under the Viceroyalty of Peru bordered the Pacific Ocean, but in colonial times it was unquestionably part of the Atlantic world. Without restricting the scope of the inquiry in some way, scholars would find it nearly impossible to design manageable research projects, given the demographic and ethnic diversity of Latin America and its territorial extent.

In addition to rival schools of thought that parallel those in the European debate about the seventeenth-century crisis, the scholarship about Latin America has other concerns. Many of the native peoples in Latin America (as in North America) did not use written records of the sort common in Europe, so scholars must be creative in finding ways to study their histories. One possibility is to use European written records, such as documents written in

Spanish and Portuguese by merchants, clerics, and bureaucrats. By their very nature, those documents rarely present a fully rounded picture of non-European peoples, let alone their points of view. Nonetheless, older generations of scholars often relied almost exclusively on such records and, many have argued, presented only the views of Europeans.

More recently, many scholars of Latin America have learned native languages as well as Spanish and Portuguese so that they can read documents created by the colonial administrations in those languages. Their work is opening a new world of evidence for topics such as the seventeenth-century crisis. Other information comes from the findings of archaeology and anthropology, which can illuminate aspects of local histories that are ignored or misrepresented in written records. All evidence, from whatever source and in whatever form, should be subjected to critical analysis. In the best recent work, scholars have used a wide range of evidence to provide subtle and nuanced views of the past from multiple perspectives. Because I am surveying scholarly work on all of Latin America, it is necessary to pick and choose carefully. As I did for Spain, Portugal, and West Africa, I discuss a few broad themes that cut across local or regional boundaries and pertain to an examination of the seventeenth-century crisis.

One of the liveliest areas of investigation of Latin America has concerned population trends and patterns of migration. Old World diseases and the effects of European conquests caused a demographic catastrophe in Latin America during the sixteenth century, with a horrifying death toll among the native populations. Intermittent waves of disease, such as the pandemic of 1616–1620, continued to recur long after the wars of conquest had ended. A consensus on numbers has yet to emerge about the size of the native populations before Europeans arrived in the Americas; estimates range from a conservative low of 14–20 million inhabitants to an improbable high of more than 100 million. Nearly all of the estimates were devised by working backward from Spanish documents of the late sixteenth century, created when officials realized the gravity of the ongoing catastrophe.[30]

By the mid-seventeenth century, the western hemisphere probably held between 4.5 million and 10 million inhabitants. By then, the population of Latin America had turned upward again, and Iberian colonial societies were evolving as a diverse mixture of Indians, Europeans, and Africans. The arrival of hundreds of thousands of West Africans, brought across the Atlantic as slaves, undoubtedly helped the population of Latin America to rebound from a century of demographic catastrophe and also contributed to economic growth in the region by providing essential labor.[31] In other words, the population of Latin America lived through a history far different from that of Iberia or West Africa during the sixteenth and seventeenth centuries, though the worst of the population crisis and the subsequent recovery seem to have occurred at roughly the same times in both Iberia and Latin America.

Besides work on population and migration, several other themes relate to the debate over the seventeenth-century crisis in Latin America. Before it faded from fashion, the subject of agriculture attracted much interest from the 1950s to the 1970s, and various prominent scholars delineated a cycle of agricultural boom and bust in sixteenth-century Mexico that was strikingly similar, at least in its timing, to the situation in Spain.[32] One respected study analyzed the Mexican cycle in explicit relationship to the Atlantic economy in terms of the changing availability of labor, the market demand for grain, and the effects of an increasing supply of money on both sides of the Atlantic.[33] There are recent signs that scholars are again turning their attention to agricultural production and its relationship to population, social structure, local government, law, finance, transport, and trade, to name just the most obvious connections. One important new article surveys tithe records for most of South America from 1681 to 1800.[34] Although it begins too late to tell us much about the onset of any crisis in the seventeenth century, the research clearly documents long-lasting economic difficulties in the region around Lima. Other scholars have shown that areas as diverse and distant as the Caribbean islands[35] and Paraguay[36] also experienced agricultural distress in varying degrees during the seventeenth century.

Given the dramatic changes in the labor force and land use during the sixteenth and seventeenth centuries, as well as the vast spaces involved, it is difficult to gauge whether climate change influenced agricultural distress in Latin America as it seems to have done in Europe and West Africa. Chronicles beginning with the arrival of the Spaniards and Portuguese often mention climate and weather. Those topics also commonly appear in administrative records such as town council minutes because they had a direct bearing on agricultural production and the tax base. By examining such records, climatologists have been able to reconstruct a detailed historical record of the phenomenon known as "El Niño," the periodic warming of the tropical Pacific Ocean that tends to arrive around Christmastime (hence its name) and which continues to have enormous implications for global weather patterns.[37]

El Niño tends to cause increased rainfall, storms, and coastal flooding from Ecuador to Peru, drought in the mountainous areas of southern Peru and in northeastern Brazil, and other weather conditions that often harm agriculture.[38] Over the very long term, El Niño conditions have tended to recur about every 5 years. According to historical records, that seems to have been the case in the period between 1550 and 1650, so that farmers presumably incorporated El Niño into their short-term plans. By contrast, beginning around 1650 and continuing to 1675–1680, El Niño conditions appeared much less frequently—in fact, less often than in any other period in the past 500 years. In the 1680s, El Niño once again became a more frequent and regular visitor, recurring every 4.5 years or so.[39] The unusual period from 1650 to 1675–1680 may have lulled farmers into complacency and out of the habit of planning for El Niño. Did they expand cultivation onto marginal lands at greater risk for drought or flood? Did they introduce unfamiliar crops that were more susceptible to ruin when El Niño returned? To many contemporary observers in Peru, the 1680s marked the start of a long downturn in agricultural production, and the tithe figures bear that out. The on-again, off-again pattern of El Niño recurrences may help to explain the trend.

Another lively area of research on Latin America concerns the voluminous records of mining production and the minting of coins. Detailed study by a number of scholars has shown that mining output in the Viceroyalty of Peru, which included the enormously rich silver mines at Potosí, rose to a peak around 1610 and declined thereafter for the next century.[40] Mining in the Viceroyalty of New Spain rose to a peak around 1592, declined slightly until about 1630, and then dropped sharply. By the 1660s, however, Mexican mining production was rebounding.[41] In 1695, the discovery of gold in Brazil further stimulated the mining of silver, whose relative value rose as Brazilian gold flooded onto the world market. In addition to studying mining, historians of Latin America have also examined the coinage of silver in various mints to get a different perspective on the output of precious metals. These records also suggest a decline in the late sixteenth and early seventeenth centuries.[42] If mining production and coinage records can serve as proxies for economic vitality as a whole—and many argue that they can—Mexico replaced Peru as the more dynamic economy in the course of the seventeenth century.

Tax collection and the flow of bullion and coined money back and forth across the Atlantic are other topics that scholars of Latin America have used to track changes in the economy, but they are difficult to interpret. The pioneering work of Earl J. Hamilton traces fluctuations in the volume of treasure from taxes and other fees remitted to the Spanish Crown in the sixteenth and seventeenth centuries.[43] He argues that bullion flows to Spain experienced a slight decline from 1591 to 1630 and a subsequent sharp drop. Methods of tax collection in Spanish America changed over time, however, so what looks like a decrease in tax receipts in a given period may in fact reflect no more than a change in the way the taxes were collected and registered.[44] Was there a decrease in tax revenues? Answers vary, depending on the author and the focus of individual studies. B. H. Slicher van Bath argues that tax revenues in Spanish America generally rose until 1650 but fell thereafter, especially in Peru.[45]

Assuming that the decline in revenue was real, rather than a product of changing collection methods, the question remains as to whether to call the phenomenon a crisis and, if so, for whom. A reduction in tax revenues in the Americas may or may not indicate economic distress; it may instead mean there was more tax evasion or a decline in administrative efficiency. If either was the case, then the documented decrease in tax revenues could be interpreted as a positive development for America but a negative one for Spain. Similarly, we know that an increasing percentage of the taxes collected in the seventeenth century remained in the Americas for fortifications and port works, roads and bridges, wages and salaries, and so on. Although this presumably had a negative effect on the Spanish economy and the government's budget, the monies retained in America arguably had a positive effect on local economies and helped them emerge from the economic contraction of the seventeenth century. A separate but related issue concerns the amount of American silver that entered Pacific trade en route to Japan and China, both officially and clandestinely. Although Pacific trade is beyond the scope of this survey, there is little question that the high demand for silver in Asia, particularly China, helped to stimulate silver production in Peru and Mexico in the sixteenth century. Changes in Asian demand may well have contributed to the seventeenth-century falloff in American silver production as well.[46]

With regard to Atlantic trade, Pierre Chaunu and Huguette Chaunu's classic study of the fleet records in Seville up to 1650 documents a growth in trade volume in the sixteenth century, which ascended to a peak in about 1609 and then declined dramatically.[47] More recent work has challenged the work of the Chaunus on several points but not in broad outline. For the period after 1650, some have argued for a recovery in the last decades of the seventeenth century,[48] whereas others say the downturn continued into the early eighteenth century.[49] The figures for specific commodities often have different timetables of expansion and contraction. Wherever we look, however, there is no escaping the conclusion that registered trade in the Iberian Atlantic suffered a major contraction during the seventeenth century.[50]

However, registered trade did not include all trade. From Spain's point of view, all trade that did not pass through official channels was illegal and thus branded as contraband or piracy. But merchants outside Iberia did not respect Spain's claimed monopoly and often succeeded in circumventing it. Spanish merchants and colonists in Latin America also participated in contraband trade to avoid taxes and high prices. How large a role did smuggled goods and piracy play in Iberian Atlantic trade? We may never know the story in full, but several scholars have made credible attempts to estimate the level of illegal merchandise and treasure and to gauge their effects on the volume of transatlantic trade. When commerce in general flourished, contraband may have accounted for no more than about 10 percent of the total. At the depths of the seventeenth-century contraction, however, illicit trade may have far exceeded official figures, so that the downturn in total trade would have been less severe than the official figures suggest.[51]

All of the economic topics mentioned so far had a social dimension as well. Some of the most exciting research on Latin American colonial society in recent decades has focused on communities, administration, religious practices, social groups, cities, and rural life, in addition to ongoing work on population and migration.[52] Studies of the ways in which individuals and social groups adapted to economic change can help us to understand what the seventeenth-century crisis meant at the personal level. For example, one recent study analyzes the role of Mexico City's merchants in economic growth from the 1590s to the 1630s, economic contraction from the 1640s to the 1660s, and the erratic recovery thereafter.[53] By following the fortunes and activities of prominent merchants, the analysis helps to explain how Mexico emerged during the seventeenth century as a semiautonomous entrepôt for both Atlantic and Pacific trade.

Examined in a broad context, problems such as the seventeenth-century crisis have the potential to reveal all of the complexity of Clio's web but only if we can find some way to weave all of its threads together. Most of the studies that proved useful in preparing this chapter use numbers to some extent. That is not an accident. Although numbers cannot fill in all of the gaps, they can answer some of our questions and in the process provide a tool for examining historical developments that are broadly comparable. For example, farming regions all over the Iberian Atlantic world were sensitive to changes in rainfall patterns during the sixteenth and seventeenth centuries, whether those regions were in southern Spain, western Africa, or central Mexico. We now know that occurrences of El Niño affect the weather virtually worldwide, though in different ways; that was presumably true in earlier centuries as well. By focusing on the effects of weather and other measurable aspects of farming and daily life in all parts of the Iberian Atlantic world, we will undoubtedly learn more about the timing, effects, and resolution of the seventeenth-century crisis.

Based on my sampling of the published literature, I hazard the following generalizations: Some sort of economic downturn seems to have occurred in the seventeenth century everywhere in the Iberian Atlantic world where we have reliable evidence. Whenever it began, however long it lasted, and whether it was a brief period of stagnation, recession, or depression or the start of a longer decline, I maintain that the crisis was real and not merely a projection of European categories onto other parts of the world.

I also suggest that the examples of crisis in various parts of the Iberian Atlantic—despite their differences in timing, depth, and extension—were related to each other in a variety of ways. If changes in the weather influenced the onset of the crisis in Iberia, as I think it did, a similar mechanism arguably affected West Africa and Latin America as well, though not necessarily in the same way. If population pressure in Portugal, Spain, and West Africa in the late sixteenth century led to emigration, voluntary or forced, the arrival of newcomers in the Americas compensated in part for the catastrophic demographic decline in native peoples there. Changing population sizes and migration patterns also affected local economies and the trajectory of the seventeenth-century crisis on both sides of the Atlantic. Transatlantic trade involved flows of money and goods in both directions. The onset, timing, duration, and eventual end of the depression in trade figures were shaped by an ongoing conversation between the Old Worlds of Europe and Africa and the New World of America, using the language of supply and demand. We know some of the dialogue already, thanks to the work of several generations of scholars, but much of it remains unclear and unstudied.

How can we deepen and broaden our understanding of the seventeenth-century crisis? In my view, the most useful studies will be narrowly focused, concentrating, for example, on local or regional communities or on a specific commodity featured in transatlantic trade. The difficulty is to define research narrowly enough to master the sources and broadly enough to address questions of general importance. Well-documented conclusions about a wide range of topics, grounded in local contexts all over the Iberian Atlantic world, will provide the basis for further debate about all aspects of the seventeenth-century crisis.

NOTES

1. JoEllen Campbell and David A. Norton worked for me as research assistants at separate stages in the preparation of this chapter. I discussed a preliminary version at the round table organized by Carla Pestana on "Europe's Crisis of the Seventeenth Century in the Wider Atlantic World" at the annual meeting of the American Historical Association, Jan. 5–9, 2001, Boston.

2. Trevor Aston, ed., *Crisis in Europe* (London: Routledge and Kegan Paul, 1965); Geoffrey Parker and Leslie M. Smith, eds., *The General Crisis of the Seventeenth Century* (London: Routledge and Kegan Paul, 1978).

3. For example, David Hackett Fischer's recent synthesis of economic cycles during the past millennium allows some validity to every possible explanation of the seventeenth-century crisis, except the Marxian construal. David Hackett Fischer, *The Great Wave: Price Revolutions and the Rhythm of History* (New York: Oxford University Press, 1997), pp. 91–102, 341–43.

4. Eric Hobsbawm, "The Crisis of the Seventeenth Century," *Past and Present* 5–6 (1954).

5. For the Dutch, see Jonathan Israel, *Dutch Primacy in World Trade, 1585–1740* (Oxford: Oxford University Press, 1989). The literature on English Atlantic trade is vast. An excellent recent summary of English interloping in the Spanish empire is G. V. Scammell, "'A Very Profitable and Advantageous Trade': British Smuggling in the Iberian Americas circa 1500–1750," *Itinerario: European Journal of Overseas History* 3(4) (2000): 135–72.

6. Colin McEvedy and Richard Jones, *Atlas of World Population History* (New York: Penguin Books, 1978).

7. Pierre Vilar, "The Age of Don Quixote," in *Essays in European Economic History*, ed. Peter Earle (Oxford: Oxford University Press, 1974). A recent example of the same line of argument is Stanley J. Stein and Barbara H. Stein, *Silver, Trade, and War: Spain and America in the Making of Early Modern Europe* (Baltimore: Johns Hopkins University Press, 2000).

8. Carla Rahn Phillips, "Time and Duration: A Model for the Economy of Early Modern Spain," *American Historical Review* 92(3) (June, 1987): 531–62.

9. The totals derive from using a multiplier of 5 to convert household counts to total population. See Vicente Pérez Moreda and David-Sven Reher, eds., *Demografía histórica en España* (Madrid: Ediciones Arquero, 1988).

10. Carla Rahn Phillips, "The Growth and Composition of Trade in the Iberian Empires, 1450–1750," in *The Rise of Merchant Empires: Long-distance Trade in the Early Modern World, 1350–1750*, ed. James D. Tracy (Cambridge and New York: Cambridge University Press, 1990), pp. 34–101.

11. A. A. Thompson and Bartolomé Yun Casalilla, eds., *The Castilian Crisis of the Seventeenth Century: New Perspectives on the Economic and Social History of Seventeenth-century Spain* (Cambridge and New York: Cambridge University Press, 1994).

12. For pioneering works in serial history, see François Simiand, *Recherches anciennes et nouvelles sur le mouvement général des prix du XVIe au XIXe siècle* (Paris: Domat Montchrestien, 1932); Earl J. Hamilton, *American Treasure and the Price Revolution in Spain, 1501–1650* (Cambridge: Harvard University Press, 1934); Jean Meuvret, "Les crisis de subsistances et la démographie de la France d'ancien régime," *Population* (Oct.–Dec., 1946): 643–50; Pierre Chaunu and Huguette Chaunu, *Séville et l'Atlantique, 1504–1650*, 8 vols. (Paris: A. Colin, 1955–1959); and Fernand Braudel and F. C. Spooner, "Prices in Europe, 1450–1750," in *The Economy of Expanding Europe in the Sixteenth and Seventeenth Centuries*, ed. E. E. Rich and C. H. Wilson, vol. 4, *Cambridge Economic History of Europe* (Cambridge: Cambridge University Press, 1967), pp. 378–486.

13. Emmanuel Le Roy Ladurie, *Times of Feast, Times of Famine: A History of Climate since the Year 1000*, trans. Barbara Bray (Garden City, N.Y.: Doubleday, 1971); H. H. Lamb, *Climate: Present, Past, and Future* (London: Methuen, 1977).

14. P. D. Jones and R. S. Bradley, "Climatic Variations over the Last 500 Years," in *Climate since A.D. 1500*, ed. Raymond S. Bradley and Philip D. Jones (London: Routledge, Chapman, and Hall, 1992), pp. 658–60.

15. F. Serre-Bachet, J. Guiot, and L. Tessier, "Dendroclimatic Evidence from Southwestern Europe and Northwestern Africa," in *Climate since A.D. 1500*, pp. 360–61.

16. Carla Rahn Phillips, "Local History and Imperial Spain," *Locus: A Historical Jour-*

nal of Regional Perspectives on National Topics 2(2) (Spring, 1990): 119–29. See also Ruth MacKay, *The Limits of Royal Authority: Resistance and Obedience in Seventeenth-century Castile* (Cambridge: Cambridge University Press, 1999).

17. Ida Altman and James Horn, "Introduction," in *To Make America: European Emigration in the Early Modern Period*, ed. Ida Altman and James Horn (Berkeley: University of California Press, 1991), pp. 1–30. Much higher figures were proposed by Vitorino Magalhaes Godinho, "Portuguese Emigration from the Fifteenth to the Twentieth Century: Constants and Changes," in *European Expansion and Migration: Essays on the Intercontinental Migration from Africa, Asia, and Europe*, ed. P. C. Emmer and Magnus Mörner (New York and Oxford: Berg, 1992), pp. 13–48.

18. Robert Rowland, "Emigración, estructura, y región en Portugal (siglos XVI–XIX)," in *Emigración española y portuguesa a América: Actas del II Congreso de la Asociación de Demografía Histórica* (Alicante, Spain: Instituto de Cultura Juan Gil Albert, 1991), pp. 137–46.

19. James Lockhart and Stuart B. Schwartz, *Early Latin America: A History of Colonial Spanish America and Brazil* (Cambridge and New York: Cambridge University Press, 1983), pp. 369–88; A. J. R. Russell-Wood, "Colonial Brazil: The Gold Cycle, c. 1690–1750," in *The Cambridge History of Latin America*, vol. 2, ed. Leslie Bethell (Cambridge and New York: Cambridge University Press, 1984), pp. 547–600.

20. Henk Ligthart and Henk Retsma, "Portugal's Semi-peripheral Middleman Role in Its Relations with England, 1640–1760," *Political Geography Quarterly* 7(4) (1988): 353–62.

21. For comprehensive overviews of the field, see David Eltis, David Richardson, Stephen D. Behrendt, and Herbert S. Klein, eds., *The Atlantic Slave Trade: A Database on CD-ROM Set and Guidebook* (New York: Cambridge University Press, 1999); and Paul Finkelman and Joseph C. Miller, eds., *Macmillan Encyclopedia of World Slavery* (New York: Macmillan Reference USA, 1998).

22. See Philip Curtin, *The Atlantic Slave Trade: A Census* (Madison: University of Wisconsin Press, 1969); P. E. Emmer, "European Expansion and Migration: The European Colonial Past and Intercontinental Migration, an Overview," in *European Expansion and Migration*, pp. 1–12; David Eltis, "Free and Coerced Transatlantic Migrations: Some Comparisons," *American Historical Review* 88 (1983): 251–80; Philip D. Morgan, "The Cultural Implications of the Atlantic Slave Trade: African Regional Origins, American Destinations, and New World Developments," *Slavery and Abolition* 18(1) (Apr., 1997): 122–45; David Eltis and David Richardson, "The 'Numbers Game' and Routes to Slavery," in *Slavery and Abolition* 18(1) (Apr., 1997): 1–15.

23. See, for example, Patrick Manning, *Slavery and African Life: Occidental, Oriental, and African Slave Trades* (Cambridge: Cambridge University Press, 1990).

24. George E. Brooks, *Landlords and Strangers: Ecology, Society, and Trade in Western Africa, 1000–1630* (Boulder, Colo.: Westview Press, 1993), p. 170.

25. See, for example, Philip D. Curtin, *Economic Change in Precolonial Africa: Senegambia in the Era of the Slave Trade* (Madison: University of Wisconsin Press, 1975), pp. 3–7, and the *Supplementary Evidence* volume, pp. 3–5, listing droughts, plagues of locusts, and famines.

26. Joseph C. Miller, "The Significance of Drought, Disease, and Famine in the Agriculturally Marginal Zones of West Central Africa," *Journal of African History* 23(1) (1982): 17–61.

27. Brooks, *Landlords and Strangers*, pp. 170–76.

28. James L. A. Webb Jr., *Desert Frontier: Ecological and Economic Change along the Western Sahel, 1600–1850* (Madison: University of Wisconsin Press, 1995), pp. 3–11.

29. Ruggiero Romano, *Coyunturas opuestas: La crisis del siglo XVII en Europa e Hispanoamérica* (Mexico: Colegio de México, 1993).

30. Two recent surveys of the population debate are David Henige, *Numbers from Nowhere: The American Indian Contact Population Debate* (Norman: University of Oklahoma Press, 1998), and Noble David Cook, *Born to Die: Disease and New World Conquest, 1492–1650* (Cambridge: Cambridge University Press, 1998).

31. John Thornton, *Africa and Africans in the Making of the Atlantic World, 1400–1800* (New York: Cambridge University Press, 1998), persuasively makes the case for African contributions to the development of the Americas.

32. Woodrow Borah, *New Spain's Century of Depression* (Berkeley and Los Angeles: University of California Press, 1951); François Chevalier, *Land and Society in Colonial Mexico: The Great Hacienda,* ed. Lesley Byrd Simpson and trans. Alvin Eustis (Berkeley and Los Angeles: University of California Press, 1963); André Gunder Frank, *Mexican Agriculture 1521–1630: Transformation of the Mode of Production* (Cambridge: Cambridge University Press, 1979).

33. Frank, *Mexican Agriculture 1521–1630*, pp. 17–18.

34. Carlos Newland and John Coatsworth, "Crecimiento económico en el espacio peruano, 1681–1800: Una visión a partir de la agricultura," *Revista de Historia Económica* 18(2) (Spring–Summer, 2000): 377–93. Kenneth J. Andrien, *Crisis and Decline: The Viceroyalty of Peru in the Seventeenth Century* (Albuquerque: University of New Mexico Press, 1985), argues that the crisis in Peru emerged from fiscal and monetary policies rather than from serious difficulties in the economy, but most other scholars do not agree.

35. Lorenzo E. López y Sebastián and Justo L. Río Moreno, "La crisis del siglo XVII en la industria azucarera antillana y los cambios producidos en su estructura," *Revista Complutense de Historia de América* 23 (1997): 137–66.

36. Mario Pastore, "Taxation, Coercion, Trade, and Development in a Frontier Economy: Early and Mid-Colonial Paraguay," *Journal of Latin American Studies* 29 (1997): 329–51.

37. El Niño (EN) is accompanied in the atmosphere by what is called the Southern Oscillation (SO). Together they are known to weather scientists as ENSO. W. H. Quinn, V. T. Neal, and S. E. Antunez de Mayolo, "El Niño Occurrences over the Past Four and a Half Centuries," *Journal of Geophysical Research* 92 (1987): 14,449–61, is the pioneering study of historical occurrences of El Niño. An updated version is W. H. Quinn and V. T. Neal, "The Historical Record of El Niño Events," in *Climate since* A.D. 1500, pp. 623–48. A sampling of work on the topic can also be found in Henry F. Díaz and Vera Markgraf, eds., *El Niño and the Southern Oscillation: Multiscale Variability and Global and Regional Impacts* (Cambridge and New York: Cambridge University Press, 1992).

38. David Enfield, "Historical and Prehistorical Overview of El Niño/Southern Oscillation," in *El Niño and the Southern Oscillation*, p. 97.

39. Henry F. Díaz and Roger S. Pulwarty, "A Comparison of Southern Oscillation and El Niño Signals in the Tropics," in *El Niño and the Southern Oscillation*, pp. 179–81.

40. David Brading and Harry Cross, "Colonial Silver Mining: Mexico and Peru," *His-*

panic American Historical Review 52 (1972): 545–79; Richard L. Garner, "Long-term Silver Mining Trends in Spanish America: A Comparative Analysis of Peru and Mexico," American Historical Review 93(4) (Oct., 1988): 898–935; Ann Zulawski, "Wages, Ore Sharing, and Peasant Agriculture: Labour in Oruro's Silver Mines, 1607–1720," Hispanic American Historical Review 67(3) (1987): 405–30.

41. Heraclio Bonilla and P. J. Bakewell, El sistema colonial en la América española (Barcelona: Editorial Crítica, 1991). For collected articles on mining production in the Americas as a whole, see P. J. Bakewell, ed., Mines of Silver and Gold in the Americas (Aldershot, UK, and Brookfield, Vt.: Variorum, 1997).

42. John Jay TePaske, Herbert S. Klein, and Kendall W. Brown, in The Royal Treasuries of the Spanish Empire in America, 3 vols. (Durham: Duke University Press, 1982), meticulously outline the bureaucratic structure of mining, assaying, and the taxation of mining production.

43. Hamilton, American Treasure and the Price Revolution in Spain.

44. Herbert Klein and Jacques A. Barbier, "Recent Trends in the Study of Spanish American Colonial Public Finance," Latin American Research Review 23(1) (1988): 43–50.

45. B. H. Slicher van Bath, Real hacienda y economía en Hispanoamérica, 1541–1820 (Amsterdam: Centro de Estudios y Documentación Latinoamericanos, 1989), pp. 122–25. See also Peter T. Bradley, The Lure of Peru: Maritime Intrusion in the South Sea, 1598–1701 (New York: St. Martin's Press, 1989).

46. Artur Attman, American Bullion in the European World Trade, 1600–1800, trans. Eva Gree and Allen Gree (Göteborg: Kungl Vetensskaps och Vitterhets-Samhallet, 1986); Dennis O. Flynn and Arturo Giráldez, eds., Metals and Monies in an Emerging Global Economy (Aldershot, UK, and Brookfield, Vt.: Variorum, 1997); Ward Barrett, "World Bullion Flows, 1450–1800," in The Rise of Merchant Empires: Long-distance Trade in the Early Modern World, 1350–1750, ed. James D. Tracy (Cambridge: Cambridge University Press, 1990), pp. 224–54.

47. Chaunu and Chaunu, Séville et l'Amérique, vols. 6–8.

48. Michel Morineau, "D'Amsterdam à Séville: De quelle réalité l'histoire des prix est-elle le miroir?" Annales: Économies, Sociétés, Civilisations 23 (1968): 178–205.

49. Antonio García-Baquero González, "Andalusia and the Crisis of the Indies Trade, 1610–1720," in Castilian Crisis of the Seventeenth Century, pp. 115–35; Antonio García-Baquero González, "Tres siglos de comercio marítimo colonial: Un balance desde la metrópolis," in Comercio marítimo colonial: Nuevas interpretaciones y últimas fuentes, ed. Carmen Yuste López (México: Instituto Nacional de Antropología e Historia, 1997), provides a good overview of the debate about trade and revenue statistics.

50. See the evidence surveyed in Phillips, "Growth and Composition of Trade in the Iberian Empires."

51. See Eufemio Lorenzo Sanz, Comercio de España con América en la época de Felipe II, vol. 2 (Valladolid, Spain: Diputación Provincial de Valladolid, 1980), pp. 142–46; Zacarias Moutoukias, "Una forma de oposición: El contrabando," in Governare el mondo: L'imperio spagnolo dal XV al XIX secolo, ed. Massimo Ganci and Ruggiero Romano (Palermo, Italy: Societa Siciliana per la Storia Patria, 1991); Antonio García de León, "Contrabando y comercio de rescate en el Veracruz del siglo XVII," in Comercio marítimo colonial, pp. 17–33.

52. For example, see Stuart B. Schwartz, *Sovereignty and Society in Colonial Brazil: The High Court of Bahia and Its Judges, 1609–1751* (Berkeley: University of California Press, 1973); and Mark Burkholder and D. S. Chandler, *From Impotence to Authority: The Spanish Crown and the American Audiencias, 1687–1808* (Columbia: University of Missouri Press, 1977).

53. Louisa Schell Hoberman, *Mexico's Merchant Elite, 1590–1660: Silver, State, and Society* (Durham: Duke University Press, 1991).

DENNIS REINHARTZ

*Establishing a Transatlantic
Graphic Dialogue, 1492–1800*

TO THE OLD WORLD of Eurasia and Africa, the world rediscovered by Christopher Columbus in 1492 was indeed new. Because this contact was to be permanent, the New World was from the beginning even more alien and exotic than the Vinland, Markland, and other territories visited somewhere across the Davis Strait from Greenland by Leif Erickson, Thorfinn Karlsefni, and the other Norse explorers nearly half a millennium earlier. On the whole, it would take the better part of four centuries or more until the closing of the American frontiers for the newness substantially to wear off and for the Old World to comprehend the New. The New World had been significantly remade in the image of the Old by the end of the nineteenth century,[1] but not without deeply affecting the remakers in the process. It was this development that makes 1492 a dividing point between the medieval and the modern.[2]

Various factors contributed to the perceived New World strangeness, especially in the first three centuries of contact until the end of the European colonial wars and the coming of the American revolutions. The distance, underscored again and again by the length of the voyages to the New World, emphasized its dissimilarities to the Old. The Americas, which were not supposed to be there in the first place, in any case were very far away from Eurasia and Africa and therefore also had to be very different.[3] Relatedly, as Peter Mason points out, "The exotic . . . is not something that exists prior to 'discovery.' . . . Discovery produces the exotic."[4]

As the Old World's geographical knowledge of the New World grew and its size increased therewith (accompanied by a comparable decrease in the size of Eurasia) in the sixteenth and seventeen centuries, the New World also intensified in diversity and curiosity. The geography of a place, especially a new place, is both real and perceived. Mental geography qualifies the understanding and exploitation of real geography. Illusions can be as significant as reality, and their power can be a major factor in the formulation of geography (e.g., the Northwest Passage), particularly at a great distance. According to J. Wreford Watson, "*The mental image is the environment we go by as true, until the true environment destroys the illusion*" (italics in the original).[5] William Brandon summarizes as follows: "Its exact dimensions notwithstanding, this gulf of difference between the two worlds, Old and New, the difference itself, within which, in the swirling mists of which, could discern all manner of contrasts, giving rise to all manner of marvels and reports, the difference itself may have been the one principal feature to strike European observers. Whether they interpreted correctly or not, whether to this day it is correctly interpreted, is perhaps less important than simply recognizing the fact of the enormous, subtle, profound, very possibly all but bottomless, all but unbridgeable, difference."[6]

The reports that the early explorers, travelers, and colonists in the New World sent back to the Old World "were for the most part factual,"[7] but most Europeans were illiterate. How then did many of them begin to formulate their understanding of the New World? They received their raw data mainly through the graphics that illustrated or complemented the written words rather than through the words themselves. From the "best-selling" accounts of Columbus's voyages onward, narratives and images of the New World were in great demand in Europe.[8]

This chapter deals principally with the visions of the New World transmitted in an important cadre of sources—the printed maps and other graphics—to Europeans during the approximately three centuries after Columbus's rediscovery. It is a study of graphic representational effect and seeks to explain how these images of landforms, Indians, and flora and fauna influenced the European conception of the New World and attitudes and policies toward it. It should be remembered here that the Vikings left behind no such graphic accounts of their discoveries but only the oral sagas in the somewhat obscure Old Icelandic and archeological remains that were not unearthed until the beginning of the second half of the twentieth century. Neither significantly influenced the rediscovery, exploration, and settlement of the Americas.[9] I do not here consider the impact on Africa or the equally interesting, though rarer and often more transitory (largely due to the absence of printing), African (e.g., Benin)[10] and Indian (e.g., Susquehannock)[11] graphic imagery reflecting the coming of the Europeans.

As Watson has further explained, when encountering new lands, illusion is as significant as reality. "The power of illusion is a major factor in the making of geography,"[12] thus helping in part to explain the persistent belief in the proximity of Asia to America or the cartographic rendering of California as an island well into the eighteenth century.[13] "So often men only see in the world the world they want to see," based on the world they know.[14] "Geography is made, then, largely in terms of the country we *perceive* or are conditioned to *perceive: the country of the mind*" (italics in the original).[15] It is a product of cultural conditioning, and the classical academic preparation of the early writers and artists with regard to the Americas was woefully inadequate in facilitating their descriptions. Consequently, illusion often begets illusion (e.g., settlement improves the land) and/or is replaced by illusion.[16] Thus multiple levels of perception are drawn upon—the "climate of the mind" influences the "country of the mind" as real climate influences real country.[17]

Nothing depicts new lands better than maps. Therefore it is perhaps best to begin with a map, one that is contemporary with Columbus's voyages. Martin Waldseemüller (1470–1521?) was a clergyman-teacher-geographer-publisher in St. Die in the Vosges Mountains of Lorraine under the patronage of Duke René II of Anjou and Lorraine. In 1513, in Strasbourg, Waldseemüller published a new edition of the classic *Geographia* of Claudius Ptolemy, accompanied by a series of maps from woodblocks drawn according to the ancient dictates of Ptolemy as recorded in his work. But he also innovated from Ptolemy in two key respects: Many of the individual maps were updated to adjust for the thirteenth-century increase in Western geographical knowledge since Ptolemy's time, and two new maps were added beyond Ptolemy's original prescription to accommodate the discovery of the New World.

The first was a planisphere world map with a representation of the New World, which Waldseemüller had already named "America" after Amerigo Vespucci on his earlier maps in 1507. In that same year he had also been the first to publish *Quaturo Navigationes,* Vespucci's account of his four voyages to the New World, and therefore honored him as "a man of great ability" who he believed to be the discoverer of the New World. Once Waldseemüller found out about Columbus, he retracted his designation, omitted it from future editions of his maps, and by way of apology sought to explain his mistake on them, all to no avail. However, other cartographers, such as Gerhard Mercator and Abraham Ortelius in the second half of the sixteenth century, picked up the usage of "America," and the name stuck.[18]

The second map was the first printed chart of the Atlantic Basin, "Tabula Terra Nova," which is found in its most refined form in the 1522 edition. It shows the extent of transatlantic Iberian discovery and exploration through the first decade of the sixteenth century. The two written statements near the center of the map make the Columbus apology and the delineation of the Gulf of Mexico, which first appeared on the 1513 map, worthy of note, chiefly since we have no accounts of gulf exploration until that of the Alonso Alvarez de Piñeda voyage of 1519 and Hernando Cortés's conquest of Mexico (1519–1521). This early rendition of the gulf perhaps hints at a previous source that is now unknown to us.

On this edition the white space of northern South America has been filled in with a charming yet telling vignette. To the left is what looks like a great she-bear. Because of the configuration of its snout, some have called it the first picture of an opossum, but with its external mammaries it is definitely not a marsupial. In addition, the first recorded mention we have of an opossum comes (in Florida) from the 1542 *Relación* of Alvar Núñez Cabeza de Vaca of his *entrada* (entry) of 1527–1537 across the southern part of North America.[19]

On the right are Indians enjoying a feast of human body parts in a natural setting. By the time of this edition of the map, there had been several, though not always reliable, accounts of Native American cannibalism. However, this image is indicative of much more. It is reflective of the crucial debate that was beginning to rage in the high councils of Spain and elsewhere in Europe about the true nature of the Indians. Who were they, and why did the Bible not account for them? Were they descendants of a lost tribe or the children of the Devil? If the former, they were children of God, had souls, and could be Christianized, as Bartolomé de Las Casas, their first great champion, a Dominican priest and a companion of Columbus (1484–1576), was arguing. In 1542, then Bishop Las Casas wrote defensively of the Indians:

God made all the peoples of this area, many and varied as they are, as open and as innocent as can be imagined. The simplest people in the world—unassuming, long suffering, unassertive, and submissive—they are without malice or guile, and are utterly faithful and obedient both to their own native lords and to the Spaniards in whose service they now find themselves. Never quarrelsome or belligerent or boisterous, they harbour no grudges and do not seek to settle old scores; indeed, the notions of revenge, rancour, and hatred are quite foreign to them. At the same time they are among the least robust of human beings: their delicate constitutions make them unable to withstand hard work or suffering and render them liable to succumb to almost any illness, no matter how mild. Even the common people are no

The brave old Hendrick the great SACHEM or Chief of the Mohawk Indians
one of the Six Nations now in Alliance with & Subject to the King of Great Britain
Sold by Cha: Bakewell opposite Birchin Lane in Cornhill.

"The Brave Old Hendrick" (c. 1740). John Carter Brown Library, Brown University.

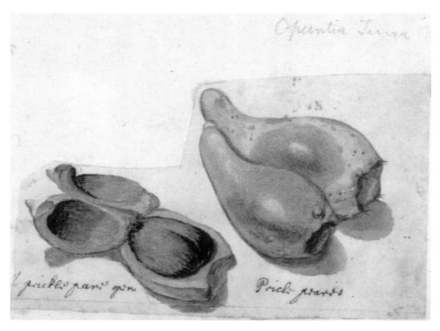

Hans Sloane, "Prickly Pear Fruit" (1707–1725). John Carter Brown Library,
Brown University.

Mark Catesby, "Bison Americanus and Rose Acacia" (1771). John Carter Brown Library, Brown University.

Maria Sybilla Merian, "Alligator and Snake" (1719). John Carter Brown Library, Brown University.

Maria Sybilla Merian, "Pineapple" (1719). John Carter Brown Library, Brown University.

tougher than princes or than other Europeans born with a silver spoon in their mouths and who spend their lives shielded from the rigours of the outside world. They are also among the poorest people on the face of the earth; they own next to nothing and have no urge to acquire material possessions. As a result they are neither ambitious nor greedy, and are totally uninterested in worldly power. Their diet is every bit as poor and as monotonous, in quantity and in kind, as that enjoyed by the Desert Fathers. Most of them go naked, save a loincloth to cover their modesty; at best they may wrap themselves in a piece of cotton material a yard or two square. Most sleep on matting, although a few possess a kind of hanging net, known in the language of Hispaniola as a hammock. They are innocent and pure in mind and have a lively intelligence, all of which makes them particularly receptive to learning and understanding the truths of our Catholic faith and to being instructed in virtue; indeed, God has invested them with fewer impediments in this regard than any other people on earth. Once they begin to learn of the Christian faith they become so keen to know more, to receive the Sacraments, and to worship God, that the missionaries who instruct them do truly have to be men of exceptional patience and forbearance; and over the years I have time and again met Spanish laymen who have been so struck by the natural goodness that shines through these people that they frequently can be heard to exclaim: "These would be the most blessed people on earth if only they were given the chance to convert to Christianity."[20]

On the other hand, if they were the Devil's spawn, then they had no souls and could be much more easily enslaved to labor in the mines and fields of the New World.[21] Was this picture of the Indians included on this map merely to fill in space and/or to entertain its user, or did its author have a definite point of view about them to convey? Such a determination perhaps does not matter since the impact of this vignette on the map's European audience was in all probability negative.

Half a century later, in Abraham Ortelius's *Theatrum Orbis Terrarum,* the picture of the Americas had changed substantially. Ortelius (1527–1598) was a cartographer who lived and worked in Antwerp in the Netherlands, and his *Theatrum,* generally recognized as the first atlas, marked a sharp departure from Waldseemüller.[22] The *Theatrum* first appeared in 1570 and ran through numerous editions in Latin, Spanish, French, German, and English until c. 1640. By book-publishing-industry standards of the day, this amazing volume was an instant best-seller and remained so through the middle of the seventeenth century.[23]

As Ortelius flourished in Antwerp, the Holy Roman Emperor Charles V abdicated in 1555 and ceded his homeland, the Burgundian Habsburg king-

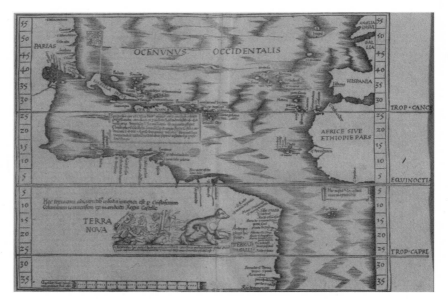

Martin Waldseemüller, "Tabula Terra Nova" (1522). Courtesy of the Virginia Garrett Cartographic History Library, University of Texas–Arlington.

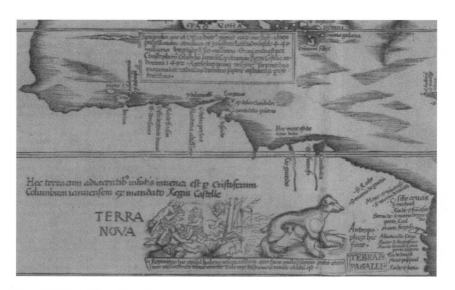

Detail, "Tabula Terra Nova."

dom of the Netherlands, to his son, King Philip II of Spain. The region was greedily incorporated into the emerging Spanish Empire, which also included rapidly increasing territories in the Americas and Asia and an important international trade center in which Ortelius then found himself. Thus, he was able to readily gather information for the *Theatrum* from Iberian and other navigators and merchants as well as scholars, other geographers such as his good friend Mercator, and the like.

The only real New World map in the 1570 first edition of the *Theatrum* is "Americae Sive Novi Orbis, Nova Descriptio," engraved by Frans Hogenberg, but parts of the Americas appear on six other maps, and others were soon added in succeeding editions. "Americae" appeared at the opening of the major colonization of the Americas and is rightly regarded as the "great Renaissance summation of the discovery and exploration of the New World."[24] It presents a significant attempt to synthesize information from other maps and the colored accounts of the conquests of Cortés in Mexico and Francisco Pizzaro in Peru in 1532 and the entradas of Pánfilo de Narváez, Núñez Cabeza de Vaca, Fray Marcos de Niza, and Francisco Vásquez de Coronado from 1539 to 1542 and Hernando de Soto and Luis de Morosco from 1539 to 1543, among others,[25] and shows both North and South America. With regard to the developing picture of North America,

> To the north of the Spanish traverses, the continent was seen as opening up like a fan, the central ribs of which were formed by the estuaries of the great Missouri-Mississippi system. The principal source of this river network was believed to be in a range of high mountains (the Rockies?), described by various Indian attestants to be somewhere to the northwest of Quivira, near the Pacific shores and not too distant from Asia. The Cíbolan domains in turn were held to be a possible offshoot of India. Another mountain chain (the Appalachians?) was seen as coming in from the east at a latitude north of Quivira. Based on this continental view, cartographers for many years wrongly portrayed the Appalachian Mountains running more east to west than north to south. At its widest, the continent stretched more than one thousand miles (still only approximately one-third of its actual size) from the Atlantic near Iceland to the Pacific near China, with a passage connecting the two oceans somewhere in the North. The northwestern coast of America was separated from China by the fabled Straits of Anian. Eventually cartographers placed Quivira, the Tontonec of the Hopis, and other lands discovered by Coronado on the eastern shore of these straits and even made the straits themselves a Northwest Passage. And though this land had many wonders, it did not seem to contain Aztec and Inca-like civilizations and their readily appropriated wealth.[26]

The original copperplate for "Americae" was replaced probably due to wear in 1579, but little more than a few decorative ships changed. In the 1587 edition of the map they greatly increased in number from three to fifteen in the Pacific and from one to eleven in the Atlantic. While undoubtedly these additions were largely aesthetic, they may also have meant to signify the growing European presence in the New World.

The original distinctive yet incorrect 1570 "potato" shape of South America also changed dramatically in 1587. More detail appeared, especially in Central and South America, as did the number of Spanish place names, reminding us of the old imperialist axiom that "to name it and to map it is to claim it." Or as J. B. Harley has pointed out, "By creating the illusion of sameness [among the maps in the *Theatrum*], the map ["Americae"] made the New World easier to assimilate into the European consciousness. . . . But with its Latinized names and Dutch conventional signs the cast is largely European. The map increases the psychological distances between America and its Indian civilizations. As an act of cultural imperialism it performs an intellectual and political appropriation of the space of the New World."[27] As if to underscore this appropriation, in the 1587 version, the elegant title cartouche is now also draped with New World fruit and vegetables.[28]

In much the same fashion, eventually in the *Theatrum* were also to be found the first printed regional maps of the New World—"Hispaniae Novae sivae Magnae, Recens at Vera Descriptio, 1579," "Culiacanae, Americae Regionis, Descriptio," and "Hispaniolae, Cubae, Aliarumque Insularum Circumiacientium, Delineato" on the same page (1584) and "Peruviae Auriferae Regionis Typus," the landmark "La Florida," and "Guastecan Reg." on the same page (1584). Thus, for example, on the cartouches of these maps, New World fruit and vegetables, toucans or parrots, and what seem to be Aztec heads intermingle with more traditional European cherubs, lions, and other symbols. With his American maps in the new atlas format, Ortelius not only ordered the geography of the New World and greatly broadened the world for his viewers and readers but also set a standard for other cartographers for presenting the New World.[29]

Before passing beyond Ortelius and his *Theatrum*, a brief mention of the American imagery on his title page is in order. Crowned and enthroned at the top of the title box of course sits Europe as the ruler of the world. Asia is a richly dressed handmaiden to the left of the title, and Africa to the right is a half-naked, hotly radiant black female. Below the title, a wholly naked reclining woman, the first allegorical representation of the New World, is America. She is an Amazon warrior armed for the hunt, and she holds a severed head that again hints at cannibalism. To her right is an incomplete bust of another naked woman, the unexplored terra incognita of the rumored southern

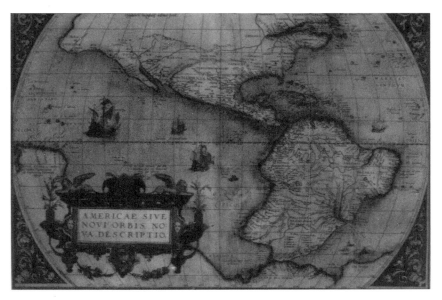

Abraham Ortelius, "Americae Sive Novi Orbis, Nova Descriptio" (1570). Courtesy of the Virginia Garrett Cartographic History Library, University of Texas–Arlington.

Ortelius, "Americae Sive Novi Orbis, Nova Descriptio" (1587). Courtesy of the Virginia Garrett Cartographic History Library, University of Texas–Arlington.

continent of Magellenica. The fire below her breasts relates to those observed by Magellan to the south as he first passed through the straits at the tip of South America in 1522 that still bear his name.[30]

More than a hundred years later, Herman Moll's large two-page, moderately famous "A New and Exact Map of the Dominions of the King of Great Britain on ye Continent of North America" from his great folio atlas, *The World Described,* not only shows the then current state of the nascent British Empire along the east coast of North America from Labrador and Newfoundland south to Carolina but also is an early example of a "booster map," encouraging British American colonization.[31] A master engraver of copper originally from Bremen, Moll (1654?–1732) created the first plates for this map in c. 1713 and on them emphasized the loss of most French fishing rights in Newfoundland to the British under the Treaty of Utrecht (1713) at the conclusion of the War of the Spanish Succession (Queen Anne's War). Likewise, far to the south, where British Carolina bordered on Spanish Florida, in a special inset Moll also indicated contemporary and projected British territorial gains at Spain's expense.

To further lure immigrants, the map depicts many of the rivers (e.g., the Potomac, James, and Rappahannock in Virginia) reaching inland from the sea apparently unimpeded, several of them from very good harbors such as Chesapeake Bay. Similarly, the map shows rather extensive references to roads, especially radiating outward from important cities such as Philadelphia, Boston, and New York. While Moll's imagery at the time was perhaps still somewhat visionary, he was describing what would become one of the real achievements of the British Colonies: their transportation and communication infrastructure.

Moll also played down the hazards of the wilderness and its native inhabitants. To the west of Pennsylvania, for example, there is abundant reference to the "Iroquois" of the Six Nation Confederacy, in which he stresses their "hearty friendship to ye English" against the French. He of course fails to mention the French allies among the not insignificant Huron Confederacy, who would play a critical role in the Seven Years War (French and Indian War) from 1756 to 1763.[32]

The promotional message of Moll's map is probably best summarized in its most famous aspect: the beaver inset at center right. In fact, over the centuries it has become the reason for this map's more popular designation as the "Beaver Map" by scholars and collectors. The scene is actually a composite of several images done almost thirty years earlier by Nicolas Guérard, an engraver for Nicolas de Fer,[33] but given his artistic talent and the widespread use and appreciation of his maps, Moll certainly was its popularizer. In this idyllic New World graphic vignette, the industrious beavers (especially with the

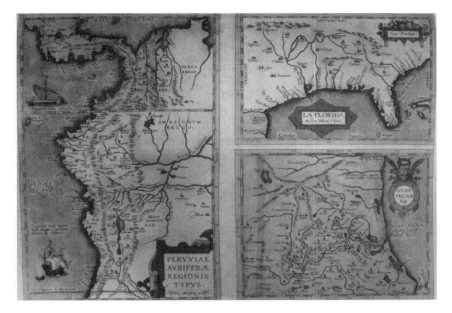

Ortelius, "La Florida" (1584). Courtesy of the Virginia Garrett Cartographic History Library, University of Texas–Arlington.

Herman Moll, "A New and Exact Map of the Dominions of the King of Great Britain on ye Continent of North America" (1715). Collection of Dennis Reinhartz and Judy Reinhartz.

development of the fur trade, the beaver was becoming emblematic of North America) are working harmoniously on a dam before a mighty waterfall, undoubtedly the powerful Niagara Falls. Its meaning for the viewer is clear: With the right outlook and effort and given its energy and promise, anything is possible in the New World.[34] In depicting the New World as an alien utopia, Moll too is here continuing in the by then well-established tradition begun by Columbus, Vespucci, the cartographer Peter Martyr, John Rastell (the adventurer brother-in-law of Sir Thomas More), and others.[35]

Nearer the end of the eighteenth century, during the later European Enlightenment, cartography like that of the French royal geographer Didier Robert de Vaugondy (1723–1786) and others had become even more widespread and more "scientific" (and therefore more authoritative) but not necessarily more accurate. For example, Vaugondy's composite "Carte de Californie" of 1772, created for the atlas of Denis Diderot's great *Encyclopédie* (1770–1779), the "ultimate" reference work, shows the part of the evolution of the contemporary state of geographic knowledge of Spanish Alta California. However, on the most modern map, Coronado's Quivira (actually at the big bend of the Arkansas River) was nevertheless shown northeast of Cape Fortuna near the Pacific Ocean, and the Seven Cities of Cíbola were located around an unnamed, nonexistent lake and along an equally nonexistent, unnamed river from the lake, leading to the Colorado River and into the Sea of Cortés.[36]

THE NEW PEOPLE

Beginning with the early images of Waldseemüller and others, the Indians and their folkways—like their lands—took on the characterization of perceptions of the Old World mind. Thus the Pawnee slave of the Tewa-speaking Pueblo Indians who led Coronado and his men to Quivira was dubbed the "Turk" because of his turbanlike headgear and *bigotes* (mustache).[37] While the cannibalism theme was a mainstay throughout the sixteenth century and into the seventeenth, other pictures of them appeared as well.

The manuscript "Plano del valle del rio de San Miguel, desde sus fuentes hasta San Francisco de Chamacuero" of 1580 in the *Archivo General des Indias* in Seville is typical of Spanish–Native American fusion cartography of the later sixteenth century coming out of Mexico.[38] The map was commissioned and probably supervised by the Spaniards but obviously drawn by Indians. Here they depicted themselves as more numerous than the Spanish and largely on the peripheries of early colonial life, engaged in mostly traditional activities such as hunting (e.g., Spanish cattle), gathering, and even warring with each other and the Spanish. Many of the Spanish are shown on horseback and armored, but all of the Indians are near naked and on foot. Both Indian and Spanish homes are depicted, some with Spanish place names. Various other features such as mountains, roads, and passes were also so labeled, perhaps by the Spanish supervisors of the cartography. Note the Indian portrayal of native fauna such as dogs, deer, and rabbits and flora such as prickly pear cactus, yucca, and probably cottonwood trees.

The Indians of Théodore de Bry (1528–1598), illustrating the various editions of *Grands et Petits Voyages* (Frankfort am Main, 1591), are generally larger and more naked and depict strange behaviors but are nevertheless physically European-like figures. In a scene from part two, Florida natives are showing reverence before French explorers in 1564 to a boundary marker left behind by an expedition two years earlier.[39] Additionally, in part two, Florida Indians are farming in nice straight rows. This pastoral sight easily brings to mind, for example, the masterful and very European *Gleaners* (1857) by Jean François Millet of almost two hundred years later.

A Fleming, born in Liège, de Bry never saw the New World or any of its diverse native population. His renditions of the Indians understandably were wholly inspired by the texts supplied to him to illustrate and/or publish, other accounts, and his imagination. His orientation therefore was primarily Old World. Similar Indian images occurred again on Capt. John Smith's map of "Virginia" (Oxford: Joseph Barnes, 1612). However, that is because, although Smith carried out some of the critical surveys for this map and was quite familiar with the Susquehannock and some other Virginia Indians, the English engraver of this map in Oxford again was not. The original for the Smith map's lone Indian figure, "A Weroan or Great Lord of Virginia," was by de Bry from Thomas Hariot's "A Brief and True Report on the New Found Land of Virginia," which was about the ill-fated Roanoke Colony, in de Bry's *India Occidentalis* (Frankfort am Main, 1590). It was based on firsthand accounts and sketches and was supposed to be a Secotan from the area of North Carolina. On the Smith map, the figure was transformed into a Susquehannock from several hundred miles to the north in present-day Virginia. This image was then at least a thirdhand account. Note also in the inset that Powhatan is holding court and exercising dominion over the Susquehannock in a very European fashion.[40]

Further in this vein, in the Library of Congress's elegant manuscript copy of José de Urrutia's 1769 map from the consequential 7,600 miles inspection of the presidios of the northern frontier of New Spain carried out by the marquis de Rubí from 1766 to 1768, the Hopi pueblos on their sacred mesas in present-day Arizona are shown as Moorish-Andalusian villages.[41] While in its content this map epitomizes the military scientific accuracy of the pro-

Théodore de Bry, "Indians Farming" (1591). John Carter Brown Library, Brown University.

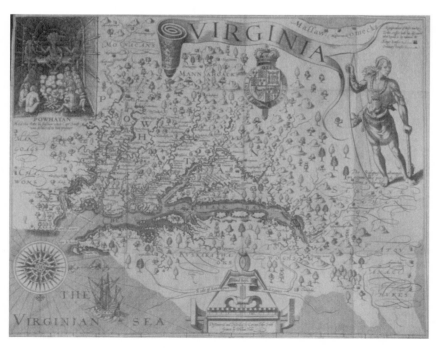

Capt. John Smith, "Virginia" (1619). John Carter Brown Library, Brown University.

duction of the Spanish Royal Corps of Engineers, in its decorative symbolization it is still partly illusional.

What's more, there are some amazing graphics depicting the actual transformation of New World natives into Old Worlders. In a "before and after" engraving from an early seventeenth-century Capuchin missionary history, two Brazilian coastal Indians who were brought to Paris in 1613 are shown at the time of their conversion to Christianity. At baptism, each one was given a Christian name, "François Carypyra" and "Louis Marie." To highlight the metamorphosis, Carypyra is shown still in indigenous regalia, including extensive body tattoos, while Marie has obviously completed the transition to a peaceful civilized Frenchman.[42]

A c. 1740 engraving from London, titled in part "The brave old Hendrick the great Sachem or Chief of the Mohawk Indians," demonstrates analogous processes at work. Hendrick, a leader of the League of Six Nations, had come to England as part of an allied Indian delegation in 1710 and stayed. Upon conversion to the Church of England, he became "Hendrick" and, by the time of this portrait, a proper Englishman. He died as a loyal ally of the British during the American Revolution at Lake George in 1775.[43]

By the time "Old Hendrick" had posed for his picture, Indians had come a long way in the European mentalité. Starting out as cannibals and even devils to be killed and enslaved, they had progressed to the status of human beings with souls ripe for conversion. In the eighteenth century, they were furthermore associated at times both with the revival of interest in the ancient Druids, especially among British intellectuals (some of whom were members of Moll's circle), and with the "noble savage" of the "state of nature" so pertinent to Enlightenment philosophy.[44] As we have seen, this entire incredible mental renovation, concerning a major expression of the New World, was aptly captured in the writings and especially the graphics of the Old World.

We are told that the Indians reacted with equal wonder during their earliest contacts with representatives of the Old World. The Aztecs saw the white Cortés astride his horse as one creature, a prophesied reincarnation of their principal deity, Quetzalcoatl. Intimidated by his ships, northern Indians initially saw Henry Hudson in a similar light. The Spanish horses apart from their riders astonished them almost as much, yet they did not achieve full mastery over them until after 1602. Moreover, the Native Americans were continuously amazed by Africans such as Estebanico, the slave who journeyed with Cabeza de Vaca and Fray Marcos de Niza; York, William Clark's slave, who accompanied him to the Pacific Ocean and back;[45] and even the "buffalo soldiers" of the late-nineteenth-century Western frontier experience in the United States. But unlike the Old World graphic and other sources

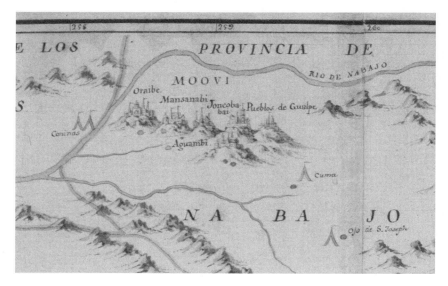

José de Urrutia, "Mapa que comprehende de la frontera de los dominos del rey en la America septentrional" (1769). Courtesy of the Geography and Map Division, Library of Congress.

Claude d'Abbeville, "François Carypyra." John Carter Brown Library, Brown University.

Claude d'Abbeville, "Louis Marie." John Carter Brown Library, Brown University.

alluded to earlier, the original New World sources recording these reactions are of the Indian oral tradition and/or were lost, only to be meagerly preserved secondarily in Old World or American reports.

NEW FLORA AND FAUNA

In the first centuries after the Columbian recontact, the accounts and pictures of unusual New World plants and animals were as abundant as those of New World peoples. Cabeza de Vaca first described the prickly pear cactus and the harvesting and eating of its "tuna" fruit in his *Relación*.[46] Coronado referred to the cacti as "thorny trees" when he encountered them on the otherwise featureless *llano estacado* ("staked plains") of the Texas Panhandle.[47] The British personal physician to the governor of Jamaica and botanist Hans Sloane (1660–1753) still called it the fruit of the "prickly pear-tree" when the latter painted it for his *Natural History of Jamaica* (1707–1725).[48]

Samuel de Champlain attested to sea dragons, Jacques Cartier called walruses "sea oxen," and the Spanish turned manatee into mermaids.[49] Cabeza de Vaca too first described the North American buffalo as "hunched-backed cows": "They have small horns like the cows of Morocco; the hair is very long and wooly like a rug. Some are tawny, others black. To my judgment the flesh is finer and fatter than those from here [Spain]."[50] Understandably therefore, never having seen buffalo but knowing of Cabeza de Vaca's and others' descriptions of them, Francisco López de Gómara naturally pictured one as a large, hairy, and humped cow in his *Primera y Segundo Parte dela Historia General de las Indias* (Zaragoza, 1553).[51] Thereafter, largely because of their reported vast herds, buffalo made quite an impression on Europeans, and even as late as the mid-eighteenth century, Moll and other distant cartographers were indicating buffalo as "beaves" on their North American maps.[52] In addition, notwithstanding the passage of time, the accumulation of reports, and his own firsthand observations, in the elegant watercolor of the "Bison Americanus and Rose Acacia" by Mark Catesby (1682–1749) from his monumental *Natural History of Carolina, Florida, & the Bahama Islands* (London, 1771), traces of the original Cabeza de Vaca account and Gómara graphic image interestingly linger.[53]

Important New World plants such as maize, potatoes, sweet potatoes, pineapples, and tobacco became well known to an increasing number of people on the eastern side of the Atlantic Basin through rather fine graphic renderings well before they were actually experienced. An early image of tobacco, "Nicotiana," was to be found in *Stirpium Adversaria Nova* by Petrus Peña and Matthias de l'Obel, printed in London in 1570 and 1571.[54] The first published picture of white potatoes, "Of Potatoes in Virginia," appeared in

Francisco López de Gómara, "Buffalo" (1553). John Carter Brown Library, Brown University.

John Gerard's *The Herball or General History of Plantes* (London, 1597). Gerard's depiction may have been based in part on specimens brought back to England by Sir Francis Drake from his Panamanian raids in 1585.[55] Early on, the English and Germans referred to potatoes as "earth [underground] apples" or "erdäpfel."

A decade later, a fine picture of Indian corn appeared in Giovanni Battista Ramusio's *Terzo Volume delle Navigationi et Viaggi* (Venice, 1606).[56] Referring to it as "Spanish Patatas," Sloane masterfully drew the sweet potato for his Jamaican natural history.[57] Columbus first came upon the pineapple on his second voyage to the New World in 1493, and, because of its unique taste, it then became quite popular. Maria Sybilla Merian (1647–1717) beautifully offered this example, surrounded by butterflies, caterpillars, and other insects (a primary interest), from her unaccompanied visit with her daughter to the Dutch colony of Surinam in South America in 1699, in her *Dissertatio de Generatione et Metamorphosibus Insectorium Surinamesium* (Amsterdam, 1719). Sloane admired her work greatly, and it appeared in Dutch, Latin, and French editions.

Merian was also fascinated by larger New World animal life, as exemplified by her spectacular portrayal of a South American alligator apparently protecting its newly hatching offspring against an intruding snake.[58] The armadillo was another creature that regularly caught the attention of early explorers. Francesco Redi's picture of a non-nine-banded South American "armadilho" appeared in his *Experimenta circa Res Diversas Naturales* (Amsterdam, 1675). Redi captured its ability, when threatened, to curl up into a ball for protection. He and others believed that the ground-up bones of its tail could act as a painkiller and cure deafness.[59] And in his *Natural History,* Catesby provided several stunning studies of the flamingo and various aspects of its rather odd anatomy.[60] With these and other wildlife representations (e.g., parrots), Catesby easily proved to be a significant prelude to the nineteenth-century achievement of the American-born (Haiti) Creole, John James Audubon (1785–1851).

CONCLUSIONS

One should bear in mind that, even with their true-to-life representations based on direct observations or even because of them, talented illustrators such as Catesby, Merian, and Sloane among others contributed greatly to the exoticism of the New World as observed in the Old mainly through maps and other graphics. The exotic is in large part a product of decontextualization.[61] So, for example, when Merian's wonderful pineapple was taken from its natural Surinam setting (i.e., a source of the exotic) into a Dutch burgher's home in Amsterdam (i.e., the ordinary) in the first half of the eighteenth century, the image and what it represented was recontextualized and in its alienness became exotic, perhaps much more so because of the artistic quality and authenticity of the representation.

Prior to the Columbian recontact, graphic imagery was rightfully acknowledged as more symbolic and artistic than realistic. This popular acceptance was to a degree reinforced by the effective use of printed graphic propaganda (Albrecht Dürer, the Cranachs, etc.) by both sides during the Protestant Revolution and succeeding religious wars in the sixteenth and seventeenth centuries. Therefore, the fruition of greater realism took time— time for the New World cultures, flora, and fauna to lose their strangeness in the awareness of the ever-less-distant Old World. In this regard, William H. McNeill astutely observed in 1992:

> Only when learned Europeans decided it was necessary for them to visit strange and distant parts in order to see things for themselves did reliably sifted and relatively complete information about animals and birds, together with geological studies of the New World become available. The voyage of Alexander von Humboldt, 1799–1803, followed by twenty years devoted to writing and publishing the new data he had gathered, constituted the first great landmark of this advance. Even more significant was the voyage of Charles Darwin on the *Beagle,* 1831–1837. Darwin needed a little more than

twenty years for digesting his observations before he published his famous book, *The Origin of Species,* in 1859, thus radically changing our notion about how God had created the natural world. Taken together, the work of Humboldt and Darwin constitute a remarkably clear example of how careful study of American data and prolonged effort to fit the novelties into existing knowledge induced a basic transformation of inherited understandings and a rather reluctant recognition of the universality of change.[62]

I would add to McNeill's insightful remarks on the achievement of this new realism the fact of the end of the Old World drive for empire in the New World and its replacement by American independence and autonomy from Europe extending from Chile to Canada in the nineteenth century. The name of Thomas Jefferson should therefore probably be added to those of Humboldt and Darwin as early instigators of the change.

Nevertheless, in the three centuries after Columbus and before the "rather reluctant recognition of the universality of change,"[63] which was founded upon new scientific attitudes and political arrangements, cartographers, engravers, and other graphic artists were largely the "defacto referees" of much of the New World information disseminated in the Old.

NOTES

1. Anthony Pagden, *European Encounters with the New World: From Renaissance to Romanticism* (New Haven and London: Yale University Press, 1993), p. 10.

2. William Brandon, *New Worlds for Old: Reports from the New World and Their Effect on the Development of Social Thought in Europe, 1500–1800* (Athens: Ohio University Press, 1986), p. 5.

3. Pagden, *European Encounters*, p. 3.

4. Peter Mason, *Infelicities: Representations of the Exotic* (Baltimore and London: Johns Hopkins University Press, 1998), pp. 1–2.

5. J. Wreford Watson, *Mental Images and Geographical Reality in the Settlement of North America* (Nottingham: University of Nottingham, Cust Foundation Lecture, 1967), pp. 3–4, 8.

6. Brandon, *New Worlds for Old,* p. 11.

7. Ibid., p. ix.

8. Ibid., pp. 9–10.

9. Watson, *Mental Images,* p. 18.

10. For example, after the Portuguese reached the kingdom of Benin on the west coast of Africa roughly in and around present-day Nigeria in the 1470s and allied with it in the slave trade, they and their technological achievements (e.g., gunpowder) were regularly portrayed in Benin bronze art. Paula Ben-Amos, *The Art of Benin* (London: Thames and Hudson, 1980), pp. 24–29, and *Royal Benin Art in the Collection of the National Museum of*

African Art (Washington, D.C.: Smithsonian Institution Press, c. 1987), pp. 54–55. In the latter work, an Edo musketeer is ably portrayed in mixed African and European regalia.

11. In his account of the Jamestown Colony in Virginia, Capt. John Smith relates how, in 1607, Powhatan, the chief of the Susquehannocks, drew a map for him expressing their worldview and accommodating England using meal, cornstalks, twigs, and a fire. The map is reconstructed and reproduced in Gerald A. Danzer, *Discovering World History through Maps and Views* (New York: Harper-Collins, 1992), S3.

12. Watson, *Mental Images*, pp. 3–4.

13. Glen McLaughlin and Nancy H. Mayo, *The Mapping of California as an Island: An Illustrated Checklist* (Saratoga: California Map Society, 1995).

14. Watson, *Mental Images*, p. 6.

15. Ibid., p. 9.

16. Kirkpatrick Sale, *The Conquest of Paradise: Christopher Columbus and the Columbian Legacy* (New York: Random House, 1990).

17. Watson, *Mental Images*, pp. 16–22.

18. Katherine R. Goodwin and Dennis Reinhartz, *Tabula Terra Nova* (Dallas: Somesuch Press, 1992).

19. John Bakeless, *The Eyes of Discovery: The Pageant of North America as Seen by the First Explorers* (Philadelphia: J. B. Lippincott, 1950), p. 39.

20. Bartolomé de las Casas, *A Short Account of the Destruction of the Indies* (London and New York: Penguin Books, 1992), pp. 10–12.

21. Goodwin and Reinhartz, *Tabula Terra Nova*.

22. Robert Sydney Martin and James C. Martin, *Contours of Discovery: Printed Maps Delineating the Texas and Southwestern Chapters in the Cartographic History of North America 1513–1930: A User's Guide* (Austin: Texas State Historical Association, 1982), p. 36.

23. Marcel van den Broecke, Peter van der Krogt, and Peter Meuer, eds., *Abraham Ortelius and the First Atlas: Essays Commemorating the Quadricentennial of His Death, 1598–1998* (Utrecht, the Netherlands: HES Publishers, 1998); Marcel van den Broecke, *Ortelius Atlas Maps: An Illustrated Guide* (Utrecht: HES Publishers, 1996); and Robert W. Karrow Jr., *Mapmakers of the Sixteenth Century and Their Maps: Biobibliographies of the Cartographers of Abraham Ortelius, 1570: Based on Leo Bagrow's A. Ortelii Catalogus Cartographorum* (Winetka, Ill.: Speculum Orbis Press, 1993).

24. Samuel Y. Edgerton Jr., "From Mental Matrix to *Mappamundi* to Christian Empire: The Heritage of Ptolemaic Cartography in the Renaissance," in *Art and Cartography: Six Historical Essays*, ed. David Woodward (Chicago and London: University of Chicago Press, 1987), pp. 42–43.

25. Dennis Reinhartz and Oakah L. Jones, "Hacia el Norte!: The Spanish Entradas into North America, 1513–1549," in *North American Exploration*, vol. 1, ed. John L. Allen (Lincoln: University of Nebraska Press, 1997), pp. 241–91ff.

26. Ibid., pp. 288–89. See also Dennis Reinhartz, "The Americas Revealed in the *Theatrum*," in *Abraham Ortelius and the First Atlas*, pp. 209–20, and Bernard DeVoto, *The Course of Empire* (Boston: Houghton Mifflin, 1952), pp. 52–57 and 61–63.

27. J. B. Harley, *Maps and the Columbian Encounter: A Interpretive Guide to a Traveling Exhibition* (Milwaukee: Golda Meir Library, University of Wisconsin, 1990), p. 113.

28. Reinhartz, "The Americas Revealed in the *Theatrum*," pp. 211–15.

29. Ibid., pp. 215–19.

30. Rodney Shirley, "The Title Pages of the *Theatrum* and *Parergon*," in *Abraham Ortelius and the First Atlas,* pp. 161–63.

31. Herman Moll, *The World Described* (London: 1709, 1717?, 1720?, 1726, 1728, 1730?, 1740?, 1754?; Dublin: 1730, 1741).

32. Dennis Reinhartz, *The Cartographer and the Literati: Herman Moll and His Intellectual Circle* (Lewiston, N.Y.: Edwin Mellen Press, 1997), pp. 131–46.

33. Edward H. Dahl, "The Original Beaver Map: De Fer's 1698 Wall Map of America," *Map Collector* (Dec., 1984): 22–26.

34. Reinhartz, *Cartographer and the Literati,* p. 37.

35. Brandon, *New Worlds for Old,* pp. 5–19.

36. Dennis Reinhartz, "*Legado:* The Information of the Entradas Portrayed through the Early Nineteenth Century," in *The Mapping of the Entradas into the Greater Southwest,* ed. Dennis Reinhartz and Gerald D. Saxon (Norman: University of Oklahoma Press, 1998), pp. 105, 140. Also see Mary Sponberg Pedley, *Bel et utile: The Work of Robert de Vaugondy Family of Mapmakers* (Tring, Herts, UK: Map Collector Publications, 1992).

37. Bakeless, *Eyes of Discovery,* p. 40.

38. Jacobo Stuart Fitz-James y Falcó, duque de Alba, *Mapas Españoles de America, siglos XV–XVII* (Madrid: Alba, 1951). My thanks to Gary Spurr, archivist at the University of Texas–Arlington, for bringing this map to my attention. See also Barbara E. Mundy, *The Mapping of New Spain: Indigenous Cartography and the Maps of the Relaciones Geográficas* (Chicago: University of Chicago Press, 1996).

39. Susan Danforth, *Encountering the New World 1493 to 1800: Catalogue of an Exhibition* (Providence: John Carter Brown Library, 1991), p. 36.

40. Laurie Glover, *The John Smith Map of Virginia: Derivations and Derivatives,* Newberry Library slide set no. 24 (Chicago: Newberry Library, 1997), pp. 1–20.

41. José de Urrutia, "Mapa, que comprende la frontera de los dominios del rey en la América septentrional" (1769), manuscript pen-and-ink and watercolor map, four pages, Library of Congress G4110 1769.U7 TIL Vault Map Collection, Geography and Map Division.

42. Claude d' Abbeville, *Historie de la Mission des Pères Capuchins en l'Iisle de Maragnan* (Paris, 1614). See also Danforth, *Encountering the New World,* p. 21.

43. Danforth, *Encountering the New World,* p. 49.

44. Reinhartz, *Cartographer and the Literati,* pp. 97–111.

45. Bakeless, *Eyes of Discovery,* pp. 71, 235–37.

46. *Castaways: The Narrative of Alvar Núñez Cabeza de Vaca,* ed. Enrique Pupo-Walker and trans. Frances M. López-Morillas (Berkeley: University of California Press, 1993), pp. 55–56.

47. Bakeless, *Eyes of Discovery,* p. 77.

48. Tony Rice, *Voyages of Discovery: Three Centuries of Natural History Exploration* (New York: Clarkson Potter, 1999), p. 55.

49. Danforth, *Encountering the New World,* pp. 6, 29.

50. *Castaways,* p. 63. Also see Bakeless, *Eyes of Discovery,* pp. 44, 107.

51. Danforth, *Encountering the New World,* p. 29.

52. For example, see Herman Moll, "A Map of the North Parts of America Claimed by France," in *The World Described* (London: 1717).

53. Amy R. W. Meyers and Margaret Beck Pritchard, *Empire's Nature: Mark Catesby's New World Vision* (Chapel Hill and London: University of North Carolina Press, 1998), p. 214.

54. Danforth, *Encountering the New World*, p. 74.

55. Ibid., p. 28.

56. Ibid.

57. Rice, *Voyages of Discovery*, p. 55.

58. Ibid., pp. 90–119. See also Danforth, *Encountering the New World*, pp. 22–23.

59. See Danforth, *Encountering the New World*, p. 29.

60. See Meyers and Pritchard, *Empire's Nature*, p. 58.

61. Mason, *Infelicities*, p. 3.

62. William H. McNeill, "Introduction," in Danforth, *Encountering the New World*, p. xx. Also see *Encountering the New World, 1493–1800* (Providence: John Carter Brown Library, 1992), VHS videotape, 15 min.

63. McNeill, "Introduction," p. xx.

DAVID BUISSERET

Urbanization in the Old World and in the New

THE ORIGIN OF THE FORMATION of towns goes back far into history, and its study would take us progressively eastward, from Asia Minor into Assyria, and from there into China. In this chapter, though, we are trying to catch the process of urbanization at a late stage, when large numbers of Europeans crossed the Atlantic Ocean into the Americas, bringing with them well-developed ideas of what towns should look like. The Africans who came also had concepts of towns, no doubt, but had little chance to put their ideas into practice.

To oversimplify, early modern Europeans had developed four main types of urban form: the "organic" town, the rectangular town, the "Renaissance" town, and the fortified town. The first of these was by far the most common, as will be evident to anyone leafing through the three volumes of town views produced by Georg Braun and Franz Hogenberg toward the end of the sixteenth century.[1] All over Europe, from the Atlantic eastward to the Elbe River, and from Scotland south to Sicily, these "organic" towns had emerged in response to the local terrain and road patterns. Thus many grew up at river crossings or where convenient passes emerged from hills, and their streets generally led out from a central area toward neighboring towns.

Cambridge (figure 1) is a good example of an organic city. It emerged at a point where the River Cam was easily bridged and where water mills could easily be constructed. One road led out westward to Huntington (bottom left), another east to Newmarket (top), and another south to Trumpington (right); within the town, these roads wandered into a central area, with lesser roads leading off them. There was no way out to the north (top left) because that way lay the inhospitable, or at any rate trackless, fens. The town was roughly divided by parishes, marked by churches, but it had absolutely no monumental feel. Such architectural distinction as it possessed came from the individual buildings of many colleges, often sited alongside the river (across the bottom, from right to left). It did have a castle, bottom left, but this played little part in the life of the town, which revolved around the life of the colleges. Just as Cambridge was a collegiate town, so other towns might be primarily for local markets, longer-distance trade, or industry; their common feature was that they had developed organically, without apparent planning. A great many have survived more or less intact into the twenty-first century in spite of bombing and economic development. Thus it is still possible to navigate the center of many western European towns, using the work of Braun and Hogenberg as a guide.

The rectangular town had different origins, and these were often military.[2] Curiously enough, Rome itself was and is highly irregular in design, but in their conquered provinces the Romans often founded towns—derived from military camps—whose chief feature was two main crossing streets, the *via principalis* from north to south and the *via decumana* from east to west. With this great cross thus established, further north-south and east-west streets could be added in each of the quarters. Originally these streets housed the elements of a Roman military camp, disposed in a common pattern, but as time went by they became the site of a variety of private dwellings. During the European Middle Ages, quadrilateral cities were sometimes erected on virgin sites, and one of the most famous of these was at Aigues-Mortes in southern France, which Saint Louis used as the base for the organization of a crusade. A late but very striking example of this kind of town is the one established at Santa Fé in Spain in 1492 (figure 2). It differs crucially from the Roman towns in that it has no *via principalis;* here the great east-west street leads to a central square, and the pattern is rigorously maintained out to the edge of the central area. Often, of course, Roman origins have been almost completely overlaid by later accretions. Thus Paris once possessed its great north-south and east-west crossing streets, but they can now be perceived only with great difficulty, buried in the street pattern of the modern metropolis.[3]

The "Renaissance" towns owed something to both Greek and Roman predecessors, but they also had a monumental quality usually absent from cities with strictly military origins. London, for instance, had been an organic city that grew up at a crossing on the River Thames as a series of small towns or villages, with Whitehall for the king's court, Westminster for the ecclesiastics, Clerkenwell for the merchants, and so forth. When a good deal of this incoherent growth had been destroyed by the great fire of 1666, Sir Christopher Wren suggested a plan that would have tied the different parts of the city together, offering magnificent vistas and views of the great churches and palaces (figure 3). This plan, proposed to the newly restored Charles II, was

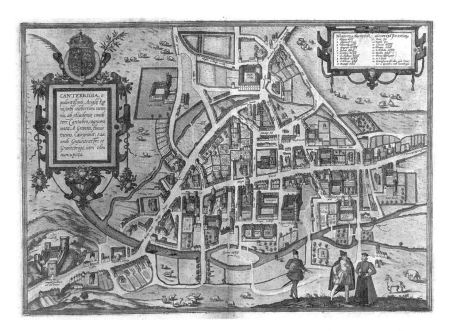

FIGURE 1. Plan of Cambridge, England, from George Braun and Franz Hogenberg, *Civitates Orbis Terrarum* (Cologne, 1595–1617). This copper engraving, derived from an unknown manuscript, gives a good impression of a little town of the organic type, with its streets and lanes irregularly wandering toward the "market hill" at the center of the town. Courtesy of the Newberry Library, Chicago.

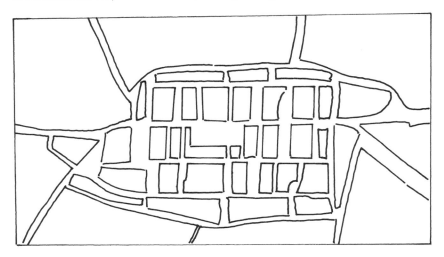

FIGURE 2. Sketch plan of the streets of Santa Fé, Spain. This sketch is adapted from an aerial photograph of the town taken in about 1958. The plan of the streets shows an early modern town before it has expanded much out of its original rectangular plan. Orange groves still hem it in, beyond the long-established street pattern.

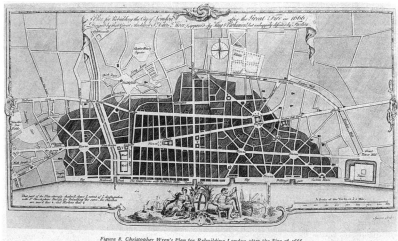

Figure 8. Christopher Wren's Plan for Rebuilding London after the Fire of 1666

FIGURE 3. Sir Christopher Wren's plan for the rebuilding of London after the great fire of 1666. This imaginative plan shows the north side of the river Thames, with the White Tower on the extreme right. Had the plan been put into effect, it would have transformed London into something like contemporary Turin, where the dukes of Savoy succeeded in transforming their medieval capital city into a good example of the triumphalist city. Courtesy of the Newberry Library, Chicago.

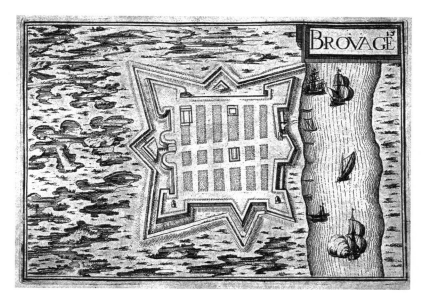

FIGURE 4. Nicolas Tassin's plan of Brouage from his *Plans et Profils* (Paris, 1634). This plan of Brouage, which was important as a great center for the production of salt, shows an example of a fortified town constructed in accordance with the plans of the sixteenth-century Italian engineers, with its bastioned fortifications and strict internal street design. Brouage conforms almost exactly to this plan today. Courtesy of the Newberry Library, Chicago.

typical of many of the period in that it celebrated the power of the sovereign and indeed required his support for it to be carried out. Visitors to the London proposed by Wren would be in no doubt that this was the capital of a great monarchy, whose majesty was here celebrated in architectural form. Similar plans could be found all over Europe, from Madrid in the west to Saint Petersburg in the east, with a particularly telling example at Turin.[4] All of these cities originated from the Renaissance idea of the state as a work of art, whose capital would be symbolically worthy of the monarch.

Fourth, there were the military cities, planned expressly to repulse assault by the newly efficient guns of the sixteenth century. Sometimes, as at Antwerp, a great new bastioned "trace" would be thrown around an existing city. But often, as at Brouage (figure 4), a completely new town would be built within the new walls. In this case the street layout is strictly rectangular (as it remains to this day), but it could sometimes be radial, as in many Renaissance cities; this might speed access to the all-important defensive artillery on the bastions. Probably the most prominent feature of these early modern military cities is their long, thick line of fortifications (the "bastioned trace"), which continued to influence the plans of many of these towns long after their military significance had diminished. At Paris, for instance, the great circular line of fortifications became the line of the "external boulevards," which now carry a great volume of traffic, and at Vienna they became the noted "Ring" and the site of many of Vienna's nineteenth-century cultural institutions.

ORGANIC NEW WORLD TOWNS

There were, then, four main possibilities for town shapes in early modern Europe. Each of these four may be found in most parts of the New World. The earliest "English" town, for instance, was probably Saint John's in Newfoundland, lying alongside the wonderful fjord that offered shelter to its fishing fleet. Here the houses were allowed to grow up pell-mell along the narrow strip of land adjacent to the harbor. These wooden shacks were vulnerable to fire, and several disastrous conflagrations of the seventeenth and eighteenth centuries eventually led to a certain measure of control over the siting of houses. By and large, though, the visitor to Saint John's can even today see the incoherent origin of its streets in the paths that connected one group of fishing huts to another.

The French towns on the St. Lawrence River, built in the early years of the seventeenth century, were less irregular in plan. Québec, Montréal, and Trois Rivières all had a certain element of regularity, often imposed by the site. The heart of Montréal, for instance, lay in a narrow strip alongside the river (figure 5). Here there was a main street, but the side streets joined it at a variety of angles, and much space was left for gardens. The whole area lay on land controlled by the seminary of Saint Sulpice, so that until the coming of the royal engineer, Chaussegros de Léry, in the early eighteenth century,[5] it was hard to impose on the growing city any plan based upon a systematic street system that was linked with the fortifications. From the start of the settlement, this lack of planning was probably the result of the existence of two great authorities, the church and state, neither of which was clearly dominant.

There was even less planning in the early settlement of the two great cities to the south, Boston and New York. Around 1630, members of the Massachusetts Bay Company, under the direction of Gov. John Winthrop, had settled on the Shawmut peninsula, hard by a fine bay that provided shelter from Atlantic gales. Here a little town arose very much as settlements had arisen in medieval England, with houses following convenient roads along the peninsula (figure 6). The names of the streets and buildings testify to their informal origin: Great Street, the Neck, Town House, Dock Square, and so forth. Clearly, the inhabitants of early Boston felt no need either to respect the ideals of some sort of urbanism or, in the naming of the streets, to flatter some distant lord proprietor. In these early days, everything developed in a way that is best called "organic." Later on, the growth of the town brought about many changes; the bays were filled, the hills fortified, and a rectangular street pattern was established. But the origins were purely rustic, as might be expected from a group of people independent of, and indeed hostile to, close state control.[6]

Much the same was true of New York, whose site on the tip of Manhattan Island was chosen around 1625 by a group of Dutch settlers. Here they wanted to establish the headquarters of the Dutch West India Company, with a little town under the protection of the great fortress designed by Cryn Frederiksen. The growing village generally followed the contours of the gently curving peninsula, whose northern extremity was closed off by a palisade along what would one day be Wall Street. By 1660, there were about 300 houses, and by 1672, after the town had passed to the English in 1664, nearly 500 had been built. However, for a century after this time, the development of New York continued to be irregular, and it was not until after the Revolutionary War that a checkerboard system began to be systematically followed.[7]

Most of the other great eastern cities—Philadelphia, Savannah, Charleston, and so on—followed a more regular pattern. Interestingly, the early cities of the English West Indies closely resembled the pattern of Boston and New York. At Port Royal in Jamaica, for instance, the English had, after 1655, allowed a town to develop on the hitherto empty site of the Spanish *cayo de*

FIGURE 5. Gaspard Chaussegros de Léry's 1724 plan of Montréal, Canada. This elegant plan, the work of a French royal engineer, brings out the way in which French urban foundations were regulated by the needs of church and state. The key, or "Renvoy," lists only religious and military institutions, all enclosed within the bastioned fortifications. Courtesy of the Newberry Library, Chicago.

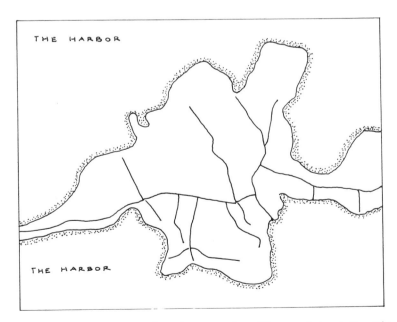

FIGURE 6. Sketch-map to show the street plan of Boston at about 1640. This sketch, copied from a contemporary plan, shows how irregularly the streets of this English town developed. Some streets led to the water's edge, while others gave access to the fields that surrounded the town. All had developed without the benefit of any central plan.

carena, or careening cay.[8] During the later seventeenth century, Port Royal developed at much the same rate as Boston, though its merchants were somewhat richer. The town itself grew along both shores of a peninsula, rather as New York was doing, until, by 1690, it had perhaps six thousand inhabitants. By then the little town was surrounded by six or seven great forts, but these had sprung up as they were needed and had not determined the line of streets in the town, which had simply expanded as economic possibilities allowed. Alas, in 1692, Port Royal was largely destroyed by an earthquake, and its survivors established a new town across the waters of Kingston Harbour. As we shall see, this town would be very differently planned from the organic Port Royal.

The other great town in the seventeenth-century British Caribbean was Bridgetown, in Barbados. This settlement had begun developing around 1630 as the major port for an increasingly important sugar-exporting island, and it was famous from the start for its incoherent plan. Built around the site known as "Indian Bridge," it had developed in response to the merchants' need for warehouses to stock their exports of sugar and imports of foodstuffs and dry goods. By 1680, Bridgetown had about three thousand inhabitants, all crowded into streets that boasted both Dutch- and English-style townhouses. Of course, such a city proved highly vulnerable to fire and suffered as well from hurricanes. Even today, however, visitors to central Bridgetown can plainly discern the original organic city on each side of Indian Bridge.[9]

RECTANGULAR TOWNS IN THE NEW WORLD

In the New World, quadrilateral cities were more numerous, and some indigenous examples of them arose in Central and South America. Nevertheless, by far the greatest number of such cities were found among the two hundred or so founded by the Spaniards during the sixteenth century. From the start, the new settlers seem to have adopted the checkerboard, even without the royal edicts that enjoined this practice in 1523 and even more fully in 1573.[10] At Santo Domingo (now the capital city of the Dominican Republic), for instance, the streets were laid out in this way around 1500, establishing as well a *plaza mayor* (main square) with a cathedral and a governor's house. A little later, Havana in Cuba followed the same example, as did San Juan in Puerto Rico in 1521 and Cartagena in 1533. These were towns founded from the ground up, though at Mexico City there seems to have been an Aztecan rectangular city that the Spaniards captured.[11] It has never been entirely clear why they, unlike the English and French, were so systematic in their early town plans, though historians have pointed not only to some peninsular royal foundations (for instance, Santa Fé, figure 2) but also to the prescriptions of Renaissance architects such as Alberti and the advice of various the-

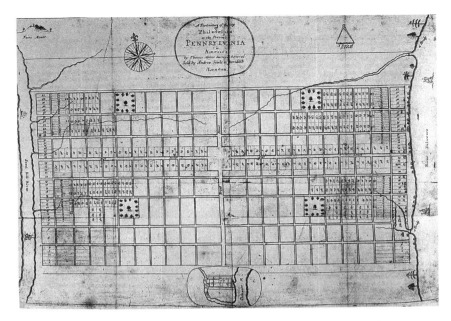

FIGURE 7. Thomas Holmes, *A Portraiture of the City of Philadelphia* (London, 1682). This engraving shows the very large area mapped out for the new city of Philadelphia, between the rivers Delaware (on the right) and Schuylkill (on the left). It would be many years before this huge space was completely filled up, but the streets of modern Philadelphia still retain the mark of their original plan. Courtesy of the Newberry Library, Chicago.

ologians. At first these quadrilateral towns lacked walls, though after the advent of English, French, and Dutch pirates in the 1580s, the great coastal towns all acquired powerful bastioned traces.[12]

An irregular form, as we have seen, was characteristic of the earliest French and English towns. However, as time went by, inspired no doubt by the great cities of the Hispanic world, the English began laying their towns out in the same way. One of the earliest was Philadelphia, established about 1681 on the peninsula between the Delaware and Schuylkill Rivers by William Penn (figure 7). The actual plan was the work of Thomas Holmes, following the ideas of Penn, who wished for a large city with lots of even size and space left for squares and churches. There was to be no fortification because these Quaker colonists would live in peace with the adjacent Indians. Nor would the streets be named after aristocratic English settlers; Penn reversed this practice in favor of homely names such as Pine, Spruce, Walnut, and Chestnut Streets. The area he set aside, more than two miles broad and more than a mile deep, would take many years to fill. Nevertheless, Penn's example led to the founding of many other quadrilateral towns in Pennsylvania.[13]

Fifty years later, Savannah was established on a more modest scale but with equal quadrilateral rigor (figure 8). In 1733, James Oglethorpe set out its plan, with twelve streets and six squares, and this model was widely followed in the rest of Georgia. Figure 8 shows how ships arrived at the Savannah River with the materials needed to build the town. Places were reserved for Anglican, Quaker, and Lutheran churches, as well as for prisons, markets, the governor's palace, and so forth; perhaps Savannah, of all the Anglo settlements, most closely followed the prescriptions of the town's Spanish founders.

Farther to the south, as we have seen, the great Caribbean Anglo centers were Port Royal in Jamaica and Bridgetown in Barbados. When Port Royal was largely destroyed by an earthquake in 1692, many of the survivors fled across the harbor to the site of what would be known as "Kingston." Here John Goffe laid out a new town, as rigorously quadrilateral as Port Royal had been organic (figure 9). The French plan shows us the way in which the new town was rapidly built, with a parade ground in the center, by the Anglican church, but with no fortifications, for control of the island depended upon control of the sea.

Port Royal, an unusual example of religious coexistence, had had Anglican, Catholic, and Nonconformist churches, as well as a synagogue, but Kingston reflected a new age of Anglican conformity. The streets were mostly named after the island's prominent citizens—Bernard, Beeston, Beckford, and so on—and still remain much as they were laid out three hundred years ago. In the rest of the island, the dozen or so parish capitals had mostly been arranged in the later seventeenth century using a quadrilateral system modified by the local terrain. In the French West Indies, the towns were generally of the fortified type. When these were not needed, however, as at Cayes and Le Cap in Saint-Domingue (now Haiti), they were rigidly quadrilateral, and this was in part due to the abundance of flat land on the island's ample plains.

The towns that we have so far been considering in the United States were all constructed before the land ordinance of 1785. After this time, a quadrilateral network of townships slowly spread across the country, beginning at the Seven Ranges of Ohio, by the Ohio River. This network of squares, six miles by six miles, slowly took in the whole country north of Texas, reaching most of Illinois, for instance, in the 1830s and the Far West much later in the nineteenth century. Once this formidable grid was in place, it was easiest for cities simply to conform to it in their planning since the roads tended to follow its north-south and east-west lines anyway. When a city lay alongside a lake, river, or railroad that was diagonally oriented, the tendency was for the streets to follow that orientation for some distance. Sooner or later, however, as the town grew, this diagonal orientation had to come to terms with the north-south, east-west grid, giving rise to the problems of adjustment that can still

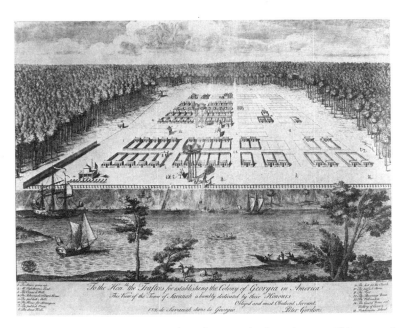

FIGURE 8. James Oglethorpe's plan of Savannah, Georgia, 1734. This engraving, which may owe something to the imagination, shows not only how supplies reached the new town, from ships moored below the high cliff, but also how the pine forests hemmed in these early southern towns—true cities in the wilderness. Courtesy of the Newberry Library, Chicago.

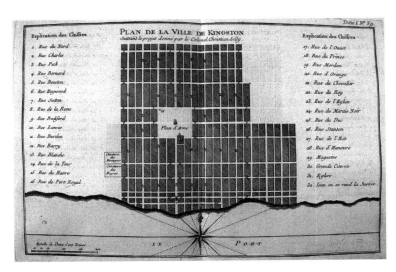

FIGURE 9. J.-B. Bellin's plan of Kingston, Jamaica, from his *Le Petit Atlas Maritime*, 5 vols. (Paris, 1764). This French engraving no doubt derives from some English original and catches the rectangular nature of the newly planned city. As time went by, the strict pattern of the historic central area was surrounded by a less formal street pattern, but the original core is still easily recognizable. Courtesy of the Newberry Library, Chicago.

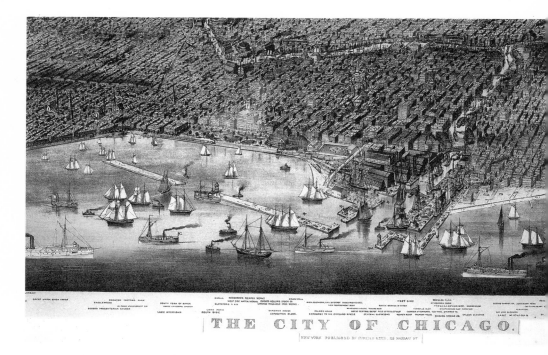

THE CITY OF CHICAGO.

NEW YORK PUBLISHED BY CURRIER & IVES, 115 NASSAU ST

FIGURE 10. Detail from *The City of Chicago* by Currier and Ives (New York, 1874). Currier and Ives have caught an image of Chicago in its frenzied stage of westward expansion, when the cardinally oriented streets seemed to be stretching forever westward into the empty prairie. North is to the right. Courtesy the Newberry Library, Chicago.

be felt by frustrated drivers in many U.S. city centers that developed in the nineteenth century.

Chicago, conveniently located along the almost perfectly north-south oriented Lake Michigan, is a good example of the way in which the land ordinance virtually dictated early development. Figure 10, oriented westward, shows the way in which, by 1892, the great city had simply expanded in that direction, using the shoreline of Lake Michigan (south to the left, north to the right) as its baseline. In the process, it jumped over the Chicago River, whose north and south branches may be seen, as if it were not there, eventually constituting an urban landscape of stunning monotony from which attempts at escape soon occurred. Many other cities went the same way, for the influence of the township-and-range grids was inescapable.

Our third category, the Renaissance, or "aesthetic" town, can be found only in regions apparently secure from military assault and consequently needing no fortifications. The most famous example is Washington itself, though here the military calculation proved faulty. After prolonged negotiations involving General Washington and Thomas Jefferson, a site was chosen, and the preliminary work entrusted to Maj. Pierre-Charles L'Enfant, a Frenchman who had served in the Revolutionary War and who in France had known both Versailles and the great monuments of Paris—the Tuileries, the Place de la Concorde, and the beginnings of the Avenue des Champs-Elysées.[14] L'Enfant produced a plan that is best envisaged from the version published by Ellicott in 1792 (figure 11). On the tongue of land formed by the Potomac River and its eastern branch, L'Enfant foresaw a huge city that would utilize the township-and-range system and at the same time incorporate the features that he knew well from Paris: the monumental squares, their diagonal links and vistas, the use of water, and so forth. This plan must have seemed absolutely quixotic at the time, and it took many years for the vacant lots to be filled. Nevertheless, L'Enfant's vision eventually informed a city of remarkable elegance and majesty, combining European and American elements in a masterful synthesis.

Washington's plan was fairly widely imitated, as John Reps sets out in a chapter called "Boulevard Baroque and Diagonal Designs."[15] Detroit and Sandusky developed particularly striking examples of this type of plan. However, there was another way to relieve the tedium of the endlessly repeated grid, and this was the means particularly developed by the landscape architect Frederick Law Olmsted.[16] He had worked at Central Park in New York during the 1850s and in the mid-1860s at the new campus of the University of California–Berkeley. In the late 1860s, he turned his attention to Riverside, a suburb about nine miles west of central Chicago. This area might have been covered by the apparently endless grid, whose beginnings are shown in figure 10. But Olmsted was alert to the need to produce town plans that somewhat respected the local topography, as those of historic European towns seemed to do, and so for Riverside he devised a plan that conformed with the gentle rolling of the land next to the river (figure 12). The house lots were varied in size and orientation, and the roads curved gently through the suburb, meeting at the railroad line, which formed the settlement's economic basis. Riverside was a great aesthetic success and remains largely unchanged to this day.[17]

Thirty years or so later, central Chicago was the site of a major urban experiment, which consciously called upon the experience of a wide variety of cities in the Old World and in the New. It began when Daniel Burnham led a

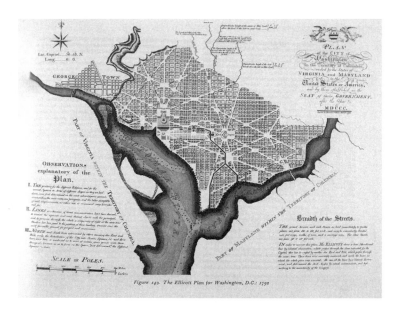

Figure 149. The Ellicott Plan for Washington, D.C.: 1792

FIGURE 11. Andrew Ellicott, *Plan of the City of Washington* (Philadelphia, 1792). This engraving shows the result of superimposing a baroque city plan on an "American" rectangular city. In spite of some very clumsy street junctions, the plan offered splendid vistas and was a remarkable forecast of developments that took many years to complete. Courtesy of the Newberry Library, Chicago.

FIGURE 12. Riverside Improvement Company, *General Plan of Riverside* (1869). This promotional map reveals the impatience of the founders of the suburb with the rectangular street pattern, by which they were soon surrounded on all sides. They wanted to show that a new community, many of whose leaders are shown, could live in some conformity with natural features like the river. Courtesy of the Newberry Library, Chicago.

team that designed the grounds and buildings of the World's Columbian Exposition, which opened in 1893. The combination of Renaissance planning devices with the most extensive landscape gardening produced a profound impression, even if some critics found the architectural style regressive. About this time the central area of Washington was also being replanned, this time with a deliberate and conscious awareness of contemporary city planning in western Europe.[18]

The same kind of international investigation preceded the production of the Burnham Plan for central Chicago. Agents reported on the style of the government buildings in London, on the height of those in Paris, on the circulation of traffic in Berlin, and so forth. In effect, what the Burnham Plan proposed was a combination of Renaissance-inspired streets and boulevards, together with the particularly American contribution made by the landscape gardeners. Even if only a portion of the plan could be carried out, including part of a bilevel street pattern in the center and a magnificent stretch of parks along the shorefront, the image still derived from many different places on both sides of the Atlantic Ocean and continued to inspire those who tried to implement Burnham's vision of the city's future.

MILITARY CITIES IN THE NEW WORLD

Military cities planned after those of early modern Europe were relatively rare in the territory controlled by the United States. Probably the most extensive fortified city in what is now the United States was "La Nouvelle Orléans," or New Orleans. Here, in 1722, the French engineer Adrien de Pauger laid out a new town in accordance with the instructions of the sieur de Bienville, the early French governor. This new city was intended to anchor the line of French fortifications running up the Mississippi River, into the Great Lakes, and out into the St. Lawrence River, so it needed to be substantially defended, both against the English colonies on the eastern seaboard and against the Spaniards in what is now west Texas. As the anonymous plan shows, New Orleans was surrounded by a bastioned trace, within which the rectangular blocks were to run eleven in number from east to west and six from north to south (figure 13). In the middle of the east-west blocks, down by the river, space was left for a great square and a cathedral.

The growth of the city meant that it soon spilled out of the fortified constraint and melded with the peculiarly French system of the *longlot*, into which the Louisiana countryside was early divided, a distinctive landholding system that marks the state even in satellite images. When the fortifications were no longer needed, their site was made into a series of boulevards, as in cities like Vienna, so that even today visitors can detect the influence of

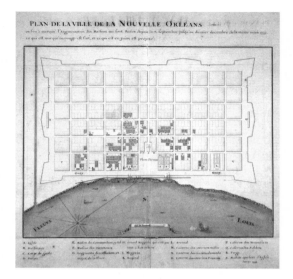

FIGURE 13. Anonymous manuscript plan of New Orleans from about 1720. Founded in 1717 as a city within a large bastioned fortification, New Orleans took many years to expand into its pattern of streets. Eventually, of course, it spilled far out of the original fortified area. Courtesy of the Newberry Library, Chicago.

Pauger's plan. Other cities like St. Louis and Mobile also had fortified elements, but none was as thoroughly carried out as that of New Orleans.

Unlike the English, who based their strategic considerations upon not losing command of the sea, the French in the West Indies laid out fortified cities like Port-au-Prince, using military engineers. Even when the English laid out a city (figure 9) that could easily have been defended by a fortified trace, they did not think that it was strategically important to add one. The French, on the other hand, envisioned a period of resistance, perhaps while a fleet was being organized. This plan had the unexpected advantage of eventually providing a good circular road, once the bastioned trace became outdated.

The only British town well defended from its genesis was Halifax, in Nova Scotia. The English had received the province at the Treaty of Utrecht in 1713, but for many years they lacked any fortress to hold in check the powerful base that the French had established at Louisbourg, where they could control the approaches to the St. Lawrence River.[19] In May, 1749, though, Col. Edward Churchill and three hundred settlers sailed for the site at Chebucto. He ordered the engineer, John Bruce, and the surveyor, Charles Morris, to set out the streets of a little town measuring about half a mile by a quarter of a mile, with square blocks. The whole village was to be surrounded by a wooden palisade in which were small forts; later on, the palisade was replaced by a stone bastioned trace that was dominated by a superb citadel that has changed little to this day. The lords of trade and plantations had controlled the work, so the streets received their names: Hollis, Bedford, Granville, Argyle, and so on. Halifax eventually became the Royal Navy's most important base in North America and played a crucial role in the Atlantic struggle of both world wars.

When the English and French laid out these fortified areas with their bastioned traces and internal square blocks, they must have been inspired by the great cities of the Spanish world: San Juan, Cartagena, Havana, and the rest. Curiously, most of these did not start out as fortified centers but as simple rectangular towns. It seems to have been the raids of the English, French, and Dutch and particularly the piratical cruise of Sir Francis Drake through the Caribbean in 1585 and 1586 that inspired the Spaniards to throw great bastioned walls around their main cities, particularly those that had to receive and shelter the *flota,* or treasure fleet, that would carry back to Spain the gold and silver upon which the empire largely relied.

To this day, in cities such as San Juan and Cartagena, the massive walls determine the urban shape of the metropolis, as they do in Callao and Havana. It is perhaps easier to appreciate the influence of the early fortification-plan in a smaller city, such as Le Cap in Haiti. Here, in the eighteenth century, the little town was surrounded by a powerful bastioned wall (figure 14). Within the walls, the streets were rigidly rectangular, as they remain to this day, and urban growth had to take account of the restraint of the walls. In such a townscape, the visitor has the feeling of walking through an area where the main

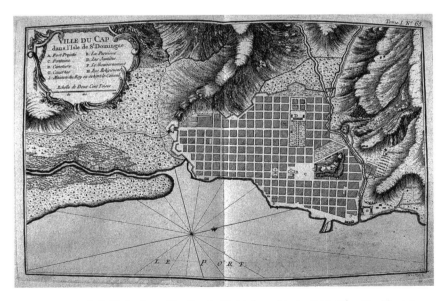

FIGURE 14. J.-B. Bellin's plan of Le Cap in Haiti, from his *Le Petit Atlas Maritime,* 5 vols. (Paris, 1764). This fortified city is typical of those established by both French and Spaniards all over the New World. Its rectangular streets are often aligned to catch the cooling breezes, and a prominent square or two is left for the great institutions of church and state—the cathedral and the governor's palace. Courtesy of the Newberry Library, Chicago.

outline has changed little since it was designed by early French engineers who were inspired both by their Spanish counterparts and indeed by the engineers of sixteenth-century Italy.

CONCLUSION

Once made, few cultural decisions leave as profound a mark on a country as those that deal with the shape of its cities. Even when, as in the case of Boston and New York, the early plan is heavily overlaid, it can almost always be detected with a little effort. The idea of a rectangular street plan has existed from China to Peru but seems to have been particularly well developed among the early Spanish settlers of the New World; the laws of the Indies in effect codified what was already a practice, one that was soon adopted by settlers from other European countries, particularly France and England.

The idea of the monumental city is a complex one with complex roots. But when monumental cities came to be built, it was to Renaissance planning that the American architects and designers looked. The eventual emergence of the skyscraper city came in stark contrast to what had been chosen for cities such as Paris and Washington and marked a stage at which the aesthetic influence of early modern Europe was clearly rejected; the tide of influence, until then flowing so strongly from the east, now began to eddy back toward Europe. Today the east-west and west-east streams have settled into a kind of equilibrium that has indeed become part of a worldwide exchange of ideas about urban design.

NOTES

1. *Civitates Orbis Terrarum,* 3 vols. (Cologne, 1595–1617); facsimile edition, ed. R. A. Skelton, 3 vols. (Cleveland: World Publishing, 1966).

2. Albert Neuberger, *The Technical Arts and Sciences of the Ancients* (New York: Barnes and Noble, 1969).

3. For a general survey, see Pierre Lavedan, *La géographie des villes* (Paris: Gallimard, 1959).

4. See the analysis by Martha Pollak, *Turin 1564–1680: Urban Design, Military Culture, and the Creation of the Absolutist Capital* (Chicago: University of Chicago Press, 1991).

5. For plans of Montreal, see André Vachon, *Taking Root: Canada from 1700 to 1760* (Ottawa: Public Archives Canada, 1985).

6. On early towns in north America, see Carl Bridenbaugh, *Cities in the Wilderness: The First Century of Urban Life in America, 1625–1746* (London and New York: Oxford University Press, 1991).

7. See Norval White, *New York: A Physical History* (New York: Atheneum, 1987).

8. For this early development, see Michael Pawson and David Buisseret, *Port Royal, Jamaica* (Kingston: University of the West Indies Press, 2000).

9. On the early English Caribbean, see Richard S. Dunn, *Sugar and Slaves: The Rise of the Planter Class in the English West Indies, 1624–1713* (Chapel Hill: University of North Carolina Press, 1972).

10. See Dora Crouch, ed., *Spanish City Planning in North America* (Cambridge, Mass., and London: Massachusetts Institute of Technology Press, 1982), and also the *General History of the Caribbean,* vol. 2, ed. Pieter Emmer (London: UNESCO Publishing, 1999).

11. Jorge Hardoy, *Pre-Columbian Cities* (New York: Walker, 1973). See also the same author's contribution, "European Urban Forms in the Fifteenth to Seventeenth Centuries and Their Utilization in Latin America," in *Urbanization in the Americas from Its Beginnings to the Present,* ed. Richard Schaedel (The Hague and Paris: Mouton, 1978), pp. 215–48.

12. These changes may be traced in a great collection of manuscript city plans from the Archivo General de Indias in Seville, the *Planos de ciudades iberoamericanas y filipinas existentes en el Archivo de Indias,* ed. Fernando Chueca Goitia and Leopoldo Torres Balbás, 2 vols. (Madrid: Instituto de Estudios de Administración Local, 1981).

13. See John Reps, *The Making of America: A History of City Planning in the United States* (Princeton: Princeton University Press, 1965).

14. H. Paul Caemmerer, *The Life of Pierre-Charles L'Enfant, Planner of the City Beautiful* (Washington, D.C.: National Republic, 1950).

15. Reps, *Making of America,* pp. 263–93.

16. See Elizabeth Stevenson, *Park Maker: A Life of Frederick Law Olmsted* (New York: Macmillan, 1977).

17. See the comparative images in David Buisseret, *Historic Illinois from the Air* (Chicago: University of Chicago Press, 1990), pp. 170–71.

18. Constance McLaughlin Green, *Washington, Capital City, 1879–1950,* 2 vols. (Princeton: Princeton University Press, 1962, 1963).

19. These developments are explained in Thomas H. Raddall, *Halifax: Warden of the North* (New York: Doubleday, 1965).

The Power of Numbers

STANLEY H. PALMER

SETTLER AND NATIVE IN IRELAND,
AMERICA, AND SOUTH AFRICA,
1600–1900

History is often simpler than the historians make it.
—SEAN O'FAOLAIN, *THE IRISH: A CHARACTER STUDY*

MORE THAN EVER BEFORE, Texas is today a state with two major languages and cultures. South Texas has "always" been "Spanish," but now the Hispanic share is swelling statewide and has risen 53 percent in just ten years. According to the 2000 U.S. Census, Hispanics now make up 32 percent of all Texans. Two of every five people in the under-18 age group are Hispanic. Forecast for future growth: The state's population will be majority-Hispanic by 2025 at the latest. Where I live, in the Dallas–Fort Worth "metroplex" (population 5.0 million), one increasingly hears two languages. The rapid cadences of Spanish or Tex-Mex vie with English, from the soft drawl of native Texans to the brisk intonations of immigrant Yankees. Over the past decade (1991–2000) in my hometown, suburban and historically "Anglo" Arlington (pop. 330,000), the Hispanic share has doubled to 18 percent of the total population while the Anglo share ("white, non-Hispanic") has plunged from 79 percent to 60 percent. The city to our west, older and larger Fort Worth, shows the same trends: The Anglo portion of the population has fallen to 46 percent of the total, while the Hispanic has grown to 30 percent. To the east, in Dallas (pop. 1.2 million), the Hispanic segment has increased in ten years from 21 to 35 percent of the city's population. People on the street remark that soon San Antonio will no longer be "Mexico's northernmost city." Historians wryly note that Mexico is simply "taking back" Texas: The tapestry of Anglo conquest (1836–1848; Sam Houston, San Jacinto, and the U.S.–Mexican War) is hardly coming unraveled, but it is being restitched.[1]

Demographic clout translates to power at the ballot box. Groups gaining in population strength seek increased access to and a greater share of political power. Because one group's gains are relative to the decline of others,' social tensions and political jostling among African Americans, Anglos, Asians, and Hispanics can be expected as a demographic outcome. Political power, old and new, is at stake. "Latinos want to make sure we get our piece of the pie," announced the president of the Texas chapter of the League of United Latin American Citizens (LULAC). A Dallas lawyer and Hispanic activist told the press, "The numbers speak for themselves. We have the figures, so we are going to demand equity. We're not going to yield what's rightfully ours."[2]

HISTORIANS KNOW that today's newspaper stories about population and politics are only the waves on the surface of the vast ocean of demographic history. What is today a struggle for power in Dallas city politics in times past more broadly involved a struggle for control of the continent.

Historians' study of that struggle is now more than a century old. The pioneer was a young historian who at the World's Columbian Exposition in Chicago in 1893 delivered a talk on "The Significance of the Frontier in American History."[3] Frederick Jackson Turner's timing was impeccable: America's frontier had just "closed" (the 1890 U.S. Census had so declared) on the very eve of the nation's celebration of the four-hundredth anniversary of Columbus's discovery of "America." Clearly, Americans did have much to celebrate: Since 1600 these transplanted Europeans had steadily, indeed rather speedily, spread the continental conquest from Boston to San Francisco.

Turner's admiring analysis of the nation's frontier history was, in large measure, the product of America's self-conscious identity at the end of the nineteenth century. A century young, past its civil war, now prosperous and powerful, the United States was clearly destined in the 1900s to become one of the world's most important nations. But how had this come about? To Turner, America was neither a former colony grown up nor a simple offshoot of Europe. In some special way America had changed those who had settled it. On the ever-advancing frontier, that "outer edge of the wave—the meeting point between savagery and civilization," settlers hacking down the forest or spreading out over the plains had time and again, in transforming moments, *become* Americans. The settler "transforms the wilderness" but so too, said Turner, does it change him. One need not look to Europe—its Middle Ages or Renaissance, its Teutonic racialism or British constitutionalism—to explain America. America's history itself was sufficient. "The existence of an area of free land, its continuous recession, and the advance of American settlement westward explain American development."[4] Turner's interpretation was as upbeat as Chicago's Columbian Exposition itself.[5] Hard work, a positive attitude, practical genius, and present-mindedness on America's expanding frontier had won for the young United States its liberty, individualism, and democracy.

If Turner's interpretation of U.S. history was novel and trailblazing, in one important area it was quite traditional. Like so many Americans at the time, people who lived in a world of color but saw only white, Turner's history was monochrome history. America's frontier he defined as a virtually endless "area of free land," whose few occupants were either invisible or two-dimensional figures, occasionally "noble" but also predictably "savage." America's history, in short, was white history. Of little or no account themselves, America's natives only stood in the way of the white settlers' westward progress. Turner's view of things seems, in fact, to have been little different from that of Gen. William Henry Harrison, who on the Indiana frontier in 1810 had lectured the Shawnee Chief Tecumseh: "Is one of the fairest portions of the globe to remain in a state of nature, the haunt of a few wretched savages, when it seems destined, by the creator, to give support to a large population, and to be the seat of civilization, of science, and true religion?"[6]

For half a century, despite emerging frontier studies elsewhere in the world,[7] the "Turnerian" view went largely unchallenged in the United States. But after World War II a professor at the University of Texas, Walter Prescott Webb, offered a more expansive view in his classic work, *The Great Frontier* (1952). Webb paid tribute to Turner the pioneer, even calling Turner's essay "the most influential single piece of historical writing ever done in the United States." Nevertheless, in a style alternately folksy and formal and usually incisive, Webb took on Turner by denying the "exceptionalism" or specialness of America's frontier history. Turner's frontier was "the new *American* land lying west of the *American* settlements," yet, argued Webb, the concept of a frontier should not be thought of as "something exclusively American, as if the United States were the only nation that had felt . . . [its] powerful influence. . . . [T]he American frontier concept . . . needs to be lifted out of its present national setting and applied on a much larger scale."[8]

Webb's "great achievement," in William McNeill's words, was to realize that America's frontier history was only "part of a global process of [European] civilizational expansion."[9] Walter Prescott Webb must be considered a pioneer of the study of transatlantic, even global, history, for he saw "the great frontier" as a *process* of interaction and exchange between what he called the Metropolis (Europe) and the Frontier (those regions discovered, explored, and settled). He was bold enough to suggest and sketch the changes in capitalism, law and government, science, the arts, and literature that, in his view, resulted from that interaction. In sum, Webb was able to break free from Turner's mononational straitjacket: America's history was not just

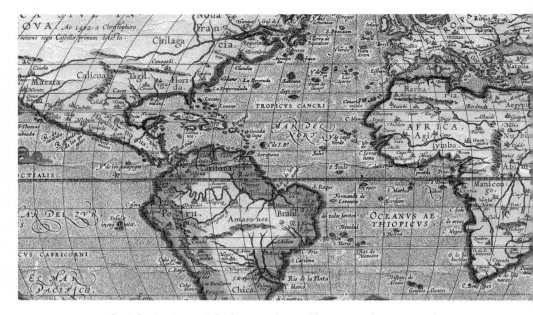

MAP 1. The Atlantic: Europe's highway to the world, c. 1600. This circumatlantic
section of Ortelius's world map of 1587 reveals the Atlantic coasts of America
and Africa. To the northwest and the south, waterway "passages"—both imagined
and real—to the wealth of "the East" later became important places of settlement.
Already on this map one can read of Spain's "Florida" and France's "Nova Francia,"
but there is not yet a "New England." South Africa is identified by "C. Bonae Spei"
(Cape of Good Hope) but of course by little else. Courtesy Special Collections,
Libraries of University of Texas–Arlington.

American history but also the result of this interactive process induced by
Europe's expansion.

Webb must also be judged as having been farsighted, for, in concluding his
book on America's frontier history, he urged the future historian to "be ready
at any time to cross the borders of his own country, or that of the one he is
studying; he must also be ready to break academic fences set up in universities to separate the so-called fields of knowledge." Webb chided his fellow
American historians—"it would seem the time has come for them to take the
lead"—to begin to produce "parallel," perhaps even comparative, studies of
those regions of the world that were also a part of "the Great Frontier." He
identified these as the Anglo-Saxon cultures (Canada, Australia, New
Zealand, and South Africa) as well as the Iberian ("the twenty republics of
Central and South America").[10]

Nevertheless, Webb's vision, like Turner's, was limited by his monocultural
emphasis on "white" progress. Since the "frontier" was, for Webb, "a vast and

vacant land without culture," the frontier process was essentially one that involved transplanted, diasporic "Europeans" evolving new and therefore young "post-European" cultures. If Webb was transnational, he was also, like Turner, Eurocentric in his view of things. No natives, apparently, peopled the American landscape. In short, for all his vision, Webb (as we all are) remained blinkered by the traditional cultural assumptions of his day. Take, for example, the following passage that, to us today, seems to reveal both new and old elements in Webb's analysis: "The concept of a moving frontier is applicable where a civilized people are advancing into a wilderness, an unsettled area, or one sparsely populated by primitive people. It was the sort of land into which the Boers moved in South Africa, the English in Australia, and the Americans and Canadians in their progress westward across North America. The frontier movement is an invasion of a land assumed to be vacant as distinguished from an invasion of an occupied or civilized country, an advance against nature rather than against men." Significantly, Webb felt compelled to add this footnote: "I am ignoring the scattered Indian population who did present some resistance but were not a major problem except for the few peoples who were in contact with them on the farthest fringes of settlement." Also significantly, he noted that the Indian population was low (date unspecified), "not more than 500,000, one Indian to about six square miles."[11]

In the past thirty years three key developments have shaped frontier studies by filling in Turner's and Webb's "vacant" frontier. First, perhaps stimulated by America's civil rights movement (c. 1955–1970), frontier historians took a big step forward by "rediscovering" marginalized minorities in America's history. Trailblazing works such as Gary Nash's *Red, White, and Black: The Peoples of Early North America* (1974)—note the plural—not only restored the roles of Indians and Africans but also made the national saga one of the interrelations of natives, settlers, and slaves. Similar stimuli—the turmoil in and later the implosion of South Africa's apartheid state (c. 1975–1994) and the ongoing crisis in Northern Ireland (from 1969 to the present)—appear to have led to fresh new "revisionist" perspectives in writing the histories of these two regions. For example, in South Africa, multicultural accounts, unthinkable a generation earlier, emerged and then became frequent; intriguingly, in Ireland, the freshness was the reaction against traditional "Irish nationalist" interpretations.[12]

A second trend, from about 1980, was the emergence of comparative studies. Wedding Webb's global (if monocultural) view of "the great frontier" to Nash's multicultural (but North American) perspective, two leading Yale historians, Howard Lamar and Leonard Thompson, produced an important edited work that was explicitly comparative. Moreover, *The Frontier in History* offered a new definition of "frontier." Since it was no longer seen as "vacant," the frontier was now described as a "zone of interpenetration between two previously distinct societies," one "indigenous," the other "intrusive." Lamar and Thompson argued that a frontier "opens" at contact and "closes" when "a single political authority has established hegemony over the zone."[13]

Finally, the third and most recent trend is a broadening notion of these concepts of contact, penetration, and emerging interrelations between indigene and intruder. Europe's outreach down and across the Atlantic to Africa and the Americas, as well as the myriad reverse flows and back eddies, today compose the scholarly field of "transatlantic history." In our era of the Internet, satellite technology, and multinational corporations, historians are rediscovering the interconnectedness of a world *before* national borders and ideologies governed the historical discourse. One result of this new transnational comparative history is that as we examine old facts in new ways, we arrive at sometimes startling new answers to questions that otherwise might not even have been asked.[14]

Indeed, so popular is transatlantic history that it now risks becoming "fashionable."[15] In January, 2000, the American Historical Association awarded its first annual "Atlantic history" book prize. The Organization of American Historians (in its *La Pietra Report*, 2000) has urged U.S. historians to become "transnational, . . . to rethink . . . American history in a global age." Across the Atlantic, a British university cooperates with a "Center for Transatlantic Studies" at a Dutch university. In the United States, Harvard University's Charles Warren Center hosts twice a year yet another meeting of the "International Seminar on the History of the Atlantic World."[16] Johns Hopkins, the University of Pittsburgh, New York University, and the College of Charleston, among others, offer courses and concentrations in Atlantic history. Atlantic history conferences pop up everywhere, including one (my favorite) at Ohio State on "transatlanticisms" (April, 1999). New doctoral programs in Atlantic history sprout in surprising locales: at Central Michigan as well as Florida International, and one even in Walter Webb's home state, at the University of Texas–Arlington (the program enrolled twenty-six students in its first three years).

IN SUM, it should by now be clear that this chapter is only a part of the broad currents in contemporary transatlantic and frontier historiography. The present work has two distinct aims: first, to discuss demography in native-settler relations in three Atlantic regions; and second, by means of the extensive endnotes to guide the reader to the accumulating rich literature on a number of related subjects. Specifically, I wish to trace in a transatlantic context the power of numbers in emerging new societies, societies where settlers (intruders) encountered natives (people already living there). William

FIG. 1. European encounters African, 1658. This early engraving—drawn only six years after Cape Town's founding—shows Dutch East India Company officials buying livestock from the Khoikhoi, a pastoral people in southwestern Africa. Thus begins modern South African history. Courtesy of Museum Africa.

McNeill has noted that "[w]hen peoples of approximately equal levels of skill, numbers, and organization meet on a frontier, drastic geographical displacements are unlikely."[17] By contrast, the intruders into native areas in Ireland, America, and South Africa *all* held the comparative advantage of coming from an advanced culture that possessed writing, science, technology, and gunpowder, were organized into nation-states, and knew about and prized the accumulation of money and capital. These were powerful weapons to bring into "primitive" regions. All these and more would be employed in the conquest. But in our three case studies, for all the things they had in common, in one area—the demography of native and settler—they differed. Trends in demography constituted just one of many historical factors, but I suggest that they helped to shape the differing outcomes in Ireland, America, and South Africa.

The word *demography* comes from two Greek words that mean, simply, "writing about people." Today the science of demography is all about statistics, counting, and analysis. The subject can be pretty dry, apparently lifeless. But numbers count. They matter because they measure. Any engineer or businessperson will tell you so. Whether it's the tolerance on a V-tech engine

South Africa fills several southern U.S. states but Ireland is smaller than New York State.

MAP 2. Physical areas compared.

or life insurance mortality tables, eye prescriptions or the bills you pay, hockey games or Florida elections—numbers *do* matter. Population numbers are important, too, for, like the "numbers" in geography and climate, they can play a basic role in historical causation.[18]

At first glance, the transatlantic societies in this chapter—Ireland, the United States, and South Africa—seem unlikely subjects for comparison. In physical size the three are vastly different: the island of Ireland (32,576 sq. mi.), the United States (3,675,633 sq. mi.), and South Africa (472,733 sq. mi.). So, too, in today's (2005) population: from tiny (Ireland, pop. 6 million), to large (South Africa, pop. 43 million), to colossal (United States, pop. 295 million). One is now the world's largest economy and indeed the only remaining political and military superpower. The second, the westernmost island off the northwest edge of Europe, is small and economically developed but politically divided (the Catholic Republic of Ireland, the Protestant government of Northern Ireland). The third is a large, racially divided, developing nation that is the economic dynamo of the African continent; historically a minority-rule settler nation, only in the past decade has it transformed itself into one of political governance by the native majority. Today these three regions may appear odd bedfellows for comparative purposes, but that oddness stems from comparing the outcomes, today's nations, not their origins.

Nearly four centuries ago, each region shared a fragile status as an embryonic settler society amid a population heavy with "natives." In the year 1600, Ireland, America, and South Africa were regions as yet unaffected by the intrusion of settlers.[19] Ireland was then ethnically Celt and Gaelic-speaking; the United States was "Indian" America; and South Africa was home to the Khoisan and Bantu. The age of European outreach and exploration and its subsequent outflow of capitalism, commerce, and people affected all three of these regions (including proximate Ireland) but in very different ways. The purpose of this chapter on the demography of native and settler is to trace and assess how these regions, similar at the start, reached very different outcomes in the shape of today's societies. By studying them comparatively, perhaps we will gain some fresh insights into their histories.

Specifically, I suggest answers to some important questions. Why in Ireland today do Northern Ireland and the Republic share governance of the island? Why in Northern Ireland do Sinn Fein and the IRA continue to squabble with Protestant Unionists? In the United States, why have the continent's natives, the "original Americans," essentially disappeared, their places taken by "Americans" largely of European and African ancestry? Why, by contrast, in South Africa after three centuries of settler rule, has the government since 1994 come to be headed by native presidents, first Nelson Mandela, now Thabo Mbeki?[20]

These are big questions and the answers complex. But sometimes the simplest or most obvious gets overlooked. Taking a peek at the differing demographic developments in these three settler societies provides us a lesson in the power of numbers. It should also give us some clues as to how and why, from small and fragile beginnings four centuries ago, these societies have traveled very different paths through history to become what they are today.

IRELAND

Lying just to the west of England, Ireland was England's first colony. The smaller of the two islands, the "Emerald Isle" is a land of rich soil but also poor rocky areas. Its green meadows and pastures, bogs, and rolling hills are well watered by rain that falls heaviest to the west. Patches of low mountains dot the island's periphery. Ireland's climate is temperate and maritime, for no part of the island is more than seventy miles from the sea.

Sailing across the Irish Sea to attack the island's vulnerable eastern flank, England's King Henry II lay claim to Ireland in the twelfth century, but it was not till the mid-1500s that Tudor monarchs pressed for total military control. The island's native people fought the English intrusion. The English army won the often bloody warfare and "planted" thousands of settlers in Ulster (1609–1610) as well as a scattering of settlers in the three other provinces. The natives staged a sanguinary uprising in the 1640s, massacring thousands of settlers, but the English Puritan leader, Oliver Cromwell, came over and conquered the whole island. He confiscated Catholic land in three provinces and sent most of the defeated Catholic landowners to live in the fourth province—poor, rocky Connacht. Forty years later, the natives rose again but were defeated in battle at the River Boyne and at Aughrim.

By 1700, the new Protestant (mostly Anglican, i.e., Church of Ireland)

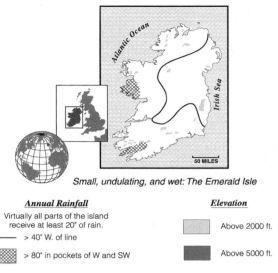

Small, undulating, and wet: The Emerald Isle

Annual Rainfall

Virtually all parts of the island receive at least 20" of rain.

——— > 40" W. of line

▨ > 80" in pockets of W and SW

Elevation

▨ Above 2000 ft.

▨ Above 5000 ft.

Note: Not shown is the political geography (border) of Northern Ireland and the Republic of Ireland.

MAP 3. Ireland (physical): rainfall and elevation.

landowners, many of them absentee, owned nearly all of the land in Ireland. The resident settlers were few in number, constituting only about one-fourth of Ireland's population. Some of the Ulster settlers, people of Scottish ancestry, were Presbyterians (i.e., Protestant but not Anglican). Nearly all of the native Catholics worked for the Protestant minority, Anglican or Presbyterian, as an underclass of tenant farmers and laborers. Seeking more rights for Catholics and independence from England, a radical group named the "United Irishmen" launched a rebellion in 1798, but the British savagely suppressed it, killing tens of thousands. England kept control of its colony, annexing it into a new British and Irish government called the United Kingdom (1801). Still, a new native leader, Daniel O'Connell, arose and demanded more rights for Catholics and repeal of the union with Britain. His cause, however, was set back by the holocaust of the Great Potato Famine (1845–1852), which destroyed the only food crop of the numerous poor Irish.

For centuries, emigration had been a part of Irish life. Both Catholics and Protestants had participated in this aspect of the island's culture. In the decades after the potato famine, emigration from the island became high and constant and aimed overwhelmingly for America (table 1).

In Ireland itself, things got better after the famine. Two factors helped: lower population pressure on the land and the continuing emigration. The British government passed laws that returned some land to native Irish own-

Table 1. Total Overseas Emigration from Ireland

Destination	1851–1890
United States	2,757,000
British North America (Canada)	228,000
Australia, New Zealand	302,000
Other	25,000
Total	3,312,000

Figures are rounded to the nearest thousand. Totals of Catholic and Protestant emigrants. Excluded are emigrants to Britain and Europe.
From data in tables in Kerby A. Miller, *Emigrants and Exiles: Ireland and the Irish Exodus to North America* (New York: Oxford University Press, 1985), p. 569, and in Donald Harman Akenson, *Small Differences: Irish Catholics and Irish Protestants, 1815–1922* (Montreal: McGill-Queen's University Press, 1988), p. 183.

ership. In touch with their kin overseas, Ireland's Catholics began to rediscover their cultural roots in a movement called the Gaelic Revival.

In the early 1900s, there was a new Irish Catholic bid for independence, the turmoil lasting from 1916 to 1921. Because Ireland's Protestant settlers, who lived mostly in the north, in Ulster, staunchly opposed this effort, the outcome in 1921 was a divided settlement called partition. Ireland's Catholics, who lived mostly outside Ulster, were granted an independent nation, the Irish Free State, which later became the Republic of Ireland. However, Northern Ireland (six of Ulster's nine counties) stayed with England. Even today the government of Northern Ireland remains a part of the United Kingdom.[21]

NATIVE

In 1600, the population of the small island of Ireland was about 1 million and overwhelmingly native Irish. By 1900, the population had quadrupled, with "natives," the Catholics, accounting for three-fourths of the total. During the three centuries after 1600, Ireland's settlers were always a minority culture ruling over a conquered, native-majority population. The long travail of Irish history is rooted in this demographic fact: British-descended settlers never did become a demographic majority.

As is well known, the island's population history is not one of unbroken sustained growth. Ireland's population doubled to 2 million by 1700 and, by 1800, had swollen to 5 million. The 1841 census enumerated 8.2 million people on the island; by mid-decade perhaps 8.5 million lived there. Then, suddenly, the Great Potato Famine changed everything: one million died of starvation and disease, and another million emigrated. Thanks to postfamine cultural patterns of late marriage or nonmarriage and heavy continuing emigration, the island's population continued to decline: from 6.5 million in 1851 to 5.1 million thirty years later and 4.4 million by 1911. Ireland was the only country in nineteenth-century Europe to lose population. Growth would return again only in the 1960s.

Given the vicissitudes of Irish demographic history, it is remarkable that Ireland remained a settler country whose population continued to be majority-native. For is it not true that over the course of three centuries Ireland's natives—its conquered Celtic, Catholic people—were in fact devastated by three major forces: warfare, famine, and emigration? Should we not expect this ongoing trauma to produce a Malthusian readjustment of the island's native-settler ratio?

Warfare, for example, took a terrible toll on the population. The island was subdued to England's rule only after brutal wars of invasion and conquest from 1550 to 1700. The eighteenth century, mostly stable and prosperous, nevertheless ended in a tumultuous, bloody final decade. In the sixteenth century "Ireland was one of Europe's frontiers, like that against the Turk, or in the New World, where the accepted rules of warfare were not always observed." Queen Elizabeth's Nine Years' War in Ulster (1595–1603) took a "horrific toll of civilians in order to deprive the Irish of food, succour, and recruits." Population losses went unrecorded but must have been substantial. Tudor scorched-earth military warfare was deemed acceptable since the Irish were perceived to be "a population of beasts and vermin." As the Earl of Surrey had informed Henry VIII (in 1521), "This land shall never be brought to good order and due subjection, but only by conquest."[22] The Ulster rising of 1641, a native assault against the intrusive settlers, brought settler reprisals against natives in "a pornography of violence"—at least 6,000 people were killed.[23] This native resistance led to Cromwell's terrorization in 1649 (severe examples were made—some 4,000 were killed—at Drogheda and Wexford) and subsequently to the famous land confiscations (1652). The turbulent century ended with the defeat of King James II's Irish supporters in 1691—7,000 were killed at the climactic battle of Aughrim alone. This final Protestant conquest ushered in a long period in which the settler ascendancy seemed unquestionably dominant over the defeated native population. Nevertheless, the eighteenth century ended in a reversion to bloodshed, as the United Irishmen's alliance with revolutionary France produced heavy-handed British government repression: a total of 30,000 deaths in the rebellion of 1798.[24] In summary, warfare over two centuries confirmed England's conquest of the island at a huge cost in lives lost: conservatively, a total of 50,000 deaths.

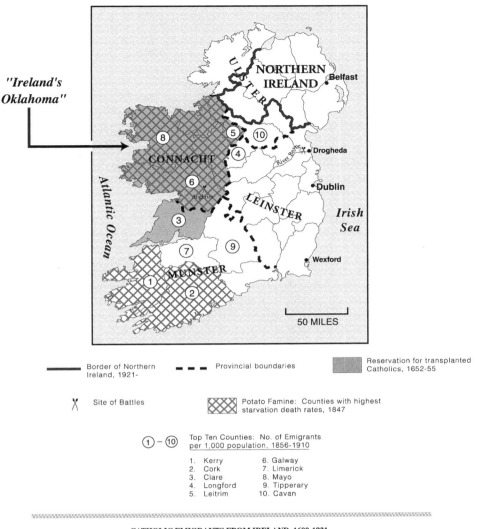

"*Ireland's Oklahoma*"

NORTHERN IRELAND • Belfast

ULSTER

CONNACHT

Atlantic Ocean

⑧ ⑤ ⑩

④ • Drogheda

River Boyne

⑥ • Dublin

Aughrim

LEINSTER Irish Sea

③

⑦ ⑨

MUNSTER • Wexford

①

②

50 MILES

——— Border of Northern Ireland, 1921-

- - - Provincial boundaries

Reservation for transplanted Catholics, 1652-55

✗ Site of Battles

Potato Famine: Counties with highest starvation death rates, 1847

①–⑩ Top Ten Counties: No. of Emigrants per 1,000 population, 1856-1910

1. Kerry	6. Galway
2. Cork	7. Limerick
3. Clare	8. Mayo
4. Longford	9. Tipperary
5. Leitrim	10. Cavan

CATHOLIC EMIGRANTS FROM IRELAND, 1600-1921

1600-1699	70,000
1700-1814	100,000
1815-1855	2,700,000
1856-1921	2,850,000

MAP 4. Native Ireland: famine and emigration.

Crop failures and famine, too, took their periodic tolls. Most famous, of course, is the apocalypse, the Great Potato Famine of 1845–1852,[25] when one million people (one-eighth of the island's population), mostly poor, native Catholics, died from disease or starvation.[26] Less well known are the numerous local and obscure food shortages that killed thousands; between 1816 and 1842, history records fourteen partial or complete "prefamine famines" (i.e., famines before the Great Potato Famine) on the island. We know the least about probably the greatest famine. In 1740 and 1741, at a time when the government kept few records, scholars suggest that as many as 400,000 native Irish—about one-sixth of the total population—perished in this early potato famine. If we push back even earlier in time, we must remember that the century of warfare, c. 1550–1650, was also one filled with famines, often caused by those long-ago, scorched-earth military policies. For example, in the late Tudor era, as part of the reduction of Ulster, the "slaughter of cattle, and burning of corn [grain] and houses was . . . horrible in the extreme." Contemporaries described people "found everywhere . . . dead of famine," and the province itself was reduced to "a desert."[27] In sum, and again to offer a conservative figure, famines in Irish history from 1700 to 1850 killed at least 1.5 million people.

Even so, by far the biggest winnower of population was emigration.[28] In Thomas Gallagher's words, Ireland functioned as "a kind of nursery for raising humans for export."[29] No European country exported its people like Ireland did. In the 250 years *before* the 1840s' potato famine, nearly 1 million Catholic Irish natives emigrated. The flight to the continent and across the Atlantic began with the emigration of 50,000 Irish soldiers defeated in the wars of the seventeenth century. While the British encouraged this emigration of Ireland's warriors "as part of the process of pacification," they also coerced the recalcitrant. A second form of emigration was the Cromwellian practice of "transportation": At least 10,000 people (some say 50,000) were shipped off to the New World, mostly the Caribbean (the population of Barbados was one-fifth Irish in 1666). Joining the coerced was a third group, the voluntary emigrants, mostly but not all "loose, idle people," who chose flight from the conquered island in the form of an indentured servitude to Virginia, Maryland, or the Caribbean.[30] Finally, partaking of each group (military, coerced, and voluntary) were some of the defeated and now dispossessed Catholic landowners. Faced with Cromwell's famous choice of going to "Hell or Connacht," more than 2,000 heads of households agreed to "exchange" their land for new real estate in the barren western province. Many others must have sensed the third, unstated option—flight—and chosen instead just to leave, most going to the Continent. In summary, the seventeenth-century emigration was crucial. Not only did some 70,000 Catholics leave the island but, more to the point, those going included disproportionate numbers of warriors, leaders, and individuals of wealth and culture. Ireland's natives lost generations of *future* leadership.

If the eighteenth century saw a lull in the emigration of native Catholics, the nineteenth century opened the floodgates. Of the 1 million native Irish who emigrated in the period from 1600 to 1845, about 600,000 left after 1815. The Great Potato Famine only sped up the process: In the years 1846–1851 1 million people fled what they called "the doomed and starving island." Recent scholars have drawn out the famine exodus to the year 1855, making the decade's total nearly 2 million Catholic emigrants. "More people left Ireland in just eleven years [1845–1855] than during the preceding two and one-half centuries." This exodus of poor, diseased natives led the *Times* of London to opine, wishfully, "In a few years more, a Celtic Irishman will be as rare in Connemara as is the Red Indian on the shores of Manhattan."[31]

This surging outflow of Ireland's poorest, pushed by the famine of 1845–1852, was startling only in its volume, for emigration had long been a part of Irish life. "[N]o other European nation saw as high a percentage of its population leave to emigrate overseas during the nineteenth century as Ireland did." Nearly all Catholic emigrants left with mixed feelings: hope for the future but also anger, bitterness, and a sense of wrong. As Kerby Miller has shown, most considered themselves exiles from their own country. In 1878, one Irishman who had immigrated to Minnesota wrote his County Carlow cousin, "Why don't you in the name of God, just shake the dust from your feet and leave your curse upon the system that exiled . . . all . . . good honest and faithful Irishmen from their native land?"[32]

The postfamine emigration of 1856–1921 emptied the island of 4.5 million people, four-fifths of them Catholic. A total of 3.5 million people, half of them young women, moved to the United States. Massachusetts became known as "Ireland's westernmost province," and New York as just "the next parish over from Galway." Moreover, the migrations were one-time, the relocations permanent. As one Irish newspaper noted, "The emigrant's chain does not draw him back but pulls forward those he has left behind."[33] Ireland's uprooted natives were being transformed into America's settlers. Overall, if we add up the human hemorrhaging from 1800 to 1921, a total of about 7 million Catholic men, women, and children left Ireland. This is a remarkable number when we recall that Ireland's total population in 1800 *and* in 1900 was roughly the same: about 5 million people.

In summary, against this background of war, famine, and emigration, as Ireland's population rose until 1846 and then fell steadily for a century, especially noteworthy is this stark fact: From 1700 to 1900, the island's native-settler ratio hovered essentially unchanged at three or four natives for every one settler. Despite the numerous and varied horrors of native Irish history, and whether in a rising or a falling population, the native-settler ratio remained largely *unchanged*. The first official religious census, done in 1834, determined that Ireland's population in that year was 81 percent Catholic and 19 percent Protestant (i.e., 10.7 percent Church of Ireland and 8.1 percent Presbyterian). Theodore Hoppen has noted the following about this 1834 census: "The great numerical fact now at last precisely revealed could not be overlooked. . . . [These] concepts of sectarian majority and minority furnished one of the central realities of modern Irish life." Most surprisingly, the demographic ratio changed little over time. In 1720, Ireland was 73 percent Catholic; in 1834, 81 percent. After the Famine holocaust, the 1861 census commissioners reported that Ireland's population was—still—78 percent Catholic. The 1901 census identified 74 percent of the island's population as Catholic.[34] In short, by a proportion oscillating between 3 to 1 and 4 to 1, the island remained overwhelmingly native and only marginally settler. A million famine deaths and the emigration of 3 million Catholics from 1851 to 1901 had dropped the Catholic proportion of the population from 80.9 to 74.2, a difference of 6.7 percentage points. The Protestant settlers were *still* heavily outnumbered.

SETTLER

How and why could this be? Why this continuing dominance in native population? This brings us to the other side of the equation: Ireland's settlers. Those British mainlanders who settled in Ireland suffered historically from four factors. The settlers were always too few in number. They were too concentrated in Ulster. There was virtually no settler in-migration after 1720. Finally, too many of the settlers and their descendants themselves joined the waves of emigration out of the island.

First, the settlers were few in number. By 1700, the English conquest was complete; war and confiscation had stripped the natives of landownership. Catholic ownership fell from 61 percent of all Irish land in 1641 to 22 percent in 1688 and 14 percent by 1704. However, Protestant landownership, often absentee, and Protestant settlement, a new invasive presence on the ground, were two different things. The number of Protestant settlers grew but never became large. The demography for this early period is still tortuous, but scholars believe that, by 1641, Ulster and Munster together had attracted about 100,000 (Protestant) migrants from Scotland and England. By this date perhaps one-sixth of the island's population was Protestant (in 1600, it had been less than 2 percent). After the Cromwellian conquest, the English parliament, in order to "civilize" the place, proposed to root 36,000 new landowners in Ireland. With the papist rebel landowners transplanted to

Connacht, their former lands (in the words of one Leinster directive of 1656) "should be thoroughly and seasonably *planted and inhabited* by protestants of this and the English nation." But talk was cheap and settlers proved scarce. Efforts to attract Protestants from England, the Continent, and even New England "came to little or nothing."[35] In the end the Cromwellian land confiscations netted (by 1670) only about 8,000 new landowners (one-fourth the number proposed); worse, many of these were absentee owners.

Still, settler growth was steady: By 1680, about 20 percent of the island's population was Protestant. After the defeat of King James II in the wars from 1689 to 1691, there would be a large (50,000–80,000 people) spurt of immigration of Scottish and northern English settlers, overwhelmingly to Ulster, in the quarter century 1690–1715. By 1730, Protestants formed 27 percent of the island's population. But then the growth stopped. Never again would the Protestant percentage be that high: By 1834, it fell to 19 percent of the total population, and by 1901, it rose to only 26 percent—essentially the same as a century and a half earlier. In sum, Ireland's dilemma was that new ownership did not translate into effective settlement. If by as early as 1700 vast acreages of Irish land were owned by (Protestant) absentees living in England, this fact did not produce a substantial settler presence. In fact, Ireland's Protestants were scattered thinly over three provinces (Leinster, Munster, Connacht), resided in Dublin or other emerging towns, and managed to concentrate as a critical mass in only part of one province.

A second key point is that most of Ireland's Protestant settlers lived in Ulster, the northernmost of the four provinces. Indeed, over time they became even more concentrated there. In 1730, three-fifths of Ireland's half million Protestants lived in Ulster. The province's eastern half, radiating from Belfast, acted as a magnet for the island's Protestants: Two-thirds of them lived in east Ulster by 1861. The failure of Ireland's Protestants to spread into the island's other provinces meant that English law and government had a very hard time growing local roots. By the nineteenth century, in many southern and western counties the Protestant percentages of total population, historically never out of the teens, had dropped below 10 percent of a county's population.

There are many reasons for the failure of Irish settlement to prosper. For one thing, from the settlers' perspective, Ireland's natives (of course with European immune systems) did not conveniently die from *diseases,* as did America's. Moreover, military conquest and land confiscations had made Ireland's natives often as surly and resentful as they were numerous. Ireland's settlers tended to live "isolated among a strange and potentially unfriendly population." The thought of being surrounded by swarms of natives deterred many from settling in Ireland. Mythology as well as history served the needs

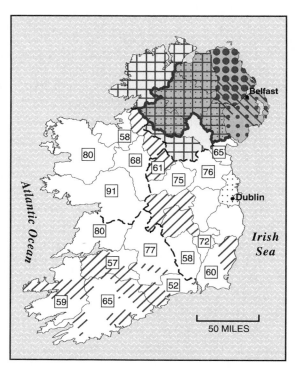

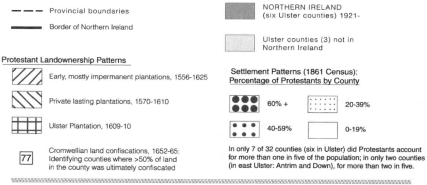

Provincial boundaries

Border of Northern Ireland

NORTHERN IRELAND
(six Ulster counties) 1921-

Ulster counties (3) not in
Northern Ireland

Protestant Landownership Patterns

Early, mostly impermanent plantations, 1556-1625

Private lasting plantations, 1570-1610

Ulster Plantation, 1609-10

77   Cromwellian land confiscations, 1652-65:
Identifying counties where >50% of land
in the county was ultimately confiscated

Settlement Patterns (1861 Census):
Percentage of Protestants by County

60% +   20-39%

40-59%   0-19%

In only 7 of 32 counties (six in Ulster) did Protestants account
for more than one in five of the population; in only two counties
(in east Ulster: Antrim and Down), for more than two in five.

PROTESTANT EMIGRANTS FROM IRELAND, 1600-1921

1600-1699	20,000
1700-1814	330,000
1815-1855	500,000
1856-1921	750,000

MAP 5. Settler Ireland: plantations and paucity of Protestants.

of "propagandists [who] expatiated on the danger and barbarism of rebellious Ireland." For instance, to drum up business, American land promoters repeated tales of Ireland's native insurrection in 1641 but downplayed the Indian threat against America's colonists. Certainly, to an Irish Protestant, America had much appeal: escape from political discrimination (in Ireland only Anglicans were full citizens), economic upward mobility ("from tenants they are become landlords, . . . and enjoy the fruits of their own industry," proclaimed the *Belfast News-Letter* in 1766), and not least, security and peace of mind. America's natives were much thinner on the ground than those in Ireland, and the growing settler density along its Atlantic seaboard made America a culturally comfortable place for settlers.[36]

A third reason for the failure of Ireland's settler experiment to thrive was that the island's seventeenth-century settlers were not refreshed by new waves of English or Scottish in-migration. The last wave of settlers into Ireland arrived in the early 1700s. The entire eighteenth century saw very little immigration. A few French Huguenots and some German Palatines and Moravians came in, but there was no in-migration of any real volume.[37] The great rebellion of 1798 and the minor threat of Emmet's rising (1803) of course did nothing to entice prospective settlers. The latter event led one Protestant woman to comment, "I begin to fear these people [Catholics], and think . . . they will regain their native land."[38] One might imagine that the aftermath of the potato famine of the 1840s—with its depopulation, land clearances, and bankruptcies—would present a "buying opportunity" for Irish and British Protestants and the British government. In fact, there were no big quasi-Cromwellian land sales, and the reverse of protestantization occurred with new demands by the natives for Catholic and Gaelic empowerment. Had there been eighteenth- and nineteenth-century waves of in-migration of English and Scottish settlers, the new settler population, added to the old, would have driven the share of settlers above its static proportion of one-fourth of the total population. Substantial settler in-migration could have filled the void created by the potato famine's killing of the most wretched, poorest native Irish and the concomitant copious hemorrhaging of Catholic emigrants out of the island. From this settler viewpoint, the history of postfamine Ireland was clearly a missed opportunity.

Because Ireland's initial settler cohorts of the seventeenth century were obviously not refreshed by new waves of settlers, historians seldom comment on the fact. Nevertheless, this "dog that didn't bark in the night" (to quote that Englishman Sherlock Holmes) is actually a crucial development in Irish history. This absence of new settlers in the two centuries before 1900 meant that both the original settlers and their descendants constantly felt themselves to be a minority under siege. One prominent Ulster Protestant in 1718 expressed his fears: "The papists being already five or six to one, and being a breeding people, you may imagine in what condition we are like to be in."

As the years passed with no prospect of settler demographic hegemony, not only were Ireland's Protestants condemned (correctly) to feel threatened but, fearing the future, they also retreated to "live in the past." Thus, nineteenth-century (and even twentieth-century) issues were fought using ancient rhetoric. In Ulster in 1886 and again in 1912, Protestants predictably opposed home rule for Ireland since politically it would empower the dominant Catholic natives and thus swamp the Protestant settler fragment. One Ulsterman in 1886 described William Gladstone's Home Rule bill as constituting "a revival of the seventeenth-century struggle between Roman Catholics and Protestants for ascendancy in Ireland, a struggle which his ancestors had twice fought to a victorious conclusion."[39] In our own time, note that familiar Ulster loyalist motto scrawled on the walls of houses in Belfast: "No Surrender," a reference to the Protestant victory over King James II at the siege of Londonderry in 1689. Recall, also, that English joke about the airline pilot on a Manchester-to-Belfast flight, instructing the passengers to reset their watches: "It is now the seventeenth century."

Fourth and finally, this basic problem of an absence of settler inflow was compounded by a second one: the considerable settler *outflow* in the eighteenth and nineteenth centuries. A total of 1.5 million Protestants left the island between 1700 and 1921. In the early and mid-1700s, whole kin groups and farmsteads of Protestants, mostly from Ulster, packed up and left for English-speaking North America, first the thirteen colonies, later the United States. The flight to America continued unabated in the first half of the nineteenth century. This denuding of Ireland of its loyalist base continued after the potato famine, as North America—Canada now as well as the United States—continued to act as a magnet for Ireland's Protestants. More than three times as many Protestants left Ireland in the seven decades after the famine than had emigrated in the seven decades before the American Revolution.

This Protestant exodus, beginning in the eighteenth and continuing throughout the nineteenth century, had enormous consequences for Irish history. Consider the implications of these two facts: (1) The Protestant population in the province of Ulster in 1700 totaled 300,000; (2) the number of Protestants from throughout the island who emigrated in the course of the eighteenth century totaled *more than 300,000*. From 1700 to 1776, 230,000 Ulster Protestant settlers, mostly Presbyterians, emigrated to colonial America. In the period from 1783 to 1814, another 100,000 Protestants left Ireland; in the thirty years after 1815, this number quadrupled to some 400,000 Irish Protestant emigrants. The allure of America combined with settler insecurities in Ireland to produce an ongoing hemorrhaging of Protestants from Ulster, a process that contributed somewhat to the success of the American Revolution and substantially to the long-term failure of the British settlement in Ireland.

The emigration of Ireland's settlers began shortly after the late-seventeenth-century Protestant conquest of the island. In the 1720s, a land agent spoke of Ulster's "Protestants being almost everywhere on the wing for America," and another Protestant observer lamented the "fatal humour" of "the dispeopleing [sic] of our country . . . our lands wasting round us, and the best of our tenants leaving us in the midst of swarms of papists." A century later this trend continued unabated. Kerby Miller has described Ireland's Protestant emigrants of the early nineteenth century as "substantial farmers and artisans," people from "business and professional backgrounds"—in short, "Protestants in fairly comfortable circumstances." As one English observer noted, "The best go—the worst remain."[40]

From early on, the British government was not blind to the consequences of this phenomenon. As early as 1730, Irish government officials were voicing fears "that northern Ireland was being abandoned to the Catholics." A privy council memo of 1762 noted that "the migration from Ireland of such great numbers of his majesty's [loyal] subjects must be attended with dangerous consequences to that kingdom." A memorial from "the noblemen and gentlemen of Ireland," significantly printed in the *Pennsylvania Gazette* in 1729, observed that "our inveterate enemies the papists . . . use all means and artifices to encourage and persuade the protestants to leave the [Irish] nation, and cannot refrain from boasting that they shall by this means have again all the lands of this kingdom in their possession."[41]

For Ireland's Protestants, emigration was escape. This denuding of Protestant Ireland before the potato famine—a half million left between 1783 and 1845—was driven by real fears. The bloody rebellion of 1798 was followed by the rise of movements to gain more rights for Ireland's Catholic natives: Catholic emancipation, the "tithe war" (nonpayment of the Anglican tithe), and repeal of the Act of Union with Britain. Because each of these popular nineteenth-century movements threatened Protestant ascendancy (two were successful), they stimulated the Protestant exodus. One emigrant Catholic servant girl in 1832 wrote home from America that most of her shipboard fellow emigrants had been "snug . . . Protestants, that found home growing too hot for them." Another new Irish American, a Protestant emigrant writing from the safety of Charleston, (West) Virginia, in 1839, explained his emigration in these words: "[B]ecause [the Catholics'] property was confiscated in times of Old . . . [we] are afraid they would try to get back their just due."[42]

If Protestant fears fed Protestant flight in the century and a half before the potato famine, how did Ireland's Protestants react to the famine and its aftermath? To many of Ireland's Protestants, the "death-dealing" potato famine represented an opportunity to improve their lot and to increase the settlers' portion of the island's population. After all, was it not the poorest and the papists who had succumbed to divine providence? Certainly the idea of post-famine Ireland as a tabula rasa occurred to the British government. Lord Lieutenant Clarendon observed that "the departure of thousands of papists [sic] Celts must be a blessing to the country they quit," for their places, he hoped, would be taken by "[s]ome English and Scottish settlers [who] have arrived." Regarding native Irish emigration, Charles Trevelyan, the British official who managed famine relief, wrote, "We must not complain of what we really want to obtain. If small farmers go [emigrate] . . . and people [who buy land] will invest capital, we shall at last arrive at something like a satisfactory settlement of the country." Historian Christine Kinealy pithily sums up: "The food shortages were regarded by these men as an opportunity to modernise Ireland."[43]

But the British government's hopes for Ireland were not to be realized. Ireland's Catholic/Protestant ratio did not change but continued to oscillate around a range of 3.5 to 1, native to settler. Not only was there no postfamine in-migration of Protestant Scottish and English settlers, but a steady exodus of the Protestant population continued through emigration. If the vast bulk (79 percent) of postfamine emigrants were Roman Catholics (2.85 million), nevertheless nearly 746,000 Protestants—a fifth of the total—also left Ireland between 1856 and 1921. Most critically, the area in Ireland with the thickest concentration of Protestants was being winnowed. Three of every four Protestants leaving—some 560,000 people—left from Ulster. The city of Belfast did grow in population, however, and the Protestant portion of Ulster's population rose from 50 percent in 1861 to 56 percent by 1911. Nevertheless, in the half century after 1861, Ulster's Protestants were in fact retreating into the laager of east Ulster; the province was demographically shrinking into what would become in 1921 the six-county state of Northern Ireland.[44] For, despite Belfast's remarkable growth, it is not often pointed out that, as in Ireland's other provinces, Ulster's population declined in the decades after the famine, dropping 21 percent from 1851 to 1911. Most of this decline was the result of Catholic emigration (that denomination's numbers were down 29 percent), but the Protestant population fell as well, the number of Presbyterians down 16 percent and Anglicans 6 percent.

In short, in Kerby Miller's words, "Ulster's urban industrial society did not stop northern emigration." Clearly, (east) Ulster was industrializing and modernizing as it became more densely Protestant. But the high levels of Protestant emigration from Ulster (more than a half million people) in the seventy years after the potato famine, combined with an absence of inflow of new settlers into Ireland, acted as a brake on generating a dominant mass of Protestants in Ireland's most Protestant province. Moreover, the export of Ireland's people, both native and settler, made North America the beneficiary. As Ireland's Catholics after midcentury headed to a land where they felt comfortable, the United States, that democratic republic that had left the British Empire in 1783, so Ireland's Protestants gravitated to Canada, that imperial dominion (1867) that some contemporaries described as "a second England."[45] Already by 1871, 35 percent of Ontario's population was of Irish descent, two-thirds of them Protestants.[46] Less than 5 percent of postfamine (1856–1921) New World Irish emigrants went to Canada, but virtually all of them were Protestants who could feel culturally comfortable in this loyalist realm of the empire. Indeed, there is abundant evidence that the Canadian government and Canada's Orange Order itself assisted in this importation of Ulster Protestants.

In conclusion, it is clear that whether Irish emigrants went to the United States or to Canada, Ireland's loss was America's gain. As for Ireland's stay-at-home settler remnant, they must have seen this postfamine emptying of Ireland as yet another missed opportunity to transform the place into a "decent," "British" Protestant society. After all, the island's unchanging ratio of three or four natives for every one settler was, in large part, the product of Protestant flight and an absence of replacement in-migration. To be transatlantic about it, North America's Protestant settlement from Ireland came at the cost, to those remaining behind, of abandoning the island to its Catholic native population, despite their own high levels of emigration.

MUSINGS

What does all this mean for Irish history? Simply put, the dynamics of native-settler demography shaped Irish history. Irish history was what it was because of this native-settler ratio. From the penal laws to O'Connell and later through Home Rule and the Gaelic League, England's governance of Ireland was always conditioned by these demographic facts: Protestant, minority rule of an alienated, often hostile, Catholic-majority population.

Because Irish society was essentially native and "papist" with a veneer of settler control, Ireland's Protestant nationalism in the late eighteenth century ("Grattan's parliament") was a weak and fragile plant, being more shallow rooted than the hardy, healthy variety in America's thirteen colonies. Had Ireland's settlers been more numerous, they would have had fewer anxieties over recurrent issues such as "rights for Catholics." Demography dictated that any Catholic (native) advances would trigger increments of Protestant (settler) disempowerment.

In the 1790s, influences from the French Revolution traumatized both sides. After the climacteric of the 1798 rebellion, Ireland's settlers protested London's solution of abolishing Dublin's parliament, but, in the end, they were relieved to get Britain's protection provided by the Act of Union (1800). For purposes of lawmaking and military support, Ireland's settlers in the nineteenth century would no longer be just a besieged minority within Ireland but rather a proud part of the United Kingdom's Protestant-majority imperial parliament in London. Inversely, throughout the nineteenth century this demographic reality would be the basis of the grievance of Ireland's Catholics: They constituted a majority of the population in their home island but were merely a disempowered minority in the London parliament that governed them.

Events in the nineteenth century offered opportunities, so Irish history might have been different. After all, the huge and continuing emigration of Catholics out of Ireland after 1800, not to mention the charnel house created by the potato famine, did strip the island of its poorest native inhabitants. Under these circumstances we might have expected nineteenth-century Ireland, under British tutelage, to morph into a modernizing West Britain. Considerable modernization did occur, but protestantization did not. Ireland did not become a less Catholic, more Protestant, society in part because of the large and growing postfamine emigration of Protestants. In turn, the fact that Ireland remained heavily native and Catholic served to dissuade prospective English and Scottish settlers from moving to Ireland. History records that the island's population was cut in half from 8.5 million in 1845 to 4.5 million by 1900. Theoretically, the emptying island was ripe for replantation. Had an increasing share of the island's people been "free-born Protestants" instead of so-called benighted papists, Irish history would have evolved differently.[47]

As the saying goes, "Opportunities are not lost; someone will take the ones you miss." Not only was there was no great protestantizing of postfamine Ireland; in fact, quite the opposite occurred. Many Catholics became active in the Gaelic revival, and some joined the Irish Republican Brotherhood (IRB). The century that had begun with the 1798 rebellion was bookended by the Southern Irish Catholic fight for independence from 1916 to 1921.[48] Meanwhile, Ireland's remnant Protestants—those who refused the option of transatlantic emigration—huddled together under siege in Ulster, where they demanded *their own* rights and protections. In 1921, the partition of the island into the Catholic Irish Free State and the Protestant government of Northern Ireland simply translated demographic realities into political ones. Those realities remain to this day.[49]

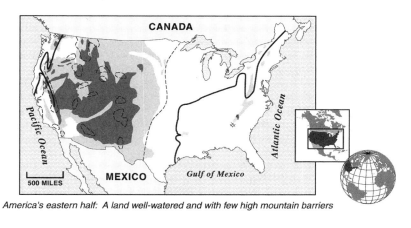

America's eastern half: A land well-watered and with few high mountain barriers

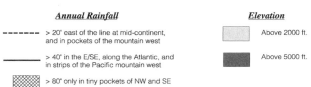

Annual Rainfall

- - - - - - - > 20' east of the line at mid-continent, and in pockets of the mountain west

————— > 40' in the E/SE, along the Atlantic, and in strips of the Pacific mountain west

▨ > 80' only in tiny pockets of NW and SE

Elevation

☐ Above 2000 ft.

■ Above 5000 ft.

MAP 6. America (Physical): rainfall and elevation.

AMERICA

More than three thousand miles to the west, across the cold North Atlantic, lay the continent of North America. For tens of thousands of years people native to this land had lived in hundreds of tribes scattered across the vast land. Since time immemorial they had been undisturbed by outside visitors. Suddenly, if slowly at first, in the decades after 1492, Spanish and French and then English visitors began to arrive. The English speakers found neither gold nor silver nor the monumental civilization that Mexico offered. Yet, in time, one lesson became clear: America had attractions that were hard to ignore. Its eastern woodlands boasted a climate and rainfall not unlike Europe's. A gentle, indented coastline gave promise of prospective harbors. Rivers wending inland offered transport to lush, fertile farmlands. Hills and valleys provided variety to the green landscape, and mountains, when encountered, were not sufficiently bleak or imposing to block access to lands that, later reports would confirm, stretched endlessly to the west.

In sum, for purposes of human settlement, North America was an attractive and accessible place. Some would come to report it as even Edenic. Starting about 1600, English-speaking intruders from Europe came in great, swelling numbers to Virginia, Massachusetts, and other colonies of settlement. Many prospered. If Ireland's history of both native and settler suffered from malign neglect, America's British Protestant settlers famously benefited from "benign neglect." These English-speaking people from Europe—to today's scholars, the "Euroamericans"—began in the eighteenth century to call themselves "Americans." Allied to the English government, these English colonists in 1763 defeated the French and the Indians in North America's war of that name. The settlers subsequently claimed on their maps, and for themselves, the vast spaces between the Appalachian Mountains and the Mississippi River.

These English-speaking "Americans" in the thirteen colonies next fought a war to separate themselves from their cultural homeland, Britain. The colonists were successful in their revolution, creating in 1783 a new country that stretched a thousand miles from the Atlantic Ocean to the Mississippi River. The territory of this new "United States of America" rapidly expanded, even at one stroke doubling in size by the Louisiana Purchase of 1803. Territorial expansion continued in the 1840s by means of a war with Mexico and a treaty with Britain: "Manifest destiny" dictated that the United States' western border was now the Pacific Ocean. In sum, very quickly, from 1783 to 1848, the territory of the new country had swollen in size and now spread from sea to shining sea.

In the process, the Indians, the original and now forgotten Americans, lost a continent. The white Americans, the settlers, signed treaties, which they broke; they fought wars, which they won. But two things principally did in the Indians: the vast, swarming, relentless tide of immigration from Europe—and disease. The Indians had no resistance to Europe's diseases. Smallpox and many other maladies helped to clear the continent of its original inhabitants.

As the new white Americans headed ever westward, the Native Americans saw the land disappear beneath them. Treaty after treaty mapped the Indian land cessions, their losses of land, according to Euroamerican law. From their original base on the Atlantic seaboard, the settlers had seeped across the Appalachians by 1783, and they had advanced well north of the Ohio River and west of the Mississippi by 1820. So numerous and land hungry were the white Americans that their U.S. government passed an Indian Removal Act (1830), whereby Indian tribes east of the Mississippi were removed to the west of that river. Most were relocated to the "Indian Territory," the present-day state of Oklahoma. As the Euroamericans continued their westward expansion, the western Indians in turn ceded more land; consequently, by 1890, with the closing of the frontier, Indians were essentially eliminated from the landscape, hidden away on small barren patches of land. Today, most Indians, only a tiny fraction of the United States' population, live intermixed or inter-married with the white settlers, though some still live on land set apart for them, land their conquerors called "reservations."[50]

NATIVE

Scholars today speculate that, in 1500, in the area north of Mexico, the Native American ("Indian") population lived in five hundred tribes and numbered anywhere from 3 to 10 million people.[51] Their total numbers we will never know. Native America was a healthy population that (by today's standards) was very, very thinly scattered across the continent.[52] Yet, unlike Ireland's, America's aboriginal population was a doomed civilization.

Two vast impersonal forces would seal the fate of America's native peoples. First, disease and death resulted from their very contact with the invasive Europeans and later America's settlers, the Euroamericans. Second, the Native Americans drowned under a massive white tide of European immigration and Euroamerican procreation. So overwhelming was this two-pronged assault on America's natives that, from a comparative transatlantic perspective, America's Indians might tragically be described as "passive victims."[53]

By far the biggest part of the American holocaust[54] was the natives' own bodies' lack of immunity to Europe's diseases. From the moment the time seal was broken in 1492, death stalked the "original Americans." Apart from disease, other less destructive forces contributed to the eradication of Indian America. Famine would not winnow the native population, as in Ireland, but emigration did. I do not mean the transoceanic type but rather the constant dislocations and removals of Indians from their ancestral lands on numerous, now obscure, occasions, both in colonial times and later within and between states. In the early colonial period, this "emigration" at times took the form of "praying towns" in seventeenth-century Massachusetts or "reservations" in Virginia. Invariably, in reaction to the English settlers' lust for land, Indian tribes were constantly moving or being moved around. The Delaware (to choose only one tribe) are found first in the state of that name, then moved to Pennsylvania and on to Ohio, thence to lands west of the Mississippi. The most famous "emigration," legitimated by the federal Indian Removal Act, is the Cherokees' "Trail of Tears" in the 1830s. In that decade one hundred thousand Indians, constituting the so-called five civilized tribes east of the Mississippi River, were rounded up and force-marched—trans-planted—to Oklahoma, America's Connacht.[55] In American history, the Indians have had their own "westward migration."

Warfare between natives and settlers was endemic because of the Euroamericans' continuous grasping for land. "The dayly fear that possest them," an early Virginian noted of the Powhatan Indians, was "that in time we by our

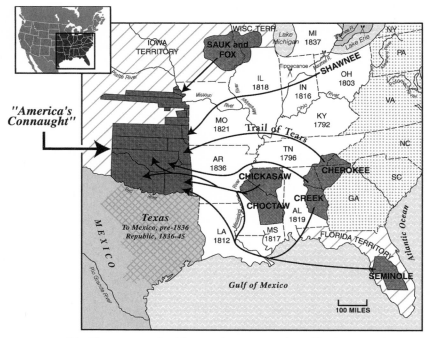

Note: Of course, many minor tribes moved or were removed as well but they are not shown on this map.

Native		Settler	
←	Indian Removal routes	– – – – –	State boundaries
X	Site of Battles	∷∷∷	United States as of 1790
▨	Indian land lost by treaty	**TN** **1796**	STATE and Date of Statehood
▨	Indian Territory (Oklahoma)	▨	U.S. Territories as of 1840
		▨	Texas

MAP 7. Indian removals from Eastern America, 1830–1840.

growing continually upon them, would dispossesse them of this Country."[56] In the early decades of contact, before they were so outnumbered, America's natives more than held their own in the fighting. For the Indians, the seventeenth-century wars were the most spectacular and the most successful in killing the European intruders. In uprisings in Virginia in 1622 and from 1644 to 1646, Indians killed 350 and 500 settlers, respectively. In King Philip's War in New England in 1675 and 1676, Indians killed 600 whites; in South Carolina's Yamassee War in 1715 and 1716, the natives killed 400 settlers. The

"Indian threat" was quite intimidating in the colonial era, not because they were better warriors than later, but because the number of settlers killed represented a relatively high proportion of the settler population.[57] This threat from Indian warfare was soon checked by the rapid rise in America's settler population. Events such as the 1704 Deerfield massacre of 54 settlers in western Massachusetts and the widespread alarm of 1754–1755 in central New York and western Pennsylvania, were traumatic to be sure, but in retrospect they represent the Indians' final and unsuccessful bid to pen up the Euroamericans in their populous, seaboard thirteen colonies.

Beyond the Appalachians and later the Mississippi, America's natives put up a strong and often clever resistance. In the 1770s, the fierceness of Indian opposition to the settlers' westward movement into Kentucky led the area to be called "the dark and bloody ground." But still the settlers came. In the Ohio territory, in a battle at the Maumee River (1791), Shawnee and Miami warriors killed 630 men of the small army (3,000 troops) the new U.S. government had put in the field against the Indians. This battle would be the most lethal military loss of settlers in America's frontier history.[58] And still the settlers came. Tecumseh rallied the Indians in what the whites called the Northwest Territory, but the death of the Shawnee leader at the battle of the Thames (1813) foreshadowed the fate of native resistance east of the Mississippi. Likewise, the Black Hawk War initially unsettled whites in the Illinois and Wisconsin territories, but only for a few years (1830–1832). Across the Mississippi, for both sides, white and red, the nineteenth-century Plains Wars were episodic, and bloodshed was more spotty than chronic.[59] To be sure, the drama was heightened when a Sand Creek massacre (about 150 Cheyennes killed, mostly women and children, 1864) alternated with a Fetterman massacre (all killed in a party of 80 soldiers, 1866).[60]

Overall, we may conclude that, however individually heroic, the Indians—weakened by disease, uncapitalized, and poorly organized—were overcome more by human numbers than military technology. The Indians rarely won and usually took punishing losses. White setbacks were rare. We remember Colonel Custer and his 225 men killed at the Little Bighorn (1876), a river in the Montana Territory, because the incident was a notorious exception.[61] Indeed, as the white wave of "civilization" washed over the continent, those who were fighting in defense of their land, the Indians, were portrayed as the "savage" aggressors. America's settlers were victimized winners, "badly abused conquerors." As Richard White has shrewdly observed, the "icons" of America's settler history "are not victories, they are defeats: the Alamo and the Battle of the Little Bighorn. We do not plan our conquests. We just retaliate against massacres."[62]

Settlers won most of the battles, of course. Most importantly, they won the war. From the early Virginians' reprisals against Indian attacks (1,000 natives killed, 1622–1624)[63] and the Puritans' terrorization of the Pequots (300–700 massacred at Mystic, Connecticut, in 1637), to the New Englanders' killing of 5,000 Indians in King Philip's War (including the beheading of Metacomet, chief of the Wampanoags), the indiscriminate killings in Bacon's Rebellion in Virginia, and the 2,000 Indians killed in South Carolina's Tuscarora and Yamassee wars—settler violence against natives in colonial America was employed firmly, episodically, and decisively. As settler America tramped westward, the story of the white man's triumph in warfare against the aboriginals—the death of Tecumseh in Canada, Andy Jackson's assault on the Creeks in the Old Southwest, the Plains Indian wars—acquired tones of inevitability and even, on occasion, the "blessing" of divine providence. Yet—and this is an important qualification—for all the thousands of Indian lives lost in battle, this mortality level pales into insignificance against Indian loss of life by disease.

By far the Indians' greatest enemy was their own bodies. That is, in the cruelest of ironies, the Indians' death warrants resulted from their long geographic isolation. The Indians simply lacked any physical immunity to the diseases of the European intruders. So wherever the whites went, they carried death with them. Native Americans had no resistance to the invisible killers—smallpox, tuberculosis, diphtheria, influenza, scarlet fever, measles. The Indian holocaust in the Americas, North and South, was "the greatest demographic disaster in history." "The most severe . . . loss of aboriginal population" in world history are the carefully chosen words of demographer Henry Dobyns.[64] In the century after the Columbian contact of 1492, Indian mortality rates approximated the devastation of nuclear warfare.

The slaughter in the Americas began, of course, with the Mayas and Aztecs. "Great was the stench of the dead," noted one sixteenth-century Mayan chronicler. "The dogs and vultures devoured the bodies. The mortality was terrible. All of us were thus. We were born to die!" As late as two centuries after the initial contact, a German missionary in Hispanic America in 1699 could observe dryly—and famously: "The Indians die so easily that the bare look and smell of a Spaniard causes them to give up the ghost." When Cortes landed in 1519, Mexico's population was about 25 million; by 1600, the "pustuled, oozing horror" had cut it to fewer than 2 million. One Yucatan native tried to put into words what pre-Columbian society had been like before his earth became a hell: "There was then no sickness; they had no aching bones; . . . they had then no smallpox. . . . At that time the course of humanity was orderly. The foreigners made it otherwise when they arrived here."[65]

For North America's natives, the dying began with the first intrusion of the English speakers. Starting in "New England" and in Virginia in the sixteenth century, death slowly spread across the continent to the Pacific Coast and, in time, to Hawaii. In settler America the killing began, predictably, at Roanoke in the 1580s. "Within a few days of our departure from . . . [their] towns, . . . people began to die very fast, and many in short space. The disease also was so strange that they neither knew what it was, nor how to cure it." In New England, as a result of contact with English fishermen, the Indian population fell by one-third *before* the Pilgrims' arrival at Plymouth in 1620. A Massachusetts settler in 1622 noted, "[They] died on heapes, as they lay in their houses. . . . [Their] Carkases ly above the ground without burial. And the bones and skulls upon the severall places . . . made such a spectacle . . . that, as I travailed in the Forrest . . . it seemed to me a new found Golgotha." During a smallpox epidemic in 1633 in Connecticut, William Bradford recorded that the Indians "die like rotten sheep."[66] Overall, scholars estimate that New England's native population dropped from 140,000 in 1600 to 10,000 by 1675.

As the whites headed inland, microbes and disease vectors—"the European's invisible ally"[67]—cleared the land of its native inhabitants. The spontaneous genocide spared no region. In the northeast, at the frontier's edge in New York, the Iroquois Five Nations lost half of their population in the seventeenth century. Southeastern tribes may have been infected as early as De Soto's travels between 1539 and 1541; we know that their populations were periodically winnowed from the late 1600s onward. One smallpox epidemic in 1738 caused the Cherokees to lose half of their population; likewise, the Catawbas of North Carolina had their population halved by disease in 1759. Settler expansion into Ohio and Kentucky brought smallpox to tribes there between 1779 and 1781.

As Euroamerican society incrementally pushed west across the Mississippi River, native populations on the plains were routinely ravaged. Epidemics in the early nineteenth century exterminated "two-thirds of the Omahas and perhaps half the entire population between the Missouri River and New Mexico." A smallpox outbreak from 1837 to 1838 killed "nearly every last one of the Mandans and perhaps half the people of the high plains." This dread disease probably reached the Pacific Northwest coast as early as 1782; a decade later the explorer George Vancouver reported that the Puget Sound area was "a general cemetery for the whole of the surrounding country, [which] at no very remote period . . . had been far more populous than at present."[68] Down the coast, in California in the five decades after 1848 (date of cession to the United States), settler shooting parties only added to the disease holocaust: That state's Indian population fell from an estimated 100,000 in 1848 to 20,000 by 1900.[69]

In summary, not only did America's natives lose the continent that had been their home for tens of thousands of years, but also demographically they were destroyed. The Indians disappeared from the landscape. In Pres. Andrew Jackson's words, "the tribes were annihilated or have melted away to make room for the whites." North America was not a "virgin land"; rather, in the clever words of historian Francis Jennings, it was a "widowed land."[70] In North America north of Mexico, an Indian population conservatively estimated at 3 million in 1500 had fallen four centuries later to a population of perhaps half a million. If we focus on land east of the Mississippi River that later became part of the United States, scholars today suggest that the Indian population there fell from 560,000 in 1500 to 250,000 by 1700. In the early nineteenth century, the settlers' new government attempted to enumerate the Indians "within the area of the United States of America": An official report (1822) offered a figure of 471,000. In 1890, the national census could find only 248,000 Indians living on U.S. territory.[71]

The dimensions of the native-settler equation leap out to us if we recall that, in 1890, the traditional date scholars assign to the closing of the frontier, the total U.S. population in forty-four states was 63 million people. Euroamerican settlers thus officially outnumbered Native Americans by 252 to 1. Three hundred years after 1600, the fatal combination of an Indian disease holocaust with a perfect storm of European immigration and Euroamerican procreation had caused America's natives virtually to vanish.

SETTLER

Arguably, the most important fact about the trend line of America's settler population is that it enjoyed an inverse relationship to that of the native population. That is, as the original Americans decreased in numbers, the new Americans dramatically increased and prospered. American history would confirm Adam Smith's dictum in *The Wealth of Nations* (1776) that "the colony of a civilized nation which takes possession either of a waste country, or of one so thinly inhabited, that the natives easily give place to the new settlers, advances more rapidly to wealth and greatness than any other human society."[72]

Of course, at first this secular trend was not clear. In the early decades natives heavily outnumbered settlers. As late as 1700, settler and native populations east of the Mississippi were roughly equal, totaling about 250,000 on each side—thus the terror of events such as King Philip's War. But very rapidly, beginning in the early eighteenth century, the settler population swelled from high birth rates and abundant immigration. Half a million Europeans, mostly Germans and (Protestant) Irish, emigrated to America during the eighteenth century.[73] Tough Scots-Irish Ulster families, long used to (and fleeing from) Ireland's "papist heathen," scrambled across the Appalachian mountains in search of lush new homesteads—and now encountered *Amer-*

Table 2. Immigration to the United States, 1821–1890 (in Thousands)

Year	Total Immigrants	Irish Immigrants	Irish as Percentage of Total	European as Percentage of Total
1821–1830	144	51	35.4	69.2
1831–1840	599	207	34.6	82.8
1841–1850	1,713	781	45.6	93.3
1851–1860	2,598	914	35.2	94.4
1861–1870	2,315	436	18.9	89.2
1871–1880	2,812	437	15.5	80.8
1881–1890	5,247	655	12.5	90.3

From data in tables in Mary Beth Norton, David Katzman, et al., *A People and a Nation*, vol. 1 (Boston: Houghton Mifflin, 1982), appendix, pp. A15 (world region), A16 (country).

ica's native peoples.[74] The Proclamation of 1763, guaranteeing trans-Appalachia to the Indians, had presented no obstacle to adventurous, land-hungry settlers. The Treaty of Paris (1783) fixed on maps the new republic's western border at the Mississippi River. And with the U.S. government's Louisiana Purchase in 1803—sometimes described as "the best real estate deal in history" ($15 million to France, or about three cents an acre)—the trans-Mississippi region was transformed from a barrier into a destination. Settlers swarmed ever westward—by river, canal, national road, and then railroad. Already by 1850, two million Euroamericans had crossed the great river, and in the next two decades 5 million more "westering emigrants" left the settled Euroamerican civilization east of the Mississippi.[75]

America was "on the move." Its population was booming. Natural increase and, most famously, in-migration swelled the settlers' ranks. Throughout the nineteenth century, huge waves of immigration from Europe brought more new Americans, again mostly emigrant Germans and Irish. As table 2 makes clear, between 1821 and 1890, some 15 million immigrants entered America. The vast majority came from Europe: After 1830, more than eight or even nine of every ten immigrants in any given year were Europeans.[76] Across the increasingly busy North Atlantic, sailing ships and later steamships in their regularly scheduled routes brought Europe's "huddled masses" on the 3,000-mile trip from Europe to New York (table 2). European in its seventeenth-century settler origins, America in the nineteenth century was now acting as Europe's "safety valve," draining off that continent's ambitious, enterprising poor as it restocked America with this new transplantation of Europeans. In the half century down to 1870, prominent among this influx of Europeans were 2.4 million Irish men, women, and children, mostly impoverished

Catholics, who accounted for one-third of all immigrants (7.4 million). Moreover, in the half century after 1870, the number of Irish immigrants remained sizeable (2.0 million, 1870–1920). Thus, since so many of those leaving Ireland were Catholic, we may observe that those who had been natives in Ireland were now settlers in America.[77]

America's population—composed of majority European (by descent or first-generation immigrant) and minority African (slave and free)—soared from 1.2 million in 1750 to 3.9 million in 1790 and 12.8 million in 1830. There was no penning up of America's settlers. The continuous Euroamerican "waves of population and civilization . . . rolling to the westward" rapidly reshaped the new nation's demography:[78] By 1830, one in every three Americans lived beyond the Appalachians. By the terms of the Northwest Ordinance of 1787, a part of the frontier could become a state when it reached a population of 60,000 "free [i.e., white settler] inhabitants," men, women, and children.[79] Thus, we can track the Euroamericans' western expansion by date of statehood. As map 8 shows, Kentucky and Tennessee became states in the 1790s, and with the entry of Ohio, Indiana, Illinois, Alabama, and Mississippi in the 1810s, the path of white conquest north and south, from Chicago to New Orleans, was clearly visible by 1820. On the west bank of the "Mother of Rivers," Missouri's entry in 1821 portended the transcontinental expansion that by midcentury would encompass Texas and California. America's original thirteen colonies (1607–1783) had, by 1820, become the United States' twenty-two states and, by 1850, thirty. In the eighty years since 1770, the nation's population (roughly four-fifths of European/Euroamerican descent) had expanded tenfold from 2.1 to 23.2 million people.

This surging flood tide, or "perfect storm," of white settlers swept before them those few, diseased, and disappearing people known as Indians. The Northwest Ordinance studiously ignored their existence. The national censuses did not include them in a state's population. From the eyes of Tecumseh the Shawnee, who died fighting at the Battle of the Thames, or Kooweskoowe, better known as John Ross, the Cherokee chief who led his force-marched people to Oklahoma—it was a flood from which there was no escape. Just look at the population of the emerging frontier states (see map 8). Ohio (which became a state in 1803) grew from a settler population of 45,000 in 1800 to 938,000 in 1830. To the south, Alabama (a state in 1819) had only 1,000 whites and black slaves in 1800; thirty years later, in 1830, Alabama's population was 310,000. A later example, the western state of California, fit the earlier demographic trends. At the time it was acquired in 1848 (Mexican cession), California had essentially no Anglo Euroamerican population.[80] Within two years, thanks to the gold rush, the region drew more than 100,000 English speakers, and California entered the Union in 1850. By 1860, the

Top 7 Cities in 1830

Rank in 1790	1830	City	Population	Future Rank in 1870
2	1	New York City*	217,600	1
1	2	Philadelphia	161,400	2
5	3	Baltimore	80,600	5
3	4	Boston	61,400	6
4	5	Charleston	30,300	n/r
n/r	6	New Orleans	29,700	8
n/r	7	Cincinnati	24,800	7

*Includes Brooklyn, NY
n/r not ranked

A Sign of the Western Boom: In 1830 St. Louis was small and Chicago non-existent, but by 1870 they would be respectively the country's 3rd (310,900) and 4th (299,000) largest cities.

Westward Expansion

⊢+⊣ Proclamation Line of 1763

Settled by 1700

Settled by 1800

Settled by 1830

Frontier Regional Populations
(in thousands)

51 Population in 1800
1,470 Population in 1830
***4,932** Population of 9 northern states in 1830
***3,581** Population of 6 southern states in 1830

Frontier States and Territories

	Population in 1800	1830
NORTHWEST		
Illinois (1818)	---	257
Indiana (1816)	6	343
Michigan Terr. (1837)	---	32
Ohio (1803)	45	938
Total	**51**	**1,470**
SOUTHWEST		
Alabama (1819)	1	310
Arkansas Terr. (1836)	1	30
Florida Terr. (1845)	---	35
Louisiana (1812)	50	216
Mississippi (1817)	8	137
Total	**60**	**728**
WEST		
Kentucky (1792)	221	688
Missouri (1821)	10	140
Tennessee (1796)	106	682
Total	**337**	**1,510**

Population in thousands
(1818) Date of Statehood.
(1837) Territory later became state in (this year).

➤ *Roughly one of every three Americans lived west of the Appalachians in 1830.*

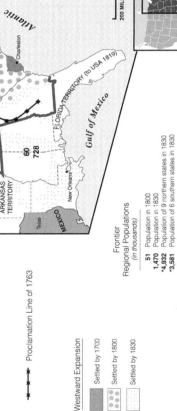

MAP 8. Settler America in 1830: The flood tide westward.

Table 3. Population of the United States, 1790–1890 (in Millions)

Year	No. of States	Population	Percentage Decennial Population Increase	Decennial Total of Immigrants as Percentage of Decennial Population Increase
1790	13	3.9	. . .	
1800	16	5.3	35.1	. . .
1810	17	7.2	36.4	. . .
1820	23	9.6	33.1	. . .
1830	24	12.9	33.5	4.3
1840	26	17.1	32.7	14.3
1850	31	23.2	35.9	27.9
1860	33	31.4	35.6	31.7
1870	37	39.8	26.6	27.4
1880	38	50.2	26.0	26.9
1890	44	62.9	25.5	40.9

From data in tables in Norton, Katzman, et al., *A People and a Nation*, vol. 1, appendix, p. A14.

state's population had swollen to 380,000. "Like locusts they swarmed," America's settlers heading "always to the west, and only the Pacific Ocean stopped them."[81]

The rate and volume of America's settler population growth was unprecedented in world history: so much land to fill up; so much land filled up. Seventy years in the colonial era (1680–1750) had produced a tenfold increase to a population of 1.2 million. Subsequent growth saw more than a doubling of the nation's population every thirty years: 4 million in 1790, 10 million in 1820, 23 million in 1850, and 50 million by 1880. Table 3 illustrates the huge role immigration played in this process of population compounding: In the 1850s, for instance, the U.S. population grew by 35.6 percent, and fully 31.7 percent of that decade's growth was due to the arrival of 2,598,000 immigrants (see also table 2). Indeed, the immigration flood tide would crest in the years from 1880 to 1920, a forty-year period when 23.5 million immigrants came in, more than twice the number (9.4 million) in the period from 1840 to 1880. America's population would continue to increase at high rates, doubling between 1880 and 1920 (pop. 106 million) and then nearly doubling again, to 203 million by 1970. By 2000, the nation's population had reached 281 million, and more Americans described themselves as being of German or Irish ancestry than of British.[82]

If the decennial U.S. censuses (from 1790 to the present) essentially tell the story of settler triumph, other evidence corroborates it. In the censuses one searches long and hard to find data on the number of Indians in unorganized territories or to see them as miniscule pieces in the ethnic puzzle of a state's population. It is important—and quite revealing—to recall that some of America's settlers (the early generations) even appropriated to themselves the word "native," calling themselves "Native Americans" or "nativists." In nineteenth-century America, in the language of both the street and the official census, "native-born" (English-speaking, mostly Protestant) American citizens wanted to keep themselves strictly separate from the hordes of "immigrants," who were described as "foreigners" or "foreign born" (Europeans). But of course both groups were of European descent: One had simply arrived more recently. My point is that the term "Native American" could carry this Euroamerican meaning because America's original natives were gone—out of sight, out of mind. America's Indians were now either long since dead, or their few and pathetic remnants were relentlessly disappearing over the western horizon.

Anyone today can quickly confirm this statistical vanishing of the original Americans. A popular recent American history textbook prints in its appendix a line graph that plots the percentage of "whites" and "nonwhites" in the U.S. population in the two centuries since the national census originated in 1790. The top line on the graph tracks the yearly percentage of majority "white" population (significantly, always above 80 percent), while the bottom line shows the minority "nonwhite" share (20 percent or less). Significantly, the "nonwhite" population comprises essentially *another* (if involuntary) immigrant group: people of African descent. The original Americans, the Indians, are so diminished, so few and negligible in numbers, that they simply cannot be shown on this graph of the population history of the United States.[83]

MUSINGS

If we step back and try to gain new insights into America's settler-native relations by adjusting to a transatlantic, comparative focus with Ireland and South Africa, the word that comes to mind is neither interaction nor even removal or extinction. It is *obstacle:* America's natives were in the way. "The settlers wanted all of the land and none of the Indians."[84]

Historically, over the long term, the native problem in America was neither essentially one of conflict nor certainly one of finding for the Indian a purpose or role (e.g., as manual laborers) in the white man's society. Rather, the small and dwindling numbers of America's native peoples confirmed their status as a secondhand superfluity. The contrast to the settler population was startling. Look at the population dynamics of the new state of Ohio: "By 1850, the 20,000 Indians who had lived there until the American Revolution were replaced by 2,000,000 white people and a small number of blacks." To nineteenth-century Euroamericans, the Indians' demographic decline was not only proof of their racial inferiority but also evidence of their expendability. Indeed, in this age of "progress" and social and scientific Darwinism, many Euroamerican commentators pronounced that the Indians' destiny was extinction. As early as 1825, Henry Clay could acidly observe of America's natives, "Their disappearance from the human family will be no great loss to the world."[85] Irish immigrants to America, themselves now become New World settlers, also embraced this American manifest destiny. Richard O'Gorman, an 1848 rebel who had fled Ireland, fearing arrest by the British, settled in New York. From there, in 1859, he wrote the following to his fellow Irishman and rebel leader, William Smith O'Brien: "Every man that can should see the United States. The progress of the country . . . is miraculous. There is the Yankee—wondrous energy, self-reliance, readiness in the use of all his powers. He has . . . work to do, and he does it. The business of the day is to till the land, cut down lumber, drain swamps, *get rid of Indians,* build railways, cities, states—and our Yankee does it with surprising speed. . . . It is refreshing . . . to find that in this effervescing process, our Irish countrymen have their share. . . . I want you to write me at once and say when you are coming."[86]

The new nation early on had achieved its independence (1783) because the thirteen colonies were so populous (already half the population of England) and because demographically the Euroamerican settlers were so overwhelmingly dominant (already, in 1790, composing four-fifths of the new nation's total population). Independence, in turn, ensured the settlers a free hand with the continent's handful of Indians. (There was no need to worry about London directives, as earlier with the Proclamation of 1763.) When family quarrels did emerge within the nation in the early nineteenth century, the issues most often related to westward expansion and concerned the heated and differing views over the extension of slavery (a problem brought on by the importation of Africans, America's demographic minority). By contrast, what to do with America's few, vanishing natives was not the stuff of major policymaking. Demography dictated that (African) slavery, not Indian-settler encounters, would produce the defining moment of the nineteenth century: the American Civil War (1861–1865).

Whether in seventeenth-century western Massachusetts, eighteenth-century trans-Appalachia, or the nineteenth-century trans-Mississippi, America's moving Indian frontier represented the conquest but not the incorporation of the Indians. Pushed westward into irrelevance and oblivion, America's natives were not so much oppressed as they were useless and in the way. Ravaged by disease and overwhelmed by European immigration and Euroamerican procreation, the Indians—outnumbered 252 to 1, according to the 1890 census—were simply not needed. Faced with a low and shrinking native population, the hardworking, go-getter white settlers, who called themselves "Americans," would "do it themselves." If the irrelevance of the Indian is a historical fact, this fact does not remove its poignancy. In a remark to British Gen. Isaac Brock in 1812, the Shawnee leader Tecumseh got it mostly right when he described to Brock their common enemy, the land-hungry Americans: "We gave them forest-clad mountains and valleys full of game, and in return what did they give our warriors and our women? Rum and trinkets and a grave."[87]

SOUTH AFRICA

Remote from Europe, far down the South Atlantic, located at the very tip of the African continent lay a third Atlantic European-settler community. Well-watered if narrow greenbelts ringed the region's south and particularly east coast, but rugged hills and daunting mountain ranges—"the great escarpment" that slices the land from northeast to southwest—blocked entry to the broad interior of grasslands, plateaus, and deserts. High elevations gave much of the region a bracing climate to accompany the splendor of its seacoasts and mountains. Yet, for all its striking physical contrasts and stunning beauty, South Africa had liabilities, too. The dramatic coastline boasted few quiet bays or navigable rivers. Rainfall was scarce: More than twenty inches a year fell only along the south and east coast and in the eastern third of the subcontinent's hinterland. A land of haunting beauty, South Africa was a challenging place physically, as one day it would be demographically and politically as well.

History records that the first European to set foot in South Africa was the Portuguese explorer Bartholomeu Dias, or one of his men, in 1488. Others followed, always on their way somewhere else. Circumnavigating the globe a century after Dias, the Englishman Francis Drake (later to be knighted for his feat) had rounded the Cape of Good Hope and—in spying Table Mountain (elev. 3600 ft.), Lion's Head, and Devil's Peak towering over the surf below— had christened it "the fairest cape in all the world." It was here, seven decades later, that the Dutch became the first Europeans to settle in South Africa. In 1652, at a time when Cromwell was carving up Ireland and English Puritans were flocking to Massachusetts Bay, a handful of Hollanders led by Jan van Riebeeck founded a small seaport that they named Cape Town.

From this base, the Dutch speakers moved inland only slowly and tenta-

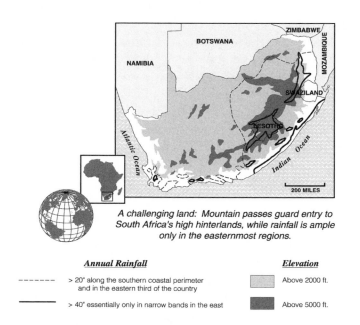

A challenging land: Mountain passes guard entry to South Africa's high hinterlands, while rainfall is ample only in the easternmost regions.

Annual Rainfall		Elevation	
-------	> 20" along the southern coastal perimeter and in the eastern third of the country		Above 2000 ft.
———	> 40" essentially only in narrow bands in the east		Above 5000 ft.

Note: The independent nations of Lesotho and Swaziland are included to show the physical geography of the region.

MAP 9. South Africa (physical): rainfall and elevation.

tively, encountering people whom they called "Bushmen" and "Hottentots." These brown-skinned natives were few in number, nomadic, and organized by kin and clan. They presented little threat to the settlers. By the late 1700s, some of the settlers were trekking farther inland, spreading in a slow process of eastern expansion. Now for the first time, in eastern South Africa, they bumped into serious adversaries: populous, mixed-farming, native African societies that were stable, not migratory, and organized into chiefdoms. In 1795, the government of Great Britain (from 1801 known as the United Kingdom) complicated things by moving in and claiming the Cape of Good Hope (Cape Colony). The British needed the Cape as a refreshment station—a half-way point—for their ships on the way to India. The stage was now set for the Great Trek beginning in the 1830s, a mythic migration into the interior by some of the original settlers of Dutch descent. To get away from the new English-speaking government at Cape Town, these *voortrekker* (pioneer) settler families crossed the mountains into lands beyond the Orange and then the Vaal Rivers, lands later to be called the Orange Free State and the Transvaal. Meanwhile, the British, who controlled the Cape Colony, also annexed coastal Natal (1843), even as the British army in eastern South Africa continued to have its hands full fighting large and powerful African tribes, first the Xhosa, then later and most famously the Zulu.

Mineral discoveries profoundly changed South Africa's history. In the late 1860s, diamonds were discovered. Twenty years later, in the Transvaal's *witwatersrand* ("white water's ridge"), gold was found in vast quantities. Soon to become South Africa's largest city, Johannesburg in the 1880s grew from a tent city into a boom town on the Transvaal High Veld (plateau region). Who would control this new wealth? To get the Transvaal's gold, the British fought the Dutch-descended settlers, who called themselves Afrikaners ("Africans"; compare to "Americans") but whom the British disdainfully called *boers,* a word in their language (Afrikaans) meaning "farmers." The British won the Boer War of 1899–1902 and took control of the Transvaal's gold. In 1910, the white settlers, new and old, British and Afrikaner, unified the Cape Colony, Natal, the Orange Free State, and the Transvaal into a single new nation, the Union of South Africa.

The frontier period was now over. But a key question remained: What about the native African people within the new country? As in Ireland, South Africa's natives greatly outnumbered the settlers, both Afrikaner and British. The union government's answer was to create numerous native reserves for the black tribes, whose adult men and women would provide labor for the nation's economy but not be citizens. This policy continued after the union became the Republic of South Africa in 1961. The apartheid government's *bantustans,* or tribal African homelands, were refinements of earlier patterns of separation and segregation.[88]

Yet, as the twentieth century deepened, the South African government's policies became increasingly controversial at home and abroad. By the 1970s, white minority rule was under siege. Could the settlers' state last? For how long could 20 percent of South Africa's population set the rules for the other 80 percent of the people?

SETTLER

If Ireland's settlers were few in a small, densely populated island and America's settlers were abundant in a land of huge physical area and a small, shrinking native population, South Africa was a big, expansive land with very few settlers. Indeed, unlike Ireland and America, South Africa was not originally intended as a settlement colony. Hugging the southwestern tip of the African continent, Cape Town had been founded in 1652 as a refreshment station for the ships of Amsterdam's *Vereenigde Oost-Indische Compagnie* (VOC, or Dutch East India Company) on their 12,000-mile route between Holland and the East Indies. Nevertheless, as adventurous and independent *trekboers* (seminomadic emigrant farmers and ranchers) roamed eastward, a colony began to grow from this "fragment" of Europe. The Cape Colony was a small, inward-looking society, one divorced by the great distance from (6,000 miles) and neglect by its culture hearth, Holland.[89] For a number of reasons the colony attracted few European immigrants: its remoteness from "civilization," VOC policies discouraging immigration, the Cape region's general aridity of climate (except along the coasts and the immediate hinterland), and an apparent absence of mineral or other economic wealth.

The lilliputian nature of this South African settler "fragment" of Europe is often forgotten. A handful of French Huguenots—156 Protestants fleeing persecution in Louis XIV's France—emigrated in 1688 to the Cape of Good Hope, where they joined the equally tiny original Dutch population. By 1700, the Cape Colony's white population—VOC employees and "free-burghers"—totaled fewer than 1,200 people (402 men, 224 women, and 521 children). In the eighteenth century a few emigrants from Germany added to the cultural mix of South Africa's settlers, who to preserve their identity (whether religious or not) called themselves "Christians" or, ironically (given the distance), "Europeans." The bulk of the settler population "apparently originated among the lower strata of European society: the urban proletariat, minor tradesmen and farmers."[90] A high birthrate, offset by the very low volume of in-migration from Europe, brought the Cape Colony's "European" population to only 20,000 by 1800. By contrast, at that date the (free, white) settler population in the United States totaled 4 million.

Great Britain's seizure of the Cape Colony in 1795 added a new dimension. Again, however, as with the Dutch VOC earlier, the British government's motives during the wars with revolutionary France were strategic. By controlling the Cape (made official by the 1814 Treaty of Paris), Britain sought only to protect its sea route to India; it had no plans for settlement yet. In 1843, for similar reasons, the British government would establish Natal as its base on the Indian Ocean coast. Britain's intrusive presence would have several important consequences: the Great Trek (1836–1854) inland by some of the Dutch settlers, the consequent opening up of lands beyond the Orange and Vaal Rivers, and the presence in the Cape and Natal of British imperial military forces that were state funded and highly organized (as opposed to the Boers' local commandos).

The settler period 1800–1870 is again important for what did *not* happen: a substantial in-migration of settlers from Europe. The original homeland (Holland) sent out no further emigrants. Other countries sent out only a few. Europe's transatlantic emigrants in their vast, seaborne numbers headed west to far closer New York or Montreal, not south to distant Cape Town. Unrefreshed by new waves of immigrants, most of the original settlers' descendants—who would come to call themselves Afrikaners—adjusted to life in the now British-ruled Cape Colony. But others, ultimately about a fifth of the Cape's "European" population, had strong feelings about preserving and

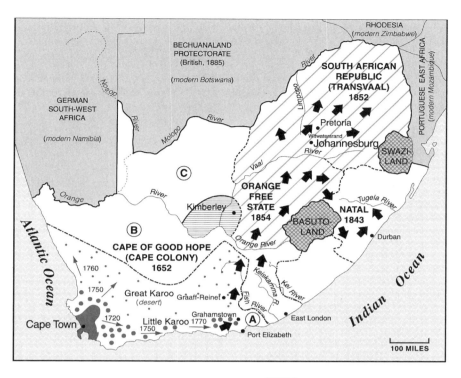

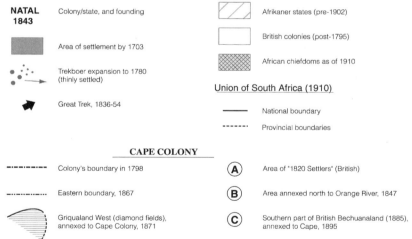

MAP 10. Settler South Africa: expansion east, then north.

protecting their customs and their evolving "African Dutch" frontier language (Afrikaans). In the 1830s, the fateful decision was made: They would begin moving away from the reach of British law, language, and culture. Trekking intermittently but steadily into the interior, beyond the Orange and then the Vaal River, these fifteen thousand "stubbornly egalitarian and anarchic" voortrekkers would establish the Orange River Colony (later named the Orange Free State) and South African Republic (Transvaal). For them and their descendants, the Great Trek would become "the central event of European man in southern Africa."[91] In the continent's High Veld interior, the Free State and the Transvaal would resist Britain's attempts in the 1870s and 1880s to incorporate them into a British Confederation of South Africa. For half a century these two small Afrikaner societies would hold onto their fragile autonomy.

Emigration from the United Kingdom brought into British South Africa— the Cape and Natal—only a trickle of new settlers. South African history textbooks highlight the "1820 Settlers," a group of British and Irish emigrant families coming into the eastern Cape Colony in Britain's "first and last government-sponsored scheme."[92] Still, these settlers totaled only 5,000 people. Between 1849 and 1851, Natal was infused with some British and a few German settlers—again totaling only about 5,000 people. From his study of the official statistics from United Kingdom ports, historian Donald Akenson has found that, from 1844 to 1876, there was an ongoing emigration to South Africa—but only on the order of 1,000–2,000 people, occasionally 4,000, each year. Overall, in the period from 1857 to 1883, a total of about 30,000 British emigrated to South Africa. Recent research indicates that these British settlers tended to come from a higher social class than the Dutch/German eighteenth-century settlers. They tended to be "urban artisans,... respectable individuals possessed of some financial means," and as townspeople they helped to expand and in many places initiate South Africa's urban development.[93]

Overall, in 1865, on the eve of the mineral discoveries, still highly rural South Africa was home to about 250,000 people of European descent. Two-thirds of them (180,000) lived in the original settlement, the Cape Colony. The Transvaal had perhaps 30,000 "Europeans," the Orange Free State maybe 20,000, and tiny Natal only 16,000. South Africa's largest city was Cape Town, whose population had grown to 30,000; the second largest, in the eastern Cape, was Port Elizabeth (pop. 9,000), whose name honored Britain's intrusion. The contrast to America was enormous. Far across the Atlantic, metropolitan New York City's population in 1860 was slightly more than one million, and young frontier towns like Cincinnati and St. Louis, each with a population of 160,000, had rapidly become major cities.

The mineral discoveries—diamonds northeast of the confluence of the Orange and Vaal in 1867 and gold in the southern Transvaal in 1886—mark the watershed event in modern South African history. Hitherto a remote pastoral land with a largely precapitalist economy, South Africa now seemed to offer a beacon for European immigration. After some hurried boundary redrawing, sparkling Kimberley (1871 pop. 25,000) was suddenly the Cape Colony's second largest city. By 1891, the British-controlled Cape, the "whitest" of the four provinces, had increased its total "European" population to 376,000, two-thirds of them Afrikaner. At this date there were 46,000 settlers in Natal, 77,000 in the Orange Free State, and 119,000 in the Transvaal. South Africa's total white population in 1891 was about 620,000.

Growth from this low settler base would be difficult. The date was late. For, even with a quickening of immigration, the task of generating quick catch-up growth was herculean. South Africa's settler population was suffering from the absence of the multigenerational "multiplier" effect that benefited other settler societies.[94] Rapid and early settler growth in America, and similar growth later in Australia, not only gave those societies a valuable "kick start" but ensured big future growth.[95] By contrast, "South Africa in her early formative period received no strong, steady stream of immigrants, which seriously retarded her rate of development."[96] When, in the mid-1830s, South Africa's Afrikaners began their Great Trek, the Cape Colony's settler population was only 65,000 (itself a big increase: up from 5,000 in 1750). Nevertheless, recall that, across the Atlantic, the United States in 1830 boasted a *white* population of 12 million—up from 1 million in 1750 and 50,000 in 1650. Here was the miracle of compounding at work.

As with the California gold rush in America a half century earlier, the lure of quick wealth brought strangers, both rowdy and respectable, to South Africa's gold fields in the 1890s. With the influx of 44,000 *uitlanders* (foreigners, i.e., not Transvaal citizens), three-fifths of them not of South African birth, golden Johannesburg quickly became a boom city (pop. 75,000 in 1899) that surpassed Cape Town in size. The decades after 1880 drew European (mostly British) immigrants to South Africa as never before. The fastest-growing province was now the Transvaal: from 40,000 "Europeans" living there in 1879 to 119,000 in 1890 and 420,000 by 1911. By the early twentieth century, South Africa's mostly British immigrants belonged disproportionately to skilled classes: the professions, commerce, and finance. Interestingly, though Irish immigrants were few, less than 5 percent of all British Isles immigrants to South Africa, they too had disproportionately high education and skill levels. "Being Irish" in South Africa did not mean at all what it meant to be Irish in America.[97]

Historically, the growth of settler South Africa had been hurt by negatives

Table 4. Population of South Africa, 1911

	European or White	Bantu
Cape Colony	582,377	1,519,939
Natal	98,114	953,398
Orange Free State	175,189	325,824
Transvaal	420,562	1,219,845
Total	1,276,242	4,019,006

Total 1911 population: 5,973,394. The Union of South Africa's census divided the population into two major categories, "European or white" and "other than European or white." This second category was then divided into "Bantu" and "mixed and other colored." The latter are omitted from this table.

South Africa's natives—so-called "pure" Africans, the Bantu—formed 85.6% of the census category labeled "other than European or white." The remainder (14.4% of nonwhites) were the 678,146 people categorized as "mixed and other colored." Two-thirds of these lived in the Cape Colony: 462,649 people of mixed race, the "Cape Colored," with nearly all the rest (142,531 people, mostly of Indian descent) living in Natal. Combining the population totals for Bantu and mixed/colored people produces the 1911 national total of 4,697,152 people officially described as "other than European or white."

From the abstract of the Union of South Africa's 1911 census, printed in D. Hobart Houghton and Jenifer Dagut, *Source Material on the South African Economy, 1860–1970*, vol. 2 (Cape Town: Oxford University Press, 1972), pp. 146–47.

such as the distance from Europe or the intimidating presence of large and powerful native tribes. By the 1890s, however, there came into focus a new and very different reason for South Africa's low volume of European immigration. On the nineteenth-century rural Afrikaner frontier, the scattered patriarchal households had always informally recruited native labor as servants and cattle herders. Now the process could be made formal, the recruitment systematic. As Transvaal gold stoked Britain's interest in the region, the overseas power of London's finance capital would tame, organize, and finally regiment an *African* workforce into an urban proletariat. The United States might have a great need for the unskilled labor of European immigrants; South Africa did not.[98]

Britain's bid to control Johannesburg's gold (already 27 percent of the world's output by 1899) triggered the Boer War of 1899 to 1902, a messy conflict in which Goliath (Britain) ultimately prevailed over David (the Afrikaners).[99] Afterward, in 1910, the victorious British united the four provinces, two Afrikaner and two British, into a new nation, the Union of South Africa, and granted it dominion status within the British Empire. Over the past forty years, South Africa's settlers had increased their numbers fivefold: The first national census (1911) recorded a population of 1.3 million "Europeans." The volume of immigration from Britain had been large enough that the original settler group, the Afrikaners, now accounted for just under three-fifths of South Africa's white population. The "white man's war"[100] had recently decided that Britain would prevail in South Africa. Now the two "European" groups, Briton and Boer, had to stop their bickering: To their mutual advantage they would rule together. "The *ultimate* end," pronounced British high commissioner Sir Alfred Milner, "is a self-governing white community, supported by *well-treated* and *justly governed* black labour from Cape Town to [the] Zambesi [River]."[101]

Nevertheless, as "the white man's" nineteenth century faded into history, new questions in a new century would emerge. In politics and power, South Africa was indeed a white man's country. Yet in population numbers it was "black." For, according to the 1911 census, the new Union of South Africa also contained 4 million native Africans (table 4). Nearly four-fifths (78.6 percent) of South Africa's population was "other than European or white." Therein lies the rest of our story.

NATIVE

In 1600, scholars suggest, the African continent was home to nearly 60 million people. Four of every five Africans lived south of the Sahara Desert, most of these in west Africa, with a secondary sub-Saharan concentration in east central Africa. Relative to other geographic regions, very few Africans lived at the southern, especially the southwestern, edge of the continent.[102]

Historically, South Africa's settlers encountered native peoples in a two-stage process. As the "European" settlers moved north and east from Cape Town from the 1650s on, they bumped into short, brown-skinned people whom anthropologists today call the "Khoisan." This modern word combines Khoikhoi (cattle-herding pastoralists) and San (hunter-gatherers). At the time, South Africa's settlers called them, respectively, "Hottentots" and "Bushmen" *(Bosjesman).*[103] The Khoisan lived a simple, austere, nomadic life and were organized in small clan and kinship groups. Numbering probably no more than two hundred thousand at the time of contact, they were thinly scattered across the arid western three-fifths of the subcontinent. Some had had contact with native neighbors to the east, but most had not. Most importantly, as it turned out, for thousands of years the San and the more numerous Khoikhoi had lived in isolation from any contact with visitors from afar.

Though the Khoisan greatly outnumbered the tiny number of Dutch settlers, they soon succumbed for two reasons. First, as with the natives of North America, diseases reduced their ranks. Isolation proved their undoing: Their bodies had no immunities to European diseases. The settlers tended to come into greater contact with the cattle-herding Khoikhoi than the reclusive, more remote San. Many Khoikhoi died in a smallpox epidemic in 1713 (the infection had come ashore with some shipboard linen to be washed) and in later ones in 1755 and 1767. Second, a series of short brutal wars, from 1659 to 1660 and between 1673 and 1677, completed the rout of Khoikhoi society. Both organized and spontaneous settler shooting parties—perhaps four thousand Khoikhoi were killed between 1775 and 1800—provided the final insults.[104] For the native survivors, there were two choices: Retreat north and east to safety in the arid interior, or stay and accept work as the settlers' domestic servants and cattle herders. By the last third of the eighteenth century, it seemed that the North American story of European dominance and native "extermination" might be repeated in the vast spaces of southwestern Africa.

In fact, the settlers' problems were only beginning. From the 1770s, the handful of Dutch trekboers trickling into the well-watered eastern two-fifths of the subcontinent encountered highly populous and politically organized societies of black-skinned people. These settled, Bantu-speaking communities practiced swidden (slash-and-burn) agriculture as well as cattle herding and metallurgy. Multilingual in the Bantu family of languages, these societies were the Mpondo, Pedi, Sotho, Swazi, Tsonga, Tswana, Xhosa, and Zulu, among others. We now know that the "Europeans" had encountered the descendants of people who nearly 1,500 years earlier had been part of a vast southward migration from the interior of the African continent. Scholars believe that these migrating Bantu tribes had reached the southeastern tip of Africa and made it their new home about 300 A.D. A Portuguese sailor, shipwrecked on the Indian Ocean coast in 1554, had described these people as tall, healthy, "very black in colour, with woolly hair." A shipwrecked Dutchman had reported the following in 1689: "The country is exceedingly fertile, and incredibly populous, and full of cattle. . . . [The people] are very civil, polite, and talkative, saluting each other, . . . whenever they meet."[105] Modern scholars have estimated that, about 1700, this Bantu population numbered between 2 and 4 million. This number means that the Bantu speakers, or native Africans, as I call them, were at least ten times more numerous than the Khoikhoi to the west.[106]

The single most important thing to remember about stage two of this native-settler contact—namely, encountering the Africans from c. 1770 onward—is that these native people were resistant to European diseases. Long contact with Arab traders in East Africa had endowed these African natives with bodily immunities to the diseases like smallpox that had ravaged the Khoikhoi. The Africans would not conveniently die off, like North America's natives. Nor would a famine holocaust remove a fourth of this African population, as happened to Ireland's natives in the 1840s.[107]

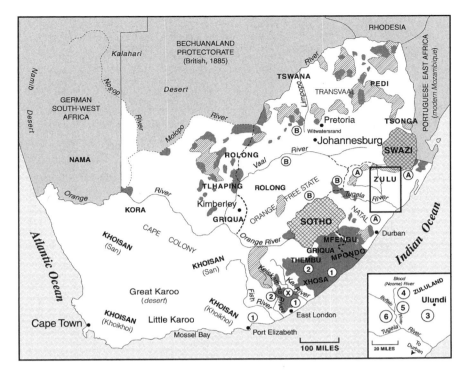

SOUTH AFRICA: A nation heavy with "natives" in its eastern half

PEDI — Location of major African chiefdoms/societies

NATAL — Settler colony

 — Fort Hare College, 1916

SHRINKAGE OF NATIVE LAND AREAS

 "Native Reserves" established by the Natives Land Act, 1913

Areas added by 1936

The overlay of a 1982 map of the South African Government's "native homelands" (*bantustans*) would reveal (at least in physical area) the power of historical inheritance: minor additions, not major reconstruction.

INTRA-NATIVE CONFLICT & TURMOIL, c. 1815-1830

(A) *Mfecane* (east of Drakensberg Mtns.)

(B) *Difaqane* (west of the Drakensberg)

SETTLER-NATIVE CONFLICT

XHOSA
(1) Eastern Cape frontier wars, 1779-1878
(2) "Great Cattle Killing," 1856-57

ZULU
Afrikaners and Great Trek
(3) Murder of Piet Retief's settler party, Feb. 6, 1838
(4) Battle of Blood (Ncome) River, Dec. 16, 1838

Anglo-Zulu War
(5) Battle of Isandhlwana, Jan. 22, 1879
(6) Battle of Rorke's Drift, Jan. 22, 1879

NATIVE 'SURVIVOR' COMMUNITIES (*not incorporated into South Africa*)

BASOTHO kingdom of Moshoeshoe (1786-1868), British colony named Basutoland 1884, later independent nation of *Lesotho* 1966

SWAZILAND, a British colony 1902, later independent nation of *Swaziland* 1968

MAP 11. Native South Africa: resistance and incorporation.

If the African peoples were largely immune to European diseases, their cattle were not. "[O]ne of the most decisive conditions which made African life so different . . . from that of . . . the Americas . . . [was] the organisation of ordinary life around cattle and sheep herds." With tribal herds often numbering in the tens of thousands, cattle constituted a prime source of African status and wealth. They were important, too, to the mobile economy of the stock-farming trekboers, many of whom were often "merely seasonal settlers." Frontier conflict thus often assumed the form of a "bloody cattle raid" between settlers and natives.[108] But since the native Africans attached great cultural importance to cattle as well, diseases could have a devastating impact on their society. Take, for example, the unintended result of an event that occurred at Mossel Bay, a small port in the eastern Cape Colony, in September, 1853. There a Dutch ship was routinely unloading its cargo, which included some imported European cattle. Alas, one of the animals, a Friesland bull, was infected, and the ensuing outbreak of "lung sickness" (bovine pleuropneumonia) devastated settler and native herds alike. Because the disease was new to the region's own livestock, the resulting "virgin soil" epidemic killed as many as 80 percent of the cattle in some chiefdoms. Another cattle pandemic occurred forty years later. With the growing globalization of the cattle trade, the spread of the ancient European and Asian infectious cattle disease, "rinderpest," to sub–Saharan Africa resulted in what can only be called cattle holocausts. In South Africa in the 1890s, for example, rinderpest destroyed not only more than 80 percent of all cattle, native and settler, but devastated herds of game animals such as buffalo and eland as well.

We now know that it was the fatal cattle disease, bovine pleuropneumonia, that led the Xhosa to their collective suicide, the great "cattle killing" of 1856 and 1857. Defeated in the Eighth Cape–Xhosa War that took place from 1850 to 1853, their morale and land shrinking, their cattle devastated by "lung sickness," many Xhosa eagerly accepted the fantastic prophecy of the sixteen-year-old Nongqawuse. Revitalization would come and the "good times" return—"the dead shall arise," ancestral warriors and healthy cattle reappear—if the Xhosa abstained from crop planting and slaughtered their diseased herds. Xhosa society was swept by chaos as the sacrifices mounted: 400,000 animals killed and, subsequently, 40,000 Xhosa dead from starvation. What an ironic and unforeseen consequence of the decision by Eastern Cape farmers to restock their herds by the importation of European cattle![109]

A few words on missionaries and their impact on native cultures are in order here. Clearly, in an important sense, in their emphasis on spreading Christianity and European values, missionaries constituted yet another assault on Khoisan and African values and belief systems. However, in contrast to Ireland and America, where mission work was either rejected or weak, respectively, the missionary tradition was strong in South Africa, notably in the Cape Colony.[110] Beginning in the eighteenth century with German Moravians and continuing in the early nineteenth with the London Missionary Society, South Africa's missionaries have had a long history of not only protesting the brutalities of settler conquest but also introducing literacy and practical training to help the natives cope with the intrusive settler culture. Missionaries founded a number of schools (including the Native College at Fort Hare, 1916). By 1928, forty-eight missionary organizations were at work in South Africa, employing 1,700 whites and 30,000 African clergy and teachers. Compared to their counterparts in Ireland or America, missionaries in South Africa's history played a much more positive role in assisting natives to adapt to the spreading settler conquest. But they neither wanted to nor could stop that conquest. As the contemporary South African joke has it, "When the whites came, we had the land and you had the Bible. Now we have the Bible and you have the land."

Warfare in South Africa in the nineteenth century was both frequent and intense. Yet it is important to distinguish its differential impacts. Settler-native conflict was preceded by intertribal native warfare, most importantly the assault of that expansionist warrior society, the Zulu, against neighboring tribes. From 1815 to 1830, Shaka Zulu's victories in the *mfecane* ("the crushing") produced untold thousands of deaths from battle and starvation and also generated waves of forced migrations of displaced tribes (the Hlubi, Mpondo, Ngwane, Sotho, and Swazi). This *difaqane,* or "the scattering," as the Sotho called it, profoundly destabilized the southeast interior of southern Africa and so depopulated it that "white travelers [had] the impression that the area was uninhabited and unclaimed."[111] It was into these lands that the fifteen thousand Afrikaner voortrekkers, fleeing the British in the Cape Colony, wandered in the 1830s and 1840s.

Unlike in America's native-settler warfare, one is struck in South Africa by the powerfulness of African resistance to the white incursions, specifically by the power of numbers: The numerousness of the natives and the paucity of settlers enabled the Africans to delay for decades the moment of total conquest. The settler advance in South Africa, unlike in America (but perhaps like in Ireland, c. 1550–1650), was characterized by "no straightforward, unilinear process by which white power became dominant."[112]

One is also struck by the differential impact of white warfare, Boer and British. The tiny Afrikaner settlements beyond the Orange and Vaal Rivers intruded on and sometimes dislocated natives but also had to constantly accommodate neighboring African tribes. The battle of Blood (Ncome) River in December, 1838, became a famous story: In a lopsided victory, settler parties totaling 468 voortrekkers circled their fifty-seven wagons in a laager and, repulsing wave after wave of attackers, killed 3,000 onrushing Zulu warriors (out of a 10,000-man Zulu army). The Afrikaners lost not a single member of their trek party.[113] Yet, of course, white technology did not always prevail over native numbers. Disaster could strike the settlers quickly and unexpectedly. For example, ten months before Blood River, Zulu warriors in a series of attacks had killed a total of 370 whites (including Chief Dingane's murder of Piet Retief and 70 of his unarmed settler party), dispatched 230 of their Khoikhoi servants, and captured 35,000 head of cattle and sheep.[114] Given such dramatics of death, whether Zulu or Boer, it is often forgotten that, more typically, Afrikaner groups became uneasy neighbors and, as needed, allies with African tribes.

When the Boers did make war, success was hardly ensured. In the Orange Free State in 1858 and from 1865 to 1868, Boer attacks on the Basotho (Basuto) came to naught. Chief Moshoeshoe not only successfully resisted but also cleverly negotiated British protection for his mountainous kingdom. (America's Shawnee chief, Tecumseh, who tried the same tactic, would perhaps have been surprised, certainly envious of this Sotho success.[115]) In the remote High Veld, the Transvaal Boers, too, precariously played the numerous, diverse tribes against each other, and when they did go to war the results were often indecisive. For instance, their 4,500-man commando (half Boer, half Swazi) was unable to defeat the Pedi in 1876. Three years later the Pedi would be conquered, but then it was by a British army allied with the Swazi.[116]

What ended the "coexistence" on South Africa's "open frontier" was the British factor. If in America the numerousness of settlers and paucity of natives early tipped the scales in favor of the former, in South Africa (with its inverse settler-native demography) it was "the power imposed by the white metropoles [that] overturned the balance."[117] Behind the massed firepower of British redcoats lay the vast financial resources and political organization of distant London (as the Boers themselves would discover between 1899 and 1902). If in the high tide of imperialism, Britain were to press a sustained commitment to control South Africa, the outcome would not be in doubt. In fact, three peoples—the Xhosa, Zulu, and Afrikaner—would learn this lesson in the thirty years after 1870. Nonetheless, all three would also put up a powerful resistance.

In the eastern Cape Colony, "the hundred years' war" between settler intruders, Boer and British, and the Xhosa natives was so relentless, if discontinuous, that scholars have attached roman numerals to the nine Cape–Xhosa Wars of 1779–1781, 1793, 1799, 1811–1812, 1818–1819, 1834–1835, 1846–1847, 1850–1853, and 1877–1878. So fierce and thick on the ground were the Xhosa warriors that the eastward advance of "civilization," decade by decade, from one river boundary to the next (Fish to Keiskamma to Kei), was neither steady nor easy.

In the final six wars British Cape officials imposed "a proper degree of terror and respect": crop burning and cattle stealing (23,000 head in 1818 and 1819) were followed by the arrest, exile, and assassination of native chiefs. Some 16,000 Xhosa were killed in the eighth conflict, Mlanjeni's War ("the War of the Axe"), from 1850 to 1853. The Xhosa were defeated only in the ninth war (1877–1878), when, allied with the Mfengu, British troops firing nine-pound cannons and new breech-loading rifles defeated 5,000 Xhosa wielding muzzle-loading guns.[118] Xhosa independence was abolished, and their homeland beyond the river (the "Transkei") annexed into the Cape Colony. Significantly, even in victory, Britain discouraged white settlement there: The Transkei would remain "African."[119]

Exhilarated by their conquest of the Xhosa and other native societies (Griqualand West and southern Bechuanaland, 1878–1879), the British now confronted the largest and most warlike African society in southern Africa. The short Anglo-Zulu War of 1879, provoked by the British, witnessed scenes of immense courage and carnage. Like America's Sioux at the Little Bighorn (1876), the Zulu would have one big victory. But, like the Sioux, they would pay the price. In January, the Zulu "massacre" of British forces at Isandhlwana (850 white soldiers and 470 native allies killed) led to Britain's revenge at Rorke's Drift (17 whites and 500 Zulu killed). Finally, in July, Britain delivered the knockout blow at Ulundi (10 whites and 1,000 Zulu killed). The power of numbers—native African numbers—did not necessarily prevail on the battlefield. Heavily outnumbered by Zulu warriors, British forces responded with scientific, high-tech killing (Her Majesty's troops expended 20,000 ammunition rounds at Rorke's Drift and 35,000 at Ulundi). Even the Zulus' "Little Bighorn," their famous victory at Isandhlwana, proved a costly one because British soldiers, fighting to the last man, were able to kill 2,000 Zulu warriors before themselves being killed.[120]

By 1880, the back of the Zulu was broken. At least four thousand warriors were dead, Chief Cetshwayo was exiled to Cape Town, the monarchy was abolished, and Zululand was cut in size by two-thirds, the homeland remnant ("British Zululand," 1887) being divided into thirteen "locations." In 1897, Britain awarded Zululand to the adjacent British settler colony, Natal, which, in 1904, opened part of it to white settlement. A final whimper of native revolt—the "rebellion" by a petty Zulu chief, Bhambatha in 1906—was speedily silenced, again with typical losses of life: More than 3,000 Zulu were killed, but fewer than 30 whites. This belated Bantu bloodbath closed South Africa's frontier.[121]

South Africa's Bantu-speaking natives, if not the Khoikhoi, had put up a valiant fight. They won some battles and lost most others and nearly all of their land. Nevertheless, they certainly did not disappear. South Africa's

Bantu were the victims of neither disease (as in America) nor emigration (as in Ireland). They were, however, demoralized and defeated. Native deaths in wars against the "European" intruders were substantial: The Cape's Xhosa and Natal's Zulu lost generations of warriors. By the dawn of the twentieth century, the "British factor"—which of course included the Europeans' powerful weapons, the Gatling (1870s) and Maxim and Nordenfelt (1890s) guns—had clearly and finally tipped the balance against South Africa's natives, most recently waves of courageous Zulus armed only with *assegais* (short spears for stabbing). Technology had thus facilitated the triumph over human numbers. Britain's "machine guns" would be the guarantors of South Africa's minority rule.

But in defeat South Africa's natives, unlike America's, had one last card to play: demography. For if the Union of South Africa (1910), a dominion in His Majesty's Empire, was a white nation, it was also a black country. Johannesburg sat on the site of an apparently bottomless supply of gold, one whose mines employed 14,000 whites and *100,000 blacks*. The "wilderness" had become by 1890 "the most businesslike town in South Africa," observed one visitor. However, in the words of another, "Johannesburg would not be Johannesburg were the nigger unknown. He is the backbone of the country."[122] The new nation's 1911 census made clear what everyone knew: Bantu far outnumbered Boer and Briton (see table 4). With the frontier's closing, South Africa's native population of 4 million was now "trapped" inside a settler society of 1 million.

"What are we going to do about the natives?" asked one commentator in 1911. "Are they to be shut off by themselves in reserves? No, because the country cannot do without their labour."[123] So how to govern postfrontier South Africa? The settler minority, now unified and backed by Britain, had triumphed over the native majority. Yet the triumph was an uneasy one, for the governance of the country in the twentieth century would demonstrate first the problems and then finally the power of numbers.

MUSINGS

Unlike America's history but like Ireland's, South Africa's history of native and settler was marked by intense interaction and dependence. Three historical factors—the settlers' great distance from Europe and lack of white immigration; second, the mineral discoveries; and third, the persistent increase of the native population—would all conspire to produce in postfrontier South Africa a century of white minority rule over the native peoples.

In retrospect, it is unlikely that the handful of early settlers and their descendants, the Afrikaners, could have permanently contained the geometrically more numerous Africans. Their numbers and resources were just too limited. The Afrikaner homesteads were "like tiny islands . . . surrounded by a sea of Africans."[124] Nor, of course, in the end could Boer beat Briton. It was the British in South Africa who ended the three-sided squabbling. In its eagerness to control South Africa's diamonds and gold, imperial Britain in the last third of the nineteenth century committed itself to both the defeat of the African and the control of the Afrikaner. From 1910 on, Britain marshaled its financial, commercial, and military resources (lately deployed against Afrikaners in the Boer War) so as to strengthen the now united white nation and regulate its needed African labor. What had been the nineteenth century's standoff between Briton and Boer became the new century's alliance against the vast majority of the country's inhabitants, whose labor was essential because of the historic low levels of settler immigration from Europe. If America's settlers wanted all of the land and none of the Indians, South Africa's victors wanted all of the land and needed the Africans.

As labor organization, infusion of (mostly British) overseas capital, and land allotment and control became set in the segregationist era (1910–1948), two key developments affecting settler and native would mark the twentieth century. The first was Afrikaner nationalism. Like its cousin, Ireland's Gaelic revival, Afrikaner nationalism promoted language preservation, political empowerment, and cultural self-esteem.[125] Both nationalisms, Irish and Afrikaner, were a response to living under the deep shadow of Anglo-Saxon triumphalism. Yet the two were strange bedfellows, for, demographically, one nationalism was that of a native majority, the other of a settler minority. Indeed, in the end, South Africa's demography of majority native and minority settler ensured that this "white African" nationalism would be most famous for its repressive pigmentocracy, the apartheid ("apartness") state that prevailed from 1948 to 1990.

The second major development, simultaneous with the first, was South Africa's central phenomenon of the twentieth century. Unlike America's, South Africa's natives were numerous, increasing, and much needed for their labor. Unlike the Indians, the Africans were not marginalized or irrelevant historical actors. Poor in income and education but strong in health and numbers, South Africa's natives formed nearly four-fifths of the country's population. Despite the white settlers' superior wealth and literacy and their government's intense organization and control of society, the power of native numbers simply could not be denied.[126] The dike would break in the 1990s, when, to the surprise of many observers, political power was transferred from South Africa's settlers to South Africa's natives without the onset of Armageddon.[127]

Table 5. Comparative Demography of Settler and Native, 1600–1900

Ireland

Population (in millions)		Date	Events
Native	Settler		
1 (est.)	0.02 (20,000)	1600	Ulster Plantation, 1609; Ulster Rising, 1641; Cromwell's confiscations, 1650s; Natives' final defeat, 1691; Natives killed in 17th-century warfare: 20,000
1.8	0.5 (500,000)	1700	Penal Laws, 1695–1730; Rising of 1798: 30,000 killed; 18th-century emigration: 300,000 Protestants to America

America

Population (in millions)		Date	Events
Native	Settler		
3 (est.)	0	1600	Jamestown, 1607; Plymouth, 1620; Indian risings, Va. and Mass., 1622–1676; diseases ravage Indians; Natives killed in 17th-century warfare: 10,000+
	0.05 (50,000)	1650	
1.5 (est.)	0.25	1700	Deerfield massacre, 1704; French and Indian War, 1754–1763; Thirteen Colonies revolt, 1775; Creation of USA, 1783; Northwest Territory, 1780s; 18th-century immigration: 500,000
	1.2	1750	

South Africa

Population (in millions)		Date	Events
Native	Settler		
2.5 (est.)	0	1600	East India Co. est. Cape Town, 1652; French Huguenots arrive, 1688; Disease and war ravage Cape Khoikhoi
3.0 (est.)	0.0012 (1,200)	1700	Afrikaner trekboers encounter Bantu, 1770s; Nine Cape Frontier Wars, c. 1780–1880; Britain seizes Cape Colony, 1795

South Africa

3.5 (est.)	0.02 (20,000)	1800	East Cape's "1820 Settlers" (Br.) arrive: 5,000
			Battle of Blood River, 1838
			Afrikaners' Great Trek, 1836–1854
			Britain annexes Natal, 1843
			Xhosa cattle killing, 1856–1857: 40,000 starve
			1860–1885 Brit./Irish immigration: 30,000 total
	0.25 (250,000) (1870)		1870–1890: diamonds, gold discovered
			Zulu War, 1879
4.0 (1911)	1.3	1900	Boer War, 1899–1902
			Johannesburg pop.: 75,000
			creation of Union of South Africa, 1910

United States

0.47 (1822)	5.3	1800	Death of Tecumseh, 1813
			Indian Removal, 1830s
	23.1	1850	Settlers' civil war, 1861–1865
			Little Big Horn, 1876
			1820–1890 immigration: 16 million
			Settlers' Oklahoma land rush, 1890s
0.25 (1890)	76.0	1900	New York City pop.: 3 million

Ireland

4.0	1.2	1800	Creation of United Kingdom, 1801
7.0	1.3	1845	Potato Famine,
5.2	1.3	1851	1846–1851: 1 million die, 1 million emigrate
			Land sales & Gaelic revival, 1870–1910
			Emigration, 1800–1921: 7 million Catholics 1.3 million Protestants
3.2	1.2	1900	Southern Ireland's war for Independence, 1916–1921
			Creation of Northern Ireland and Irish Free State, 1921

From our transatlantic tour we have seen that the historical demography of native and settler has helped to shape a society's development and character. Disease and war, famine and migrations all cause historical change, but the dimensions of change—the power of numbers—are of great importance. The contest between natives and settlers was perceived as one of "us" versus "them," civilized versus savage, Christian against heathen, European against native. "There was no medium but that either we or they must be undone."[128] These words of William King, the Anglican bishop of Derry, in Ulster in 1691, tersely reflect settler attitudes in Virginia and the Cape Colony as well.

Numbers in a sporting event, say, a football game, record how one side is doing against the other. The score, in turn, not only determines the contest's outcome but also affects the attitudes of the players.[129] If at halftime, for instance, your side—let's call them "the U.S. settlers"—is ahead 31 to 0, or, in Ulster's contest, the settlers are close to "them" (the Catholics) at 14 to 10, or in the South African match the settlers are way behind the natives, outscored 56 to 7, then each different "team" of settlers has different attitudes and expectations because of the score. Here our score refers to the size of population groups, settler and native. But of course we must add other dimensions by putting behind the numbers other facts and assumptions of the time. For instance, the settlers' sense of racial and cultural superiority to the natives; their access to capital and commerce; their levels of literacy and technology; and so on. Settlers can thus be behind in population numbers but ahead in technology—or ahead in *both* numbers and technology. An emerging society is shaped by a wide array of variables.

For America, what stands out in retrospect is the relative ease and the stunning rapidity of white settler expansion from sea to shining sea in the three centuries after 1600. Manifest destiny, indeed. The Euroamerican intruders—swollen by an immigration that seemed to empty Europe into America—invaded, conquered, displaced, and even appeared unconsciously to exterminate a perceived inferior race, scarce in numbers and scattered across the continent. In this dramatic story one basic fact has long puzzled modern scholars: How could America's pioneer frontier historians so blatantly have ignored the presence of the Indians?

Scholars today fault Frederick Jackson Turner and Walter Prescott Webb for their characterization of the frontier as "vacant" land. After all, "Native Americans" did long occupy it, only to be dispossessed by waves of the white intruders. Part of the answer, of course, is that Turner and Webb told only half of the native-settler story because America's "Indian history" both before and after 1492, or 1607, held little interest for them. "Turner's history was a story of free land, the essentially peaceful occupation of a largely empty continent, and the creation of a unique American identity."[130] For this earlier generation of scholars, America's history began only at Jamestown and Plymouth. They tended, therefore, to ignore or discount historical factors such as the powerful role that epidemic diseases had played in thinning America's native or "presettler" population.

Nevertheless, I think it would be mistaken and unfair to explain the empty, "Indian-less" frontier of Turner and Webb as a product only of the Eurocentric attitudes and focus of their generation. These two scholars were blind to the Indians because they were American historians writing *American* history. What I mean by this is that, since at least the mid-eighteenth century, certain basic facts drove that history. Set against the fast-growing, westward-expanding Euroamerican society was its native contrast: the paucity of Indians, their shrinking numbers and low density on the land, and their nonparticipation in the settlers' society and economy. This combination, positive and negative, settler and native, conspired to make America's receding Indian frontier seem unimportant, even "vacant." In Webb's words, "[T]he scattered Indian population . . . were not a major problem except for the few peoples who were in contact with them on the farthest fringes of settlement."[131] That is, the "problem" of the Indians could be overlooked because America's native history was not central but peripheral; it produced no seismic shifts affecting settler society as the 1798 Rebellion did in Ireland or the gold discoveries (with their demand for native mine labor) did in South Africa.

If Webb's view of the marginalization of America's natives was a Eurocentric assumption on his part, the assumption itself was a product of American history. Webb's mistake was to confuse product with process. The disappearance of the Indians—the product or outcome—made Euroamericans forget the process, namely the historical existence, the rise and decline, of the Native Americans. Increasingly out of sight and out of mind, America's Indians seemed invisible, not quite real. Disappearance and irrelevance became the destiny and the unfortunate status of the American Indian. Turner the American historian never changed his national vision of the frontier, but Webb the emerging transatlantic historian was in his last years moving toward comparative frontier history. Had he lived to produce a sequel to *The Great Frontier*, Webb might even have brought America's Indians more to the foreground.[132] Nevertheless, the facts of American history—including the "disappearance" of the Indians—would not have allowed Webb to alter his tone and thesis of (in today's parlance) Euroamerican settler triumphalism.

If indeed the rout of the natives gave to American settler history a self-righteous sense of satisfaction, even inevitability, that is missing in the Irish and South African settler accounts, then four final observations occur to me.

First, because of their early dominance, some of America's settlers, unlike Ireland's or South Africa's, tended spatially and temporally to sentimentalize the enemy as victim. The further the Indians receded and the more unreal they became, the greater was this tendency to romanticize America's "noble savages." Nineteenth-century New England could piously criticize Andy Jackson's removal of the Tennessee Cherokee, for in New England in the 1830s, unlike in the 1670s, the Indian existed only as a symbol. The "Indian threat" around Deerfield had long since been crushed.

A second observation is that, given this overwhelming dominance by America's settlers, might we not expect some areas east of the Mississippi to have been left for the Indians? After all, there were so few of them. Did the settlers need *all* of the land?

Third, and indeed compounding this insensitivity, the settlers appropriated not just the land but also the Indian names for it. This is odd: Winners, after all, tend to use their own names to commemorate victory and confirm the conquest. In the new Irish Free State after 1921, Sinn Fein's native Catholic "winners" renamed Sackville, Dublin's main street, O'Connell Street. And in South Africa today the renaming has only begun. Natal has become KwaZulu-Natal. The Eastern Transvaal is now Mpumalanga Province (containing the world-famous Kruger National Park, which as yet retains the Afrikaner leader's name). The capital city of Pretoria (a name synonymous with the now extinct apartheid regime) still precariously retains its name—though it does find itself inside the new, Africanized province of Gauteng. An educated guess is that in the near future a major city will be renamed "Mandela."[133] In the United States, we find too that the names of the "winners" fill the landscape. The settler conquest is amply represented by towns and cities, counties and states all named for Euroamerican leaders (Washington and Jefferson, Jackson and Lincoln) or mother-country monarchs (thus, Jamestown, Charleston, or Georgia)—or more broadly simply evoke the original English culture hearth (Boston, Exeter, Norwich, Birmingham, and Manchester).

Yet, remarkably, in America, its native people—the Indians—are widely memorialized by the names of places they lost long ago. In America, rhetoric as well as real estate has been part of the conquest. State names such as Massachusetts, Ohio, and Mississippi (to name three of more than two dozen) and cities such as Chicago, Omaha, Kansas City, and Tallahassee (to name only a few) are but samples of the Indian-derived names of numerous Euroamerican states and cities. Today these names, whispers of vanished Indian civilizations, blandly mark the conquerors' maps. Adding insult to injury, America's corporations have widely appropriated Indian names to market their products to Euroamerican consumers.[134] We Americans use Indian names for our athletic teams (Washington Redskins), for our cars (Jeep Cherokees), and even for recreational vehicles. Everyone knows what Winnebagos are; tourists and retirees tour comfortably around the country in them. But how many know that this huge, deluxe RV is named for a small Wisconsin tribe that in the nineteenth century signed seven land treaties and was forcibly relocated six times? Buy a Winnebago: It gives you great mobility.

A fourth and more substantive point is that with the Indians' disappearance, the settlers' imported African labor force moved to center stage. African Americans were destined to play an outsized historical role because of the demographic negligence of the native factor in America. Indeed, African Americans arguably become surrogate natives, for, like Ireland's and South Africa's natives, they developed into a labor force for the settler community. A central theme of nineteenth-century American history is this intertwining of settler, native, and slave: Western expansion and the coming of the Civil War were the result of white lust for land, red cessions of it, and the extension of black slavery into it. With slave emancipation (1863) and the frontier's closing (c. 1890), America's ongoing ethnic tensions would not be, as in Ireland or South Africa, the legacy of native and settler but rather of the two immigrant groups, the one voluntary, the other coerced.

Our second case, Ireland, has historically had a mixed outcome for natives and settlers. That has been the problem. In Ireland the settlers were always outnumbered by the natives. Despite the trauma of war, famine, and emigration, the island's natives historically maintained a 3 to 1 numerical dominance over the settlers, who were concentrated in only part of one province (East Ulster). This unchanging ratio of natives to settlers did little to attract prospective new settlers to Britain's western island. A second consideration for prospective British emigrants—ordinary people intending to start a new life somewhere, own some land, have some independence—was that Ireland was geographically and culturally just too close to Britain. History reminded that that government—Anglican monarchy and landowning, heavily aristocratic parliament—could impose its will when needed. Moreover, European geopolitics argued against London's granting Dublin any real measure of independence. By contrast, for both Irish Protestant and Irish Catholic, distant North America beckoned because of its freedom, abundance of land, lack of Old World ways, and conveniently disappearing aboriginals.

Third, in a postfamine Ireland marked by massive emigration and no immigration, native and settler generated their own separate cultures. The natives' Gaelic revival, with its rediscovery of the worth of Celtic culture, was a movement fueled by the dollars, anger, and homesickness of America's Irish Catholic immigrants. As this Gaelic self-esteem increased, along with demands for (Catholic) Irish nationhood, Ireland's Protestants, Anglican and Presbyterian, physically and culturally retreated into that northeast corner of

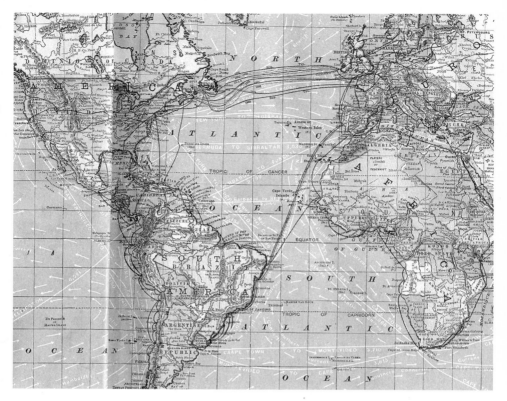

MAP 12. The Atlantic: a world filled in, c. 1900. The impact of Europe's three-century outreach is evident in this American-produced 1902 political map (Mercator projection). Lines delineating steamship routes (solid white lines) and submarine telegraph cables (dark lines) demonstrate the density of east-west transatlantic linkages between Europe and North America; by contrast, north-south Atlantic connections are tenuous and fragile. The Union of South Africa (1910) and the partition of Ireland (1921) do not appear on this map, as both still lie in the future. Courtesy, Special Collections, Libraries of University of Texas–Arlington.

the island where the settler graft had "taken." Unlike the upbeat, can-do attitude of America's self-congratulatory settlers, attitudes among Ulster's Protestants tended to be edgy and defensive, a settler remnant under siege. They were not being paranoid. The Easter uprising (1916) and war for independence (1919–1921) sought by force of arms to bring the whole island under native, Catholic governance. Only a compromise called "partition," dividing Ireland into the government of Northern Ireland and the Republic of Ireland, preserved a small settler North while granting independence to the native South. Partition was a political deal, but its rationale was based on the historical demography of native and settler.

Historically, the mixed outcome in Ireland, with neither native nor settler prevailing, is what has conferred on the Irish case its intractable, bewildering, and irritating qualities. Native and settler have literally divided up the island. Conflict endures because history has declared no clear winner but rather two "winners," the governments in Dublin and Belfast.

But if numbers—demography—dictated one outcome in 1921 (a six-county Northern Ireland), they can write another story in the future. Change is inevitable, and the 1921 settlement is not necessarily permanent. The island of Ireland may one day have one government. For the first two-thirds of the twentieth century the Protestant North and Catholic South remained very different cultures. Nevertheless, the past thirty years have seen rapid changes. Three factors argue for future changes in political governance. First, Britain is serious in its insistence on power sharing in the north, and the Dublin government is actively involved in ongoing talks. The signing of Northern Ireland's Good Friday agreement (1998) reinstated regional representative government, yet this cautious optimism was subsequently canceled when London reimposed direct rule four times, most recently in October 2002.[135] Second, economy and society in the Irish Republic, still overwhelmingly (92 percent) Catholic, have rapidly altered. The rural, Gaelic, church-centered society has morphed into a fast-paced cosmopolitan one where divorce is now legal and the church no longer dominant and high-tech transnational companies such as Dell and Intel dot Dublin's burgeoning suburbs.[136] Southern Ireland has hardly abandoned its past, but it has moved beyond any notion of self-identity fixed exclusively on Catholicism or Gaelicism. In short, circumstances and culture in the south have potentially become more appealing to many Protestants in Northern Ireland.

The third factor—and perhaps the trump card—is demography. Northern Ireland was created as an avowedly "settler" state; three of Ulster's most Catholic counties were purposely left out (conceded to the south) in order to buttress Protestant dominance. Catholics accounted for only 33 percent of Northern Ireland's population in 1921 and, as late as 1961, no more than 35 percent. However, a higher Catholic birthrate and lessening Catholic emigration have raised the Catholic portion to 39 percent in 1981, 42 percent in 1991, and 45 percent in 2001. Is it only a matter of time before the Protestant state has a Catholic-majority population?[137]

Today the Irish Republic and Northern Ireland share governance of an island whose total population of 5.8 million is 79 percent Catholic and 21 percent Protestant. If one day the island has one government, then a long-deferred dream of Irish nationalists will be realized. In the meantime, settler and native in Northern Ireland will have to learn tolerance and peaceful coexistence, practice power sharing, and experiment with integration. Ironically, in the Catholic, culturally cozy South, now eighty years deep into its own independence and identity, many citizens today are unsure of the desirability of an all-island government, entailing as it does the incorporation within its borders of a potentially dissident minority—Ulster's settler remnant.[138]

South Africa's history of native and settler was the polar opposite of America's and was in some ways similar to Ireland's story, yet different from it in others. Of the three countries, South Africa was the most distant from its culture hearth, Europe. America's North Atlantic sea lanes were closer to Europe and more heavily trafficked than the route down the South Atlantic. As America's natives decreased in number year by year, South Africa's increased, and, unlike Ireland's natives, they did not leave the country at all. As America attracted a flood tide of European immigrants, South Africa enticed only a trickle. But at least South Africa had some incoming settlers, compared to Ireland's negative situation of settlers *leaving* the country. Nevertheless, historically, the number of Europeans emigrating to South Africa was not nearly enough to affect the country's heavily unbalanced ratio, four natives for every settler.

If American triumphalism took the form of early national autonomy and the settlers' demographic hegemony, Ireland and South Africa shared a condition of being settler societies dependent on Britain. Each was a society heavy with natives and light on settlers. Settler control in each was insecure enough that, in the end, Britain's intrusion and continued presence was more needed than resented. The union acts, Ireland's of 1800 and South Africa's of 1910, helped to secure settler dominance in each country. Ireland's Protestants in the late eighteenth century, like the Afrikaners in the Boer War, had flirted with notions of political independence and cultural autonomy. Their efforts failed. Nevertheless, the settlers' status as demographic minorities in native-majority societies made them content to settle for the benefit of Britain's protection from the native threat. In short, in South Africa, as in Ireland, the British factor was crucial in long maintaining settler dominance.

But the power of numbers ensured that, in time, the dike would burst in both countries. There were too few settlers—and too many natives to police. In South Africa, when it came (the 1990s), the transition to a native-majority government was not, as in Ireland in 1921, marked by partition, namely, the concomitant creation of a small settler statelet. Some white conservatives talked about it, and others may have wished for it, but the native-settler demography was simply against it. By 1991, South Africa's settlers formed only 14 percent of the total population, down from 21 percent eighty years earlier. Nor were they concentrated in a white laager. South Africa's demographically outnumbered and geographically dispersed settlers did not have the option of creating a white statelet, of retreating into an "East Ulster." In South Africa there would be no Northern Ireland.

The outcomes of the long history of these interactions between native and settler are replete with ironies. For example, the mixed outcome in Ireland—the two states and the standoff in the north—is to a large extent the result of Irish emigration, both Catholic and Protestant, to other portions of the globe, not least to America. The 7 million Irish people who left the small island in the three centuries after 1600 were clearly, and mostly, America's gain, but so too were they Ireland's loss. Nation building abroad, not to mention individuals' countless successful personal careers, came in immeasurable ways at the expense of Ireland's well-being and national development. As for the descendants of those who chose to stay at home in (what became) the partitioned island, they would have to take sides and try to solve political problems that, in the absence of Ireland's continuous hemorrhaging of people, might never have existed or been mitigated.

We have also learned that where the natives neither die off nor emigrate and where settler immigration is low, in the end the contest goes to the natives. This is the recent lesson of South African history. It, too, is a lesson full of ironies. White South Africa becomes black. The apartheid state becomes, in Pres. F. W. de Klerk's words, a "multicultural country," a "New Society." Finally freed in 1990, Nelson Mandela, "the world's most famous political prisoner," was elected president of South Africa in 1994, garnering 63 percent of the first nonracial national vote. In pursuit of "truth and reconciliation" the new nation, native and settler, publicly confronted the horrors of its recent past.[139] The "rainbow nation" is now a multiracial democracy with eleven official languages (English, Afrikaans, and nine African) and possesses the most comprehensive written bill of rights—political, social, and economic—of any nation in the world. The dramatic recent changes are not just domestic. Whereas the "old" South Africa, a land of white-minority rule, was seen by some as an outpost of Europe in Africa, a legatee of Europe's ages of discovery and imperialism, the "new" South Africa of black-majority rule is fast becoming a lightning rod in the current global debate between the world's nations, rich and poor, north and south. Former and current presidents Mandela and Mbeki are leading South Africa into the prominent role of speaker and advocate for the world's developing nations. For example, in 2001, the city of Durban hosted the UN's "World Conference against Racism," and a year later 100 heads of state and 40,000 delegates descended on Johannesburg for the UN's "World Summit on Sustainable Development."[140]

However, now of all times, the future is ironically clouded in post-apartheid South Africa. The advent of freedom for natives has been followed by an ongoing brain drain of settlers, a "white flight" of skilled professionals out of the country.[141] The arrival of ballot-box democracy has not erased a number of domestic problems: very high crime rates, widespread domestic unemployment that is exacerbated by an influx of foreign migrant labor, and the ongoing severe inequalities in wealth distribution between native and settler.[142] Added to the anxieties are the rumblings of thunder to the north. Does the storm in famine-wracked Zimbabwe—namely, the government's bid to confiscate white farmers' lands and restore them to "the true owners . . . Zimbabweans"—signal the start of a "next stage" in South Africa's recent revolution?[143]

Even more immediately, critically, and unexpectedly, there is a new plague in the land. Nowhere does the HIV and AIDS epidemic rage more fiercely than in sub–Saharan Africa, a region where 70 percent of the world's cases are concentrated (only 2 percent are in North America). South Africa itself has the world's largest population of HIV-positive people: 5 million. No nation has a higher rate of HIV infection: one in every five adults and much higher among teenagers. One-fourth of all deaths in South Africa today are the result of AIDS. In 2003, 370,000 South Africans died from AIDS, and the number is expected to grow each year. One study has predicted that the disease will kill 6 million South Africans over the decade 2000–2010. A 1999 UN study projected that the holocaust in South Africa will drop "average life expectancy at birth" from 68 years in 1998 to 48 by 2010. A U.S. study in 2000 was even more pessimistic, predicting a life expectancy of 36 by 2010. A 2002 U.S. government survey reported life expectancy in South Africa in 2001 to average 48.09 years; the South African government estimated it at 44.2 years in 2004. AIDS deaths appear to be decreasing the population far faster than was predicted in the late 1990s. Because of AIDS deaths and the associated falling fertility rates, the population of South Africa (and of neighbors Botswana and Zimbabwe) has begun to decline: It fell 0.25 percent in 2004.[144]

In sum, history's ironies can certainly be cruel. If America's story has been one of continuous setbacks for its native peoples, not least of all their demographic disappearance due to European-imported disease, the outcome of South Africa's native-settler story is both shocking and bittersweet. Three centuries after European encounter, conquest, and subjugation, South Africa's disease-free natives finally achieved political power. Then, almost immediately, the African-majority society was swept by a sexually transmitted epidemic that one doctor has described as "undoubtedly the most serious infectious disease threat in recorded human history."[145] Yet history may offer lessons as well as ironies. Given America's long-ago native disease holocaust, what in the twenty-first century are the moral and humanitarian duties (obligations?) of developed nations to deal with a worldwide HIV/AIDS crisis whose ground zero is southern Africa? More to the point, because of America's native-settler history, does the United States—its government and its major pharmaceutical companies—have any special responsibility to get low-cost, antiviral drugs to modern-day HIV and AIDS sufferers?[146]

In the long view of history, however, it must be stressed that South Africa's natives are still around. Their present disease holocaust, unlike that of smallpox, is often volitional (indeed some call it a "war on women"). In time, the disease may be mitigated or eliminated by discoveries in modern science and medicine. By contrast, America's natives are gone, disappeared into history, their ancestors too often killed off by long-ago pandemics. Let me be clear. By "gone," I do not mean that there are none left. Rather, I mean that the Indians essentially have no importance or influence in America today because there are so very few of them. They constitute less than 1 percent of the total population of the United States.[147]

In a democracy, population determines (or is perceived to determine) power in the voting booth. But in a democracy the power of numbers can be perverse: The lower your population, the less your political power. Given America's native-settler history, it is ironic that the United States is today a society dedicated to "diversity" and "multiculturalism." In promoting these noble aims, Americans too often are unaware that our present population is in fact a "replacement" population. Historically, the United States grew very rapidly as a result of the flood tide of immigration, European and African, that inundated the continental graveyard of America's natives, the Indians, who (ironically) themselves were descendants of ancient Asian immigrants. (The volume of recent Asian immigration to the United States only compounds the irony.[148]) America's story, in short, is both triumph and tragedy. *Triumph* for the settlers: world's biggest economy, sole superpower, beacon for democracy. *Tragedy* for the natives: Their loss was so total that most Americans never even think about our holocaust. If it's invisible, it doesn't exist—and never did. But I, for one, see dead people.

AND "WHAT IFS"?

Let me close this long chapter by posing some questions, not offering answers. Like comparative transatlantic history itself, counterfactual speculation can yield some intriguing, occasionally compelling, insights. For instance, what would the shape of American history be if America's Indians had *not* been destroyed by disease? Clearly, the story would have come out differently—but how much so? Even a healthy native population numbering nearly 5 million in 1600, scattered in tribes across the vast continent, would in time have been impacted by the very high levels of immigration of newcomers arriving from Europe (see table 2). America's native-settler story would certainly have been slowed but, in the end, not stopped.

Alternatively, what if the native-settler facts had been these: a large and healthy native population confronted over time by only a small influx of newcomers? With a native-settler ratio clearly favoring the former, American history would have been stood on its head. Would an "Irish" or "South African" scenario have unfolded?

Or, again, what if America's settlers-to-be had arrived from the west, not the east? If the newcomers had traveled across the Pacific Ocean, on landing they would not have encountered cozy harbors and plenteous rivers. Similarly, moving steadily inland, they would not have enjoyed abundant rainfall or found fertile soil, woodlands, and rolling hills. Rather, the newcomers would soon have confronted few and unnavigable waterways, high mountain ranges, semiarid plateaus, and deserts. Euroamerican settlement would have been slowed, if not stopped. America's Rocky Mountain west is quite different from America east of the Mississippi River.

Finally, what historical scenarios would have developed for our settler community if we combined the two—native demography and physical geography? Factors such as numerous and healthy natives, great distance from the homeland's culture hearth, and a challenging climate and landscape would clearly have affected the development of any new settler society. Low levels of newcomer immigration would have had serious long-term effects: the development of only a small settler population. The reader will recognize that this American counterfactual historical scenario is the actual scenario—the history—of South Africa.

America's history of natives and settlers was, in short, the opposite of South Africa's. Or was it? For if America's natives disappeared, America's slaves—the imported Africans—came to function as America's surrogate natives.[149] In those parts of America where African Americans, slave or free, came to be very numerous or even outnumbered whites—in parts of the lower South, both ante- and postbellum—the slave codes and segregationist laws look remarkably similar to Ireland's eighteenth-century penal laws or South Africa's twentieth-century apartheid system.

However, of course the South was only one of America's regions: Population dynamics were different in the north and west. The South seceded and fought the Civil War to preserve slavery and white rule. Had the Confederate States of America won the war in 1865, or had President Lincoln in 1861 told the departing South, "Goodbye, good riddance," then a new South African–type state in the American South would have governed its black slave system, significantly, by laws already in force there. (As comedian Jay Leno once joked on late-night TV, "If the South had won the Civil War, what would they have named their capital? Johannesburg.") Of course, America's northern states won the war, yanking the stepchild white South back into the Union. Thus, the South's large black slave minority (37 percent of total population) became the United States' black minority, forming 17 percent of the nation's population in 1860. Even with postwar constitutional civil rights guarantees, the battered but reunited nation cobbled together a system of race separation— Southern Jim Crow laws and Northern discrimination—that became the law of the land until just half a century ago.

In short, and to sum up, America's natives, the Indians, were only a negligible factor in our history, yet America's hegemonic settlers treated them very shabbily. African Americans, disempowered through slavery and then discrimination, were also treated poorly. Yet these two groups together formed less than a fifth of the U.S. population, hardly a threatening ratio from an Irish or South African settler perspective. My point is that, given the ratio of settlers to natives and slaves, America's white settlers *should* have treated both groups better. After all, and to speak bluntly, the numerous settlers could afford to be humanitarian to the dispossessed and disempowered since there was no risk of any real transfer of political power to these two minority groups.

WHAT OF THE "WHAT IFS" in Irish history? In Ireland the historical reality is that a native population—diminished by famine, disease, and emigration and burdened with an uncomfortable proximity to Britain—was yet able, finally, to break free of British rule in 1921. But what if Irish history had been different?

The key factor in Ireland's history has been its nearness to England, the dominant political entity on the larger eastern "mainland" island (Britain) in that archipelago that maps label as the "British Isles." Given this English hegemony, the history of Ireland might have been tranquil if, like Scotland or Wales before it, Ireland had gone quietly—that is, by the early eighteenth century had essentially succumbed to incorporation by England.[150] What if the "United Kingdom" (to use the phrase created by the Irish Act of Union, 1800) were really so? What if Ireland, following its reconquest in 1649 and 1691, had undergone a mass popular conversion to British culture? If Ireland early on had morphed into a "West Britain," with modernization proceeding apace with little or no famine or disease, the distinction between Irish native and British settler would have blurred. Can we expect that an Ireland that became less foreign and more comfortably British to its settlers would probably have enticed more of them to the island?

A second, and very different and much harsher, scenario that assumes proximity to Britain but also sustained hostility by the native population produces a dominant British outcome, a clear-cut winner, only by the harshest of measures.[151] Presuming military conquest and land confiscation, aided by voluntary native emigration, an uncontested and overwhelming British triumph might have resulted if the following had obtained:

- A sustained uprooting of the entire native population, not just warriors and landowners, and the transporting of them overseas ("Barbados-ing") had had the effect of severely reducing the number of aboriginals and demoralizing any native remnant. (The British had done something similar when they moved the Acadians from Nova Scotia to Louisiana in the 1750s.) As necessary, continue this thorough process into the eighteenth century in order to clear the land for resettlement.
- Epidemic disease and/or famines had recurrently winnowed the native population, dropping it steadily, even rapidly, to the point of near extinction.
- Incessant warfare, well beyond the seventeenth century, had severely thinned the native population.

Had any or all of these British policies of "thoroughness" been both persistent and lethal in their effects, Ireland would have been reduced to a virtual tabula rasa. This "American solution" would have facilitated the remaking of Ireland into a society culturally comfortable to those British settlers who could then flock in—creating a "New England" in East Munster?

A third intriguing scenario writes Irish history with British intervention but without famine, disease, or even emigration (the "safety valve" to America). This scenario of a rising, stay-at-home population presumes, however, that Irish society had the ability to support this demographic growth. British governance of Ireland would have required focused, ongoing improvements in the society's infrastructure. Had that improvement occurred, still there was a limit to the population the small island could sustain. Improvement to Ireland's social and economic conditions would, in turn, have stanched the urge to emigrate and might have induced a slower population growth. But absent the Malthusian checks of famine, disease, and emigration, Ireland would have remained heavily native. Furthermore, if we presume no widespread popular conversion to British culture, Ireland's swollen native population would have intensely discouraged any future in-migration of settlers. In this scenario Ireland's fateful proximity to Britain again is critically important. Confronted by a populous country that is close geographically but does not share its cultural values or is downright hostile, Britain could then not have afforded to let this island on its western flank become an ally of, or serve as a staging ground for, any of Britain's European enemies. Here we realize that we are leaving fantasy and encountering actual historical events.

In this scenario, Britain's best option may well be invasion, conquest, and a brittle "settler" rule over the native majority.

FINALLY, WHAT ARE THE "WHAT IFS" for South Africa? Here the tyranny of distance is a key factor in that nation's history. The "goldilocks" factor seemed to favor America: If Ireland was too close to its dominating parent, South Africa was just too far from its home and cultural base, Europe. America's distance from Europe was "just right": a well-trafficked, westerly sea route half as long as that to Cape Town. Space enough for postadolescent independence (America), but not close enough for smothering (Ireland) or so distant as to invite neglect (South Africa).

Of course, the story of South Africa was essentially the combination of paucity of settlers with abundance of natives. However, what if history had unfolded differently? Would Europe's settlers have established even a toehold on the tip of the continent if the first natives they encountered, the Khoikhoi, had not been few in number? What if they had not been susceptible to European diseases? Would a large and healthy native population in the southwest corner of the Cape Colony, or a Khoikhoi society that had been organized along the advanced lines of the Zulu, have been able to intimidate or even expel the small infant settler colony?

If the lilliputian Dutch East India Company settlement had survived and its descendants spread inland (as they did), and assuming little settler immigration and low native mortality rates (as happened), what would the Boers' fate have been if Britain had *not* shown up? That is, instead of South Africa's triangular history of Boer, Briton, and Bantu, how would the dual story of Boer and Bantu have come out? Absent the "British factor," would the small Afrikaner settlements have been able to sustain uneasy and separate relations with the numerous surrounding native peoples? Would these "white Africans," scattered rural ranching families, have been able to prevail in sustained warfare against tribes like the Xhosa and Zulu, as the British military had done? Or would the power of numbers have caused the Afrikaners to "disappear," that is, to meld with the native African tribes around them? A startling thought, indeed.[152]

As the foregoing suggests, the British factor appears to be crucial in determining the course of South Africa's history, the way it actually turned out. Given the importance of this British factor, let us for the moment leave aside the dominant issue in South Africa's history, the native question. Rather, let us simply consider whether the region's history might have been dramatically different had the "mineral revolution" happened earlier. For instance, what if vast deposits of gold and diamonds had been discovered not in the last third of the nineteenth century but instead a century earlier—in the late eighteenth century? Britain's interest in South Africa would have been sped up, in turn causing far earlier investment in and European emigration to the region. Just as in America, where the gold rush of 1849 caused the Euroamerican settlement of California virtually overnight (which, in turn, hastened the pace of history, including the onset of the Civil War), so an early discovery of South Africa's vast mineral wealth—perhaps a few hundred miles from Cape Town?—might well have set in motion a European exodus to South Africa. As we know from the "multiplier effect" in American history, such heavy and early immigration would have created a settler community in South Africa far more populous than the one we read about in history books.

We come to perhaps our most provocative scenario by posing a final series of questions. What if South Africa's broad and dramatic landscape had *not* been the home of numerous native peoples? Or, assuming that the subcontinent was home to large numbers of native Africans, what if the natives had succumbed massively to Europe's diseases? Had the Bantu-speaking peoples of eastern South Africa been susceptible to settler diseases, as the Khoikhoi were, then the death toll would have extirpated or marginalized the large Xhosa and Zulu populations. This "American solution" would clearly have altered South Africa's history, for, as we know, the tabula rasa of "widowed" lands historically was a lure to prospective immigrants from Europe.

To be sure, traveling such a great distance physically and psychologically from its culture hearth did argue against a level of European emigration on the scale of that to America. Still, South Africa would have had strong appeal to Europeans, for, lying at 25–35 degrees south latitude, it was a temperate, not a tropical, land. A South Africa without natives, or with few, might have generated a sizeable if not huge "Euroafrican" settler population. After all, even farther away from Europe, across the Indian Ocean and straddling those same southern latitudes, was that largely arid island-continent whose conveniently few and disappearing aborigines were being replaced by a numerous settler population, mostly of British and Irish descent. But Australia's history is Australia's, and to strip South Africa of its Africans or its Afrikaners is of course not merely fanciful; it also leaches the color, complexity, and pathos from South Africa's history. In the end, such speculations, however stimulating, are about as useful as putting huge numbers of Indians into America's history.

ACKNOWLEDGMENTS

I would like to thank Don Kyle for a timely suggestion, Steven Reinhardt for his patience, and my graduate students for their insights in our colloquium on comparative transatlantic frontiers. I am grateful to Joel Quintans of the Office of Publications, University of Texas–Arlington for his talents in graphic design and his good humor in meeting the author's endless demands in map production. (I designed maps 2–11, and Joel then composed them on a computer. To create the maps, I drew on data and/or maps from the sources cited; thus, I alone am responsible for any errors that may have crept in.) As always, my biggest debt is to my wife, Elizabeth Palmer. Both my Webb Lecture slide talk and this much longer chapter are dedicated to the memory of my father, Robert R. Palmer (1909–2002).

NOTES

Epigraph Source: Sean O'Faolain, *The Irish: A Character Study* (Old Greenwich, Conn.: Devin-Adair, 1949), p. ix.

1. The growth of the Hispanic population in Texas reflects a larger national trend. The 2000 census revealed that the United States' Hispanic/Latino population increased over the past decade by 58 percent (to 12.5 percent of the nation's population). In 2005, Hispanics are expected to displace African Americans as the country's dominant minority. The state of Texas is expected by that year to have a majority of minorities—Hispanic, African, and Asian American (*Arlington* [edition of *Fort Worth*] *Star-Telegram,* Feb. 10, 2000, p. 1E; Mar. 17, 2001, p. 1A; Mar. 19, 2001, p. 1A). The youth factor is of course a predictor of the future: Hispanics have now essentially pulled even with Anglos in enrollment in all of the public schools in Texas. From 1991 to 2000, the number of Hispanics grew from 34 to 41 percent, Anglos declined from 49 to 42 percent, and African Americans remained unchanged at 14 percent of total student enrollment ("ethnic breakdown" table compiled by the Texas Education Agency, in "Changing the Face of Education," in ibid., Sept. 15, 2002, p. 26A).

2. Respectively, Vincent Ramos and Adelfa Callejo, quoted in "Census Figures Give Hispanics Greater Clout," in ibid., Mar. 19, 2001, pp. 1A, 9A. The article noted that only 2 of 15 Dallas City Council members were Hispanic, as was only one school board member, though Hispanics accounted for 53 percent of the children in the Dallas Independent School District.

3. Frederick Jackson Turner, "The Significance of the Frontier in American History," *Annual Report of the American Historical Association for the Year 1893* (Washington, D.C.: American Historical Association, 1894), pp. 199–227. His writings are available in Frederick J. Turner, *Rereading Frederick Jackson Turner: "The Significance of the Frontier in American History" and Other Essays,* commentaries by John Mack Faragher (New Haven: Yale University Press, 1998). Despite (or because of) the lambastings of revisionists, writings about Turner and his legacy continue to abound. For a beginning, see Ray Allen Billington, ed., *The Frontier Thesis: Valid Interpretation of American History?* (New York: Holt, Rinehart, and Winston, 1966); Richard Hofstadter and Seymour Martin Lipset, eds., *Turner and the Sociology of the Frontier* (New York: Basic Books, 1968); Donald K. Pickens, "Westward Expansion and the End of American Exceptionalism: Sumner, Turner, and Webb," *Western Historical Quarterly* 12 (1981): 409–18; Gerald D. Nash, *Creating the West: Historical Interpretations, 1890–1990* (Albuquerque: University of New Mexico Press, 1991); Wilbur Jacobs, *On Turner's Trail: 100 Years of Writing Western History* (Lawrence: University Press of Kansas, 1994); and Richard W. Etulain, ed., *Does the Frontier Experience Make America Exceptional?* (Boston: Bedford/St. Martin's, 1999).

4. Turner, "Significance of the Frontier," in *Frontier Experience*, pp. 17–43, quotations on pp. 19, 20.

5. Chicago's "world's fair" of 1893 drew 27 million visitors, a number representing about one-fourth of the nation's population at that time ("Chicago Day" alone drew 700,000). The heart of Chicago's World Columbian Exposition was the "White City." Erected at a cost of $28 million and occupying more than 500 acres in Jackson Park on Lake Michigan's waterfront, the White City was a dazzling place of parklike grandeur. In this model urban utopia, fourteen immense exhibit halls of stunning Beaux Arts architecture were arranged amid a wonderland of canals, ponds, lagoons, and the Grand Basin. To keep the White City white, the use of coal as an energy source was banned. For a virtual tour of the exposition, created by University of Virginia graduate student Julie K. Rose, go to http://xroads .virginia.edu/~MA96/WCE/tour.html.

Visitors to the serene and ordered elegance of the White City marveled at the modern wonders of science and technology. The signs of progress were everywhere. Among the many structures that housed some sixty-five thousand exhibits, fairgoers were most impressed by the "Electricity Building." Americans were of course proud to celebrate their past—exhibits included Whitney's cotton gin, McCormick's automatic reaper, and Remington's more recent (1874) "typewriter," but they were especially excited by the exhibits of "electricity," which promised the country a bright future. Clearly, electric trains (Chicago's famous "El," the elevated railway, would convert from steam to electric power in 1898), "moveable sidewalks," phonographs, kinetoscopes (early movie projectors), burglar alarms, and, not least, incandescent lights all pointed to a future easing of the lot of humankind. In short, for six months in 1893, Americans toured Chicago's White City in a mood of satisfied and serious self-congratulation. The evidence was undeniable: Americans had not only tamed but also "improved" the continent. Clearly, civilization had triumphed over savagery.

But fairgoers wanted fun, too. (Another of the exposition's legacies would be consumerism and mass entertainment: the amusement and theme parks—Coney Islands and Disneylands—of America's future.) Chicago's 1893 visitors found "fun" either just outside the fairgrounds at "Buffalo Bill's Wild West Show" or on site in the Midway Plaisance, a narrow, 80-acre strip of land linking Jackson and Washington Parks. On the "Midway" (a name so popular that later fairs all had "midways"), the visitor could consume novelties (Juicy Fruit gum or a "carbonated soda" and hamburger), watch "Aunt Jemima" (fifty-seven-year-old former slave Nancy Green) advertise "her" new pancakes and syrup, take a ride on the world's first "Ferris wheel," or leer at the infamous belly dancer, "Little Egypt."

The polar opposite of the White City, the Midway was a noisy, rowdy, dirty, "unrespectable" place. Among the numerous things to see and do were exhibits of "real and typical representatives of nearly all the races of the earth." Most appealing, apparently because the most exotic, were those of "Asiatic and African and other forms of life." Celtic Ireland's "Blarney Castle" (complete with kissing stone) attracted big crowds, to be sure, but fairgoers were most drawn to the displays of a "Dahomey village," a "street in Cairo," and an American "Indian village." Such exhibits featuring real humans in "natural" settings were intended to educate as well as entertain the public. Arranged according to degrees of societal "primitiveness," the Midway exhibits "certainly emphasize the value, as well as the progress of our civilization," one visitor told the *New York Times*. "The denizens of the Midway certainly . . . give the observer an opportunity to investigate these barbarous and semi-civilized people without the unpleasant accompaniments of travel through their countries and contact with them."

Chicago's carnival-barker display of the world's "lesser races" was typical of the era's social Darwinism. Four years later, the 1897 World's Fair in Brussels, Belgium, erected a "pygmy village" complete with 267 live specimens—men, women, and children specially imported from the Belgian Congo. The 1904 St. Louis World's Fair showcased "wildmen of the world, the races that had been left behind." Among them was an exhibit of America's Indians; another featured a 103-pound man named Ota Benga, who was advertised (correctly) as a "genuine" Congo Pygmy. Two years later, New York's Bronx Zoo displayed Benga, "the wild man of Africa," in a cage with an orangutan as a demonstration of the zoo's commitment to both modern science (Darwinism) and making money. A poem in the *New York Times* lauded Ota's good fortune: "From his native land of darkness/To the country of the free/In the interest of science/And of broad humanity." Black clergymen later rescued Benga from his cage; he stayed on in America, living there for ten years before committing suicide in Virginia in 1916.

As to Chicago's 1893 festivities, one final point is worth noting. Chicago's White City was of course a place for white people only—that is, people of European descent (and ideally, of north European, Protestant, Saxon, and Teutonic "race"). African Americans were not welcome. They were not a part of the "American story." African Americans did, however, have one fair day set aside especially for them: Jubilee Day, or "Colored Peoples' Day," Aug. 25, 1893. Fair officials announced that free watermelon would be distributed to all visitors. The Chicago Exposition thus offered one last, if minor, cause for the great abolitionist Frederick Douglass (1818–1895). Working with Ida B. Wells, Douglass coauthored a pamphlet titled "The Reason Why the Colored American Is Not in the World's Columbian Exposition" (Aug., 1893; repr., ed. Robert W. Rydell, Urbana: University of Illinois Press, 1999, pp. xlviii, 84). This short work chastises white America for its treatment of "Afro-Americans" and points out that their relegation to Midway sideshow status at the exposition was essentially a metaphor for their mistreatment throughout American history (see chap. 4, "Lynch Law"). Significantly, Wells and Douglass argue that the "Negroes" deserve full civil rights *because* they are civilized, not savage (see chap. 5, "The Progress of the Afro-American since Emancipation," including the state-by-state statistical table of "his wealth and business interests," p. 52). The pamphlet says not one word about "Native Americans," although Douglass, eloquent as always, might as well have been writing about them. He described Chicago's 1893 exposition as "a whited sepulcher fair without and full of dead men's bones within" (ibid., p. xlviii n53.)

Sources. See David F. Burg, *Chicago's White City of 1893* (Lexington: University Press of Kentucky, 1976), and Robert Muccigrosso, *Celebrating the New World: Chicago's World's Columbian Exposition of 1893* (Chicago: Ivan R. Dee, 1993). On the larger issue of the interrelation of culture, capitalism, and chauvinism, see Robert W. Rydell, *All the World's a Fair: Visions of Empire at American International Expositions, 1876–1916* (Chicago: University of Chicago Press, 1984). The quotation from the visitor to the Midway Plaisance is from an interview with Chauncey M. Depew (president, N.Y. Central Railroad, and a future U.S. senator), in the *New York Times,* June 19, 1893, p. 5. On Ota Benga, see Adam Hochschild, *King Leopold's Ghost: A Story of Greed, Terror, and Heroism in Colonial Africa* (New York: Houghton Mifflin, 1998), pp. 175–77; and Phillips Bradford and Harvey Blume, *Ota Benga: The Pygmy in the Zoo* (New York: St. Martin's Press, 1992).

6. Harrison quoted in Roderick Nash and Gregory Groves, *From These Beginnings: A Biographical Approach to American History,* vol. 1, 6th ed. (New York: Harper and Row, 2000), p. 169. Harrison's statement embodied common Euroamerican thinking at the time. Compare these words from Pres. Andrew Jackson's State of the Union Address, Dec. 6, 1830: "What good man would prefer a country covered with forests and ranged by *a few thousand* savages to our extensive Republic, studded with cities, towns, and prosperous farms, embellished with all the improvements which art can devise or industry execute, occupied by more than 12,000,000 happy people, and filled with all the blessings of liberty, civilization, and religion?" Quoted in Theda Perdue and Michael D. Green, eds., *The Cherokee Removal: A Brief History with Documents* (New York: Bedford/St. Martin's Press, 1995), pp. 119–20, emphasis added.

7. Eric A. Walker, *The Frontier Tradition in South Africa* (London: Oxford University Press, 1930); W. K. Hancock, *Survey of British Commonwealth Affairs* (London: Oxford University Press, 1940), chap. 1; Fred Alexander, *Moving Frontiers: An American Theme and Its Application to Australian History* (Melbourne: Melbourne University Press, 1947); and Archibald Grenfell Price, *White Settlers and Native Peoples: An Historical Study of Racial Contacts between English-Speaking Whites and Aboriginal Peoples in the United States, Canada, Australia, and New Zealand* (1950; repr., Westport, Conn.: Greenwood, 1972).

8. Walter Prescott Webb, *The Great Frontier* (Boston: Houghton Mifflin, 1952), pp. 6, 7, italics in the original; the book was reissued unrevised after Webb's death (Austin: University of Texas Press, 1964, with an introduction by Arnold J. Toynbee). On the evolution of Webb's thinking on the frontier, see ibid., pp. 405–12. Before the war Webb had produced his prize-winning study, *The Great Plains* (Boston: Ginn, 1931), a regional report on the American West.

9. William H. McNeill, *The Great Frontier: Freedom and Hierarchy in Modern Times* (Princeton, N.J.: Princeton University Press, 1983), p. 8. Originally delivered as the Charles Edmunson Historical Lectures, 1982, at Baylor University.

10. Webb, *Great Frontier,* pp. 411–12.

11. Ibid., pp. 3, 3n3, 8. Of course in Webb's lifetime (1888–1963) white Americans rarely encountered an Indian in Texas. By the late nineteenth century, Texas' native peoples either had been driven north of the Red River into Indian Territory or lived west of the state's "settled" areas. Webb's text in *The Great Frontier* runs to 418 pages; "Indians" are discussed on nine pages.

12. Gary B. Nash's *Red, White, and Black: The Peoples of Early North America* (1974; 4th ed., Upper Saddle River, N.J.: Prentice Hall, 2000) began the sea change in American historiography. James Axtell's writings have had a huge influence as well: See his article "Europeans, Indians, and the Age of Discovery in American History Textbooks," *American Historical Review* 92(3) (June, 1987): 621–32, and, among his many books, *Beyond 1492: Encounters in Colonial North America* (New York: Oxford University Press, 1992). In Sept., 1986, Nash's university, UCLA, hosted an important Newberry Library (Chicago) conference on "The Impact of Indian History on Teaching the U.S. History Survey." Now two decades old, the first explicitly multicultural survey of U.S. history was *Natives and Strangers: Blacks, Indians, and Immigrants in America* (New York: Oxford University Press, 1979; 2d ed., 1990), coauthored by Leonard Dinnerstein, Roger Nichols, and David Reimers. For the revised 3d (New York: Oxford University Press, 1996) and 4th editions (New York: Ox-

ford University Press, 2003), befitting student demand and the mood of the era, the authors retitled their survey as *Natives and Strangers: A Multicultural History of Americans*.

On South Africa's historiography, see Harrison M. Wright, *The Burden of the Present: Liberal-Radical Controversy over Southern African History* (Cape Town: David Philip, 1977); Christopher Saunders (University of Cape Town), *The Making of the South African Past: Major Historians on Race and Class* (Cape Town: David Philip, 1988; Totowa, N.J.: Barnes and Noble Books, 1988); Ken Smith (University of South Africa), *The Changing Past: Trends in South African Historical Writing* (Johannesburg: Southern Book Publishers, 1988; Athens: Ohio University Press, 1989); and Paul Maylam, *South Africa's Racial Past: The History and Historiography of Racism, Segregation, and Apartheid* (Aldershot, UK: Ashgate, 2001). Describing itself as "the first popular history published simultaneously in English and Afrikaans," *An Illustrated History of South Africa*, ed. Trewhella Cameron and S. B. Spies (Johannesburg: Jonathan Ball, 1986), alerted readers that "a number of myths of South African history are exposed" and that new findings were presented on "the motives, actions, and reactions of *all* members of South African society" (p. 7, emphasis added).

On Ireland, see J. G. A. Pocock, "The Limits and Divisions of British History: In Search of the Unknown Subject," *American Historical Review* 87(2) (Apr., 1982): 311–36; Brendan Bradshaw, "Nationalism and Historical Scholarship in Modern Ireland," *Irish Historical Studies* 26 (Nov., 1989): 329–51; Ciaran Brady, ed., *Interpreting Irish History: The Debate on Historical Revisionism, 1938–1994* (Dublin: Irish Academic Press, 1994); and D. G. Boyce and Alan O'Day, eds., *The Making of Modern Irish History: Revisionism and the Revisionist Controversy* (London: Routledge, 1996). Revisionism developed from the emergence in Ireland of the first professional historical journal, *Irish Historical Studies*. Founded in 1938, based at Trinity College Dublin, and reacting against policies of Gaelicization in Eamon De Valera's Irish Free State, the journal's budding revisionists sought to tackle tough historical questions by substituting "neutral," rigorous analysis for reflexive anti-English emotionalism, patriotism, and romantic nationalism.

13. Howard Lamar and Leonard Thompson, eds., *The Frontier in History: North America and Southern Africa Compared* (New Haven, Conn.: Yale University Press, 1981), p. 7. Two years earlier, comparative frontier studies (New Spain, New France, Brazil, South Africa, and Australia) formed the subject of the Fourteenth Annual Walter Prescott Webb Lectures (1979) at the University of Texas–Arlington (the lectures were published as *Essays on Frontiers in World History*, ed. George Wolfskill and Stanley Palmer (College Station: Texas A&M University Press, 1983). Forays from 1977 to 1979 by Oklahoma's program in frontier studies had been only partially successful from a lack of focus and definitions: See David H. Miller and Jerome O. Steffen, eds., *The Frontier: Comparative Studies*, vol. 1 (Norman: University of Oklahoma Press, 1977), and William W. Savage Jr. and Stephen I. Thompson, eds., *The Frontier: Comparative Studies*, vol. 2 (Norman: University of Oklahoma Press, 1979).

14. For instance, in his Pulitzer Prize–winning *Guns, Germs, and Steel: The Fates of Human Societies* (New York: W. W. Norton, 1997), Jared M. Diamond asks, "Why weren't the Incas the ones to invent guns and steel swords, to be mounted on animals as fearsome as horses, to bear diseases to which Europeans lacked resistance . . . ?" (p. 81). On encounters between intruders and indigenes, see Urs Bitterli, *Cultures in Conflict: Encounters*

between European and Non-European Cultures, 1492–1800, trans. Ritchie Robertson (Stanford: Stanford University Press, 1989); Colin G. Calloway, *New Worlds for All: Indians, Europeans, and the Remaking of Early America* (Baltimore: Johns Hopkins University Press, 1997); and Peter C. Mancall and James Hart Merrell, eds., *American Encounters: Natives and Newcomers from European Contact to Indian Removal, 1500–1850* (New York: Routledge, 1999). For the European cis-Atlantic background, see Barry Cunliffe, *Facing the Ocean: The Atlantic and Its People, 8000 BC–AD 1500* (Oxford: Oxford University Press, 2001). For introductions to transatlantic history, see Paul Butel's colorful saga, *The Atlantic* (London: Routledge, 1999); Thomas Benjamin, Timothy D. Hall, and David Rutherford, *The Atlantic World in the Age of Empire* (Boston: Houghton Mifflin, 2001); Bernard Bailyn and Philip D. Morgan, eds., *Strangers within the Realm: Cultural Margins of the First British Empire* (Chapel Hill: University of North Carolina Press, 1991); and David Birmingham, *Trade and Empire in the Atlantic, 1400–1600* (London: Routledge, 2000), a study of Iberian seafaring and commerce.

15. In July, 2002, an online computer search of world library catalogues—FirstSearch Online Computer Library Center (OCLC) WorldCat, http://firstsearch.oclc.org—reported that in the eight years from 1995 to 2002, a total of 349 books were published with the word "transatlantic" in their titles; "Atlantic history," 127 titles. Whereas old "transatlantic" staples were subjects like ocean liners, NATO, or the African slave trade, nowadays a very large number of books carry titles or subtitles such as "transatlantic fashion trade," "transatlantic poetry," or "transatlantic theology." There is even one titled *Berlin: The New Capital in the East. A Transatlantic Appraisal,* vol. 7, ed. Frank Trommler (Washington, D.C.: American Institute for Contemporary German Studies, 2000). However, my favorite remains *The Transatlantic Capability Gap: A General Assessment,* by William E. Cralley (Alexandria , Va.: Institute for Defense Analyses, 2000).

16. The first "AHA Prize in Atlantic History" was awarded to Jeremy Adelman (Princeton) for his book *Republic of Capital: Buenos Aires and the Legal Transformation of the Atlantic World* (Stanford: Stanford University Press, 1999). *La Pietra Report: Project on Internationalizing the Study of American History* (New York: Organization of American Historians, 2000), pp. 1–24; and see also Carl J. Guarneri, "Out of Its Shell: Internationalizing the Teaching of United States History," *Perspectives: American Historical Association Newsletter* 35(2) (Feb., 1997): 1–8. The UK's University of Central Lancashire has ties to the Maastricht Center for Transatlantic Studies at the University of Maastricht, The Netherlands. Papers on a variety of transatlantic subjects at the center's conferences have been edited for publication by two Central Lancashire historians; see Will Kaufman and Heidi Slettedahl Macpherson, eds., *Transatlantic Studies* (Lanham, Md.: University Press of America, 2000), and Heidi Slettedahl Macpherson and Will Kaufman, eds., *New Perspectives in Transatlantic Studies* (Lanham, Md.: University Press of America, 2002). Harvard University's semiannual Atlantic history workshops and annual August seminar are announced regularly in the American Historical Association's *Perspectives.* The program's director is Bernard Bailyn, author of *Atlantic History: Concept and Contours* (Cambridge: Harvard University Press, 2005).

17. McNeill, *Great Frontier,* p. 9.

18. This will come as no surprise to Texans, who know that a difference of only 10 degrees Fahrenheit in daily high (and low) temperatures can account for either a scorching (i.e., typically Texas) summer or a milder northern one. On climate and latitude, see Dia-

mond, *Guns,* pp. 138–41, 176–91, and David S. Landes, *The Wealth and Poverty of Nations: Why Some Are So Rich and Some So Poor* (New York: W. W. Norton, 1998), pp. 3–16.

19. A note to the reader: In this chapter I use the word *Ireland* to refer to the whole island, not its two political entities, the Republic of Ireland and the government of Northern Ireland. Similarly, and with apologies to Amerigo Vespucci and a plea for indulgence from Latin American and Canadian scholars, I use the word *America* to refer to only those parts of North America that later became part of the United States (thus excluded are Canada and Mexico). Finally, for reasons of shorthand and convenience, I use the term *South Africa* for those regions of Southern Africa (Cape Colony, Natal, Orange Free State, Transvaal) that later composed the Union (1910) and Republic (1961) of South Africa (thus excluded are Botswana, Lesotho, Namibia, Swaziland, and Zimbabwe).

20. In recent multiracial national elections, voters have overwhelmingly rejected candidates of the Pan-African Congress (PAC), whose motto is "one settler, one bullet," in favor of African National Congress (ANC) leaders Mandela and Mbeki.

21. The tension between native and settler is a perennial, if often implicit, theme in surveys of Irish history. A solid overview is Thomas Hachey, Joseph Hernon Jr., and Lawrence J. McCaffrey, *The Irish Experience,* rev. ed. (Armonk, N.Y.: M. E. Sharpe, 1996). In addition to J. C. Beckett's elegant, dispassionate classic, *The Making of Modern Ireland, 1603–1923* (London: Faber and Faber, 1966), the reader is referred to R. F. Foster's magisterial *Modern Ireland, 1600–1972* (London: Penguin Press, 1988). Economic history is the emphasis in L. M. Cullen's *The Emergence of Modern Ireland, 1600–1900* (New York: Holmes and Meier, 1981) and Cormac Ó Gráda's *Ireland: A New Economic History, 1780–1939* (Oxford: Clarendon Press, 1994); political history, in Alvin Jackson's *Ireland, 1798–1998* (Oxford: Blackwell, 1999). A brief but incisive interpretive study is Kevin Collins, *The Cultural Conquest of Ireland* (Dublin: Mercier Press, 1990). On the island's status in the Atlantic world, see Kenneth R. Andrews, Nicholas P. Canny, and P. E. H. Hair, *The Westward Enterprise: English Activities in Ireland, the Atlantic, and America, 1480–1650* (Detroit: Wayne State University Press, 1979). In *Kingdom and Colony: Ireland in the Atlantic World, 1560–1800* (Baltimore: Johns Hopkins University Press), Nicholas Canny assesses the island's transition in political status in Britain's burgeoning empire. On Northern Ireland, see Thomas Hennessey, *A History of Northern Ireland, 1920–1996* (New York: St. Martin's Press, 1996), and David Fitzpatrick, *The Two Irelands, 1912–1939* (Oxford: Oxford University Press, 1998).

22. Grenfell Morton, *Elizabethan Ireland* (London: Longman, 1971), pp. 129 ("Turk"), 136 ("good order"); and Foster, *Modern Ireland,* p. 34.

23. Foster, *Modern Ireland,* p. 86. The mortality levels in the Ulster rising produced a mythic historiography and, to many, offered "proof" of the savagery of the native Irish. The starting point of the enduring myth is Sir John Temple, *The Irish Rebellion: or, An History of the Beginnings and first Progresse of the General Rebellion raised within the Kingdom of Ireland, . . . together with the Barbarous Cruelties and Bloody Massacres which ensued thereupon* (London: S. Gellibrand, 1646). Presenting his book as a gothic horror story, Temple concludes that, from 1641 to 1643, some "300,000 British and Protestants [were] cruelly murthered in cold blood, destroyed some otherway [*sic*], or expelled out of their habitations" (p. 6). Scholars today offer credible figures. Patrick J. Corish argues for 4,000 "murdered" and 8,000 subsequently dead from "privations" (Corish, "The Rising of 1641 and the Confederacy, 1641–1645," in *Early Modern Ireland 1534–1691,* vol. 3, *A New History*

of Ireland, ed. T. W. Moody, F. X. Martin, F. J. Byrne [Oxford: Clarendon Press, 1976], pp. 291–92). A recent scholar suggests that the number of killings in Ulster may have totaled 12,000; see Hilary Simms, "Violence in County Armagh, 1641," in *Ulster 1641: Aspects of the Rising,* rev. ed., ed. Brian Mac Cuarta (Belfast: Institute of Irish Studies, Queen's University, 1997), pp. 133–34. The total that I suggest—6,000 killed—seeks middle ground between most scholarly estimates (4,000) and Simms's figure.

24. The Irish death totals, accumulated in just fifteen weeks from late May to early September, are stunning by comparison to other contemporary events. In France, the Jacobins' twelve-month-long Reign of Terror (1793–1794) claimed 35,000–40,000 lives. Eight years of fighting in America's Revolutionary War (1775–1783) produced for both sides a total of 34,000 deaths, half of them on the battlefield. Thomas Pakenham, *The Year of Liberty: The Great Irish Rebellion of 1798* (London: Hodder and Stoughton, 1969), pp. 342, 349–50, 401nn40–41. On the Irish rebellion's origins, see Nancy J. Curtin, *The United Irishmen: Popular Politics in Ulster and Dublin, 1791–1798* (New York: Oxford University Press, 1994). In his important recent study, *United Irishmen, United States: Immigrant Radicals in the Early Republic* (Ithaca, N.Y.: Cornell University Press, 1998), David A. Wilson notes that émigrés fleeing the failed 1798 rebellion helped both to democratize politics in America and to keep alive, across the Atlantic, the embers of Irish nationalism.

25. Scholars and other writers have dated the great famine variously (e.g., 1845–1849, 1846–1851, 1845–1852), depending on subjects covered (crop failure, hunger onset, relief, etc.) and even interpretive biases. I have chosen the broadest range, from the onset of crop failure to the restoration of "normalcy." Interestingly, both a classic revisionist account (downplaying the famine) and a postrevisionist work (emphasizing its horrors) can agree at least on the dating: See, respectively, R. D. Edwards and T. D. Williams, eds., *The Great Famine: Studies in Irish History, 1845–1852* (New York: New York University Press, 1957), and Christine Kinealy, *This Great Calamity: The Irish Famine, 1845–1852* (Dublin: Gill and Macmillan, 1994).

26. See Cormac Ó Gráda, *The Great Irish Famine* (London: Macmillan, 1989), and *Black '47 and Beyond: The Great Irish Famine* (Princeton, N.J.: Princeton University Press, 1999); Peter Gray, *The Irish Famine* (New York: Harry N. Abrams, 1995); Cathal Poirteir, ed., *The Great Irish Famine* (Dublin: Mercier Press, 1995); Chris Morash, *Writing the Irish Famine* (Oxford: Clarendon Press, 1995); Christine Kinealy, *A Death-dealing Famine: The Great Hunger in Ireland* (London: Pluto Press, 1997); L. A. Clarkson, E. M. Crawford, Liam Kennedy, and Paul S. Ell, *Mapping the Great Irish Famine: A Survey of the Famine Decades* (Dublin: Four Courts Press, 1999); and James S. Donnelly Jr., *The Great Irish Potato Famine* (Phoenix Mill, Gloucestershire: Sutton, 2001). Both Donnelly's authoritative account and Gray's succinct survey are visually stunning examples of modern book production.

27. Famines: Foster, *Modern Ireland,* p. 320, and Kinealy, *Death-dealing Famine,* pp. 42–48. G. A. Hayes-McCoy, "Tudor Conquest and Counter-Reformation, 1571–1603," in *Early Modern Ireland,* pp. 131 ("horrible"), 135 ("everywhere"); and R. A. Butlin, "Land and People, c. 1600," in ibid., p. 147 ("desert").

28. Preeminent in the field is Kerby A. Miller's prize-winning masterwork, *Emigrants and Exiles: Ireland and the Irish Exodus to North America* (New York: Oxford University Press, 1985). A recent excellent study is Kevin Kenny, *The American Irish: A History* (New York: Longman, 2000). Still useful is William Forbes Adams, *Ireland and Irish Emigration*

to the New World from 1815 to the Famine (1932; repr., New York: Russell and Russell, 1967). Recommended also are George W. Potter's classic, *To the Golden Door: The Story of the Irish in Ireland and America* (Boston: Little, Brown, 1960); David Fitzpatrick's short study, *Irish Emigration, 1801–1921* (Dundalk, Ireland: Economic and Social History Society of Ireland, 1984); and Donald H. Akenson's *The Irish Diaspora: A Primer* (Toronto: P. D. Meany, 1993).

29. Thomas Gallagher, *Paddy's Lament: Ireland 1846–1847, Prelude to Hatred* (New York: Harcourt Brace, 1982), p. 118.

30. New England refused to take Irish papists. On the seventeenth-century emigrants, see Harman Murtagh, "Irish Soldiers Abroad," in *A Military History of Ireland,* ed. Thomas Bartlett and Keith Jeffery (Cambridge: Cambridge University Press, 1996), p. 295 ("pacification"); John Childs, "The Williamite War, 1689–1691," in ibid., p. 209; Peter Berresford Ellis, *Hell or Connaught! The Cromwellian Colonisation of Ireland, 1652–1660* (Belfast: Blackstaff Press, 1975), pp. 40–43; and Miller, *Emigrants,* pp. 139, 140–41 ("idle people"). Ellis notes that while 10,000 were officially transported, "the exact number of Irish [in the 1650s] who were 'Barbadosed' or sent to the other English colonies in the New World will never be known. It was probably in the region of 50,000" (*Hell,* p. 154). Also arguing for this latter figure is Sean O'Callaghan, *To Hell or Barbados: The Ethnic Cleansing of Ireland* (Dingle, Kerry, Ireland: Brandon Books, 2000), pp. 85–88, who quotes a Catholic petitioner as describing the island as that "desolate vault, the Protestant Purgatory, Barbados" (p. 95).

31. Miller, *Emigrants,* p. 291 ("more people"); and Kinealy, *Death-dealing Famine,* p. 148 ("Manhattan").

32. "European": Chris Curtin, Riana O'Dwyer, and Gearoid Ó Tuathaigh, "Emigration and Exile," in *Irish Studies: A General Introduction,* ed. Thomas Bartlett, Chris Curtin, Riana O'Dwyer, and Gearoid Ó Tuathaigh (Dublin: Gill and Macmillan, 1988), p. 64; and Minnesota immigrant quoted in Miller, *Emigrants,* p. 344.

33. *Cork Examiner,* June 22, 1871, quoted in Gallagher, *Paddy's Lament,* p. 119.

34. Miller, *Emigrants,* pp. 346–49, 569–71; and K. Theodore Hoppen, *Ireland since 1800: Conflict and Conformity* (London: Longman, 1989), p. 60. For statistics enumerating Catholics, Anglicans, and Presbyterians in Ireland in 1834 and in five decennial Irish censuses from 1861 through 1901, see Donald Harman Akenson, *Occasional Papers on the Irish in South Africa* (Grahamstown, South Africa: Rhodes University Institute of Social and Economic Research, 1991), table, p. 17.

35. Quotations in Patrick J. Corish, "The Cromwellian Regime, 1650–1660," in *Early Modern Ireland,* pp. 373–74, emphasis added. To study Irish demography before the mid-eighteenth century is to walk in a minefield. "The best [contemporary] estimate we have" (Corish, p. 357) is Sir William Petty's *Political Anatomy of Ireland* (1691), which can be alarmingly specific (e.g., he argues for some 616,000 people killed in the period from 1641 to 1652). For a beginning, see L. M. Cullen, "Economic Trends, 1660–1691," in *Early Modern Ireland,* pp. 387–90; Jane H. Ohlmeyer, " 'Civilizinge of those Rude Partes': Colonization within Britain and Ireland, 1580s–1640s," in *The Origins of Empire: British Overseas Enterprise to the Close of the Seventeenth Century,* ed. Nicholas Canny, vol. 1, *The Oxford History of the British Empire,* 5 vols., ed. William Roger Louis (Oxford: Oxford University Press, 1998), pp. 139–40; and T. C. Barnard, "New Opportunities for British Settlement: Ireland, 1650–1700," in *Origins,* pp. 310–12, 322–26; and Foster, *Modern Ireland,* pp. 70–73, 107n., 130–31.

On the new settlements, see Michael MacCarthy-Morrogh, *The Munster Plantation: English Migration to Southern Ireland, 1583–1641* (Oxford: Clarendon Press, 1986); Raymond Gillespie, *Colonial Ulster: The Settlement of East Ulster, 1600–1641* (Cork, Ireland: Cork University Press, 1985); Ciaran Brady and Raymond Gillespie, eds., *Natives and Newcomers: Essays on the Making of Irish Colonial Society, 1534–1641* (Dublin: Irish Academic Press, 1986); John P. Prendergast's still useful *The Cromwellian Settlement of Ireland* (1865; repr., London: Constable, 1996); and Karl S. Bottigheimer, *English Money and Irish Land: The Adventurers in the Cromwellian Settlement of Ireland* (Oxford: Clarendon Press, 1971). A magisterial recent study of pre-Cromwellian settlements is Nicholas P. Canny, *Making Ireland British, 1580–1650* (Oxford: Oxford University Press, 2001).

36. T. C. Barnard, "New Opportunities," in *Origins,* pp. 313 ("isolated"), 322 ("barbarism"). American land promoters: Nicholas Canny, "England's New World and the Old," in *Origins,* p. 164. *Belfast News-Letter,* June 3, 1766, quoted in R. J. Dickson, *Ulster Emigration to Colonial America, 1718–1775* (1966; repr., Belfast: Ulster Historical Foundation, 1988), p. 17.

37. In the 1780s, one "bizarre" project, New Geneva, proposed the settlement of Swiss families near Waterford. "Colonies of Genevese were expected to implant . . . watchmaking skills and the Protestant work ethic. A university was to be built, and a land reclamation scheme begun. But they never arrived and the place became a barracks" (Foster, *Modern Ireland,* pp. 216–17).

38. Sister of United Irishman William Drennan, 1803, quoted in Miller, *Emigrants,* p. 186.

39. Archbishop William King to Archbishop Wake, February 6, 1718, quoted in Dickson, *Ulster Emigration,* p. 35; 1886 Ulsterman quoted in Beckett, *Making of Modern Ireland,* p. 399.

40. Patrick Griffin, *The People with No Name: Ireland's Ulster Scots, America's Scots Irish, and the Creation of a British Atlantic World, 1689–1764* (Princeton, N. J.: Princeton University Press, 2001), pp. 77 ("America"), 79 ("fatal"); and Miller, *Emigrants,* pp. 170–71, 201 ("the best go"). See also Dickson, *Ulster Emigration,* chaps. 2–6; Griffin, *People with No Name,* chap. 3; and Graeme Kirkham, "Ulster Migration to North America, 1680–1720," in *Ulster and North America: Transatlantic Perspectives on the Scotch-Irish,* ed. H. Tyler Blethen and Curtis W. Wood (Tuscaloosa: University of Alabama Press, 1997), pp. 76–117.

41. Miller, *Emigrants,* p. 153 ("abandoned"), and Dickson, *Ulster Emigration,* pp. 35 ("inveterate"), 192 ("dangerous").

42. Letters of 1839 and 1832, respectively, quoted in Miller, *Emigrants,* pp. 233, 234.

43. Kinealy, *Death-dealing Famine,* pp. 146 (Clarendon), 148 (Trevelyan), 149; Donnelly, *Potato Famine,* pp. 101, 115, 124–25, 130–31, 156, 166. It was in reaction to such cold, blunt talk about "modernization" and the need for society's "improvement" that Benjamin Jowett, Anglican clergyman and master of Balliol College, Oxford (1870–1893), made his famous remark: "I have always had a certain horror of political economists since I heard one of them say that the famine in Ireland would not kill more than a million people, and that would scarcely be enough to do much good" (quoted in Donnelly, p. 15).

44. Between 1861 and 1911, Ulster's Protestant population fell only 2 percent in the six counties that would later compose the government of Northern Ireland, but it dropped 44 percent in the three southern and western counties that would become part of the Irish Free State in 1921. Miller, *Emigrants,* p. 378; see also idem, pp. 346, 350, 370–71.

45. Ibid., pp. 371 ("urban"), 380 ("second England"), a phrase that could be admiring or disapproving, depending on the speaker. On Canada, see Bruce S. Elliott, *Irish Migrants in the Canadas: A New Approach* (Kingston, Ontario: McGill-Queen's University Press, 1988), a study of 775 Protestant immigrant families in the period from 1818 to 1855; and Cecil J. Houston and William J. Smyth, *Irish Emigration and Canadian Settlement: Patterns, Links, and Letters* (Toronto: University of Toronto Press, 1990).

46. Overall, in the four original provinces of the Dominion of Canada, the 1871 census showed that people of Irish descent accounted for 24.3 percent of the nation's population, behind those of French descent (31.1 percent) but ahead of those of English descent (20.3 percent); Donald Harman Akenson, *Small Differences: Irish Catholics and Irish Protestants, 1815–1922* (Montreal and Kingston, Ontario: McGill-Queen's University Press, 1988), pp. 90–91. See also Akenson's *The Irish in Ontario: A Study in Rural History* (Montreal and Kingston, Ontario: McGill-Queen's University Press, 1984).

47. When schemes were proposed, they tended to emphasize the subtraction of natives, not the addition of settlers. For example, in the midst of the potato famine there were numerous native emigration-assistance plans. Probably the most notorious was the one (memorialized by 80 signers, including 27 English noblemen and 18 members of Parliament) that urged Prime Minister Russell to implement, over a three-year period, the transfer of nearly two million of Ireland's Catholics to the vastness of Canada, where they could dwell next to their French Catholic brethren (see Gallagher, *Paddy's Lament,* pp. 146–48). The proposal was never acted upon.

48. See John Hutchinson, *The Dynamics of Cultural Nationalism: The Gaelic Revival and the Creation of the Irish Nation State* (London: Allen and Unwin, 1987); David George Boyce, *Nationalism in Ireland,* 3d ed. (London: Routledge, 1995); W. F. Mandle, *The Gaelic Athletic Association and Irish Nationalist Politics, 1884–1924* (Dublin: Gill and Macmillan, 1987); Tom Garvin, *Nationalist Revolutionaries in Ireland, 1858–1928* (Oxford: Clarendon Press, 1987); and Robert Kee, *The Green Flag: A History of Irish Nationalism* (1972; London: Penguin Books, 2000). Still useful for the impact of emigration on postfamine Irish society is Arnold Schrier's lucid early study, *Ireland and the American Emigration, 1850–1900* (1958; repr., Chester Springs, Penn.: Dufour Editions, 1997). A brilliant, monumental study of the linkage between an emerging nation's literature and its developing national consciousness is Declan Kiberd's *Inventing Ireland* (Cambridge: Harvard University Press, 1996).

49. See Dennis G. Pringle, *One Island, Two Nations? A Political Geographical Analysis of the National Conflict in Ireland* (New York: John Wiley and Sons, 1985).

50. In a cultural about-face, the (male) "whiteness" of U.S. history textbooks of forty years ago has been replaced by "technicolor," which frequently focuses on race, gender, and class. Nowadays it is rare for a survey text *not* to have some sort of "multicultural" theme. Among the best of today's multiauthored surveys are Paul S. Boyer, Clifford E. Clark Jr., et al., *The Enduring Vision: A History of the American People,* 5th ed. (Boston: Houghton Mifflin, 2005); Mary Beth Norton, David Katzman, et al., *A People and a Nation: A History of the United States,* 7th ed. (Boston: Houghton Mifflin, 2005); and John Mack Faragher, Mari Jo Buhle, et al., *Out of Many: A History of the American People,* 4th ed., (Upper Saddle River, N.J.: Prentice Hall, 2003). For persistence of the "red-white-black" theme throughout their pre–Civil War volume, two textbooks stand out: Gary B. Nash, Julie Roy Jeffrey, et al., *The American People: Creating a Nation and a*

Society, 6th ed. (New York: Longman, 2003); and Jacqueline Jones, Peter Wood, et al., *Created Equal: A Social and Political History of the United States,* 2d ed. (New York: Longman, 2005).

51. Historians coined the term "Native Americans" to refer to Indians as part of the useful revisionism of the 1970s, which was a reaction against the reigning Eurocentrism of American historiography. Nowadays most textbooks use "Native American" in their index and/or say "see specific tribes." Still, the word "Indian" is "undoubtedly the most enduring misnomer in American history." I use the two terms more or less interchangeably, though I think that with the way American history unfolded, "Native American" applies best to the first century of encounter. Many "Indian" tribes, in "an understandable bit of ethnocentrism," simply called themselves in their own language "the people" (and see note 103). A common-sense discussion of this issue of terminology is in Gregory H. Nobles, *American Frontiers: Cultural Encounters and Continental Conquest* (New York: Hill and Wang, 1997), pp. xiii–xiv ("enduring").

Since the 1970s, the American reading public has developed a strong interest in Native American history. The approach of the Columbian quincentennial only stimulated the production of a number of fine popular histories. Among the best are Alvin Josephy Jr. and Frederick E. Hoxie, eds., *America in 1492: The World of the Indian Peoples before the Arrival of Columbus* (New York: Alfred A. Knopf, 1992); Betty Ballantine and Ian Ballantine, eds., *The Native Americans: An Illustrated History* (Atlanta: Turner Publishing, 1993); and Alvin Josephy Jr., *500 Nations: An Illustrated History of North American Indians* (New York: Alfred A. Knopf, 1994). Also valuable is the handsome *Time-Life* series on Native American history: *The American Indians,* 15 vols., ed. Henry Woodhead (Alexandria, Va.: *Time-Life* Books, 1992–1994). Good introductions that are less lush but more academic are Frederick E. Hoxie, ed., *Indians in American History* (Arlington Heights, Ill.: Harlan Davidson, 1988), and Philip Weeks, ed., *The American Indian Experience: A Profile, 1524 to the Present* (Arlington Heights, Ill.: Forum Press, 1988), and Weeks's survey, *Farewell, My Nation: The American Indian and the United States, 1820–1890* (Arlington Heights, Ill.: Harlan Davidson, 1990).

Early scholarly writing, often sympathetic, approached America's aborigines as subjects for anthropology. For example, see Edward S. Curtis, *The North American Indian,* 20 vols., ed. Frederick W. Hodge, foreword by Theodore Roosevelt, and research patronage by J. Pierpont Morgan (1907–1930; repr., New York: Johnson Reprint, 1970). The first serious academic synthesis was Angie Debo's *History of the Indians of the United States* (Norman: University of Oklahoma Press, 1970; variously reprinted, including, most recently, Mattituck, N.Y.: Amereon, 2004). Recent decades have produced a cornucopia of outstanding, often prize-winning scholarly monographs investigating the interactions of the Native Americans and English-speaking settlers. Among the best are Neal Salisbury, *Manitou and Providence: Indians, Europeans, and the Making of New England, 1500–1643* (New York: Oxford University Press, 1982); Karen Ordahl Kupperman, *Settling with the Indians: The Meeting of English and Indian Cultures in America, 1580–1640* (Totowa, N.J.: Rowman and Littlefield, 1980) and *Indians and English: Facing Off in Early America* (Ithaca, N.Y.: Cornell University Press, 2000); several of the numerous books by master essayist James Axtell, including *The European and the Indian: Essays in the Ethnohistory of Colonial North America* (New York: Oxford University Press, 1981), his Chinard Prize–winning *The Invasion Within: The Contest of Cultures in Colonial North America* (New York: Oxford University Press, 1985), *After Columbus: Essays in the Ethnohistory of Colonial North America* (New York: Oxford University Press, 1988), and most recently his *Natives and Newcomers: The Cultural Origins of North America* (New York: Oxford University Press, 2000); James H. Merrell's 1990 Bancroft Prize–winning *The Indians' New World: Catawbas and Their Neighbors from European Contact through the Era of Removal* (Chapel Hill: University of North Carolina Press, 1989); Richard White's 1992 Parkman Prize–winning *The Middle Ground: Indians, Empires, and Republics in the Great Lakes Region, 1650–1815* (New York: Cambridge University Press, 1991); Daniel K. Richter's *Facing East from Indian Country: A Native History of Early America* (Cambridge: Harvard University Press, 2001), which earned him the honor of being a finalist for the 2002 Pulitzer Prize; Elliott West's 1999 Parkman Prize–winning *The Contested Plains: Indians, Goldseekers, and the Rush to Colorado* (Lawrence: University Press of Kansas, 1998), a balanced, elegantly crafted analysis of native and settler cultures and encounters; and Patricia N. Limerick's *The Legacy of Conquest: The Unbroken Past of the American West* (New York: W. W. Norton, 1987), a brilliant and controversial work whose emphasis on regionalism, not chronology (she finds the 1890 closing of the frontier irrelevant), would have much intrigued Walter P. Webb.

Two extensive bibliographic essays (citing books and articles) may be found in Nobles, *American Frontiers*, pp. 251–74; and for the period 1600–1780, in Nash, *Red, White, and Black*, 4th ed., pp. 323–55. Finally, on the philosophic difficulties inherent in Indians and whites understanding each other at all, see *The American Indian and the Problem of History*, ed. Calvin Martin (New York: Oxford University Press, 1986).

52. A very rough estimate: only 1 person per square mile. In 1500, perhaps 3 million Native Americans lived on land totaling 3.02 million square miles (to use the area of the United States' forty-eight contiguous states). By contrast, Ireland's natives were densely packed: 23 people per square mile. That island's native population, estimated at 0.75 million in 1500, was crowded into 32,000 square miles (an area the size of Maine or South Carolina).

53. The phrase is Gary Nash's. From his North American (but not comparative) perspective Nash argues, reasonably enough, that the Native Americans were engaged historical actors, on some occasions resisting the settlers and on others adapting to their culture. In Nash's words, they were *not* "passive victims" of the European intrusion (*Red, White, and Black*, 4th ed., p. 3).

54. I borrow this phrase from David E. Stannard's *American Holocaust: The Conquest of the New World* (New York: Oxford University Press, 1993).

55. On Indian forced emigrations, see Grant Foreman, *Indian Removal: The Emigration of the Five Civilized Tribes of Indians* (1932; repr., Temecula, Calif.: Textbook Publishers, 2003) and *The Last Trek of the Indians* (Chicago: University of Chicago Press, 1946); Angie Debo, *And Still the Waters Run: The Betrayal of the Five Civilized Tribes* (1940; repr., Norman: University of Oklahoma Press, 1984); Bernard W. Sheehan, *Seeds of Extinction: Jeffersonian Philanthropy and the American Indian* (Chapel Hill: University of North Carolina Press, 1973); Ronald N. Satz, *American Indian Policy in the Jacksonian Era* (Lincoln: University of Nebraska Press, 1975); Michael D. Green, *The Politics of Indian Removal: Creek Government and Society in Crisis* (Lincoln: University of Nebraska Press, 1982); Louis Filler and Allen Guttmann, eds., *The Removal of the Cherokee Nation: Manifest Destiny or National Dishonor?* (Melbourne, Fla.: Krieger, 1988); James A. Clifton, *Old Northwest Indian Removal, 1825–1855: A Bibliography* (Ann Arbor, Mich.: Books on Demand,

Univ. Microfilms, 1988); Perdue and Green, eds., *Cherokee Removal;* and Robert V. Remini, *Andrew Jackson and His Indian Wars* (New York: Viking Penguin, 2001).

Indian displacements of course affected tribes there already—see David La Vere, *Contrary Neighbors: Southern Plains and Removed Indians in Indian Territory* (Norman: University of Oklahoma Press, 2000). Paula M. Marks offers a detailed, three-century overview in her work titled *In a Barren Land: American Indian Dispossession and Survival* (New York: William Morrow, 1998). Ironically, Indian land losses continued once Euroamericans discovered the value of "nature" and need for "vacations"; national park sites became yet another area of contention between natives and settlers. See Mark D. Spence's highly original *Dispossessing the Wilderness: Indian Removal and the Making of the National Parks* (New York: Oxford University Press, 1999).

Finally, Indian removal has generated much writing, fiction and nonfiction, some of it quite good, for the general reading public and for young adult (ages 16–18) readers. (Is removal a "safe" subject because it raises moral issues without power struggles in today's politics?) Among the best written for these two audiences are, respectively, John Ehle, *Trail of Tears: The Rise and Fall of the Cherokee Nation* (New York: Doubleday, 1989), and Anthony F. C. Wallace, *The Long, Bitter Trail: Andrew Jackson and the Indians* (New York: Hill and Wang, 1993).

56. Edward Waterhouse of the Virginia Company, 1622, quoted in Axtell, *After Columbus,* p. 217.

57. The 1622 Indian rising in Virginia claimed the lives of 14.0 percent of the settler population (2,500); King Philip's War, 1.5 percent, in Massachusetts (pop. 40,000); and the Yamassee War, 2.7 percent, in South Carolina (pop. 15,000).

58. On the battle at the Maumee River (1791), see Wilbur Edel, *Kekionga! The Worst Defeat in the History of the U.S. Army* (Westport, Conn.: Greenwood, 1997).

59. The historical literature on "Indian wars" is almost embarrassingly abundant: A July, 2002, OCLC WorldCat online search uncovered 4,445 books (in English) on "Indians of North America—Wars," 1,044 of them treating the period 1866–1895 but only 298 for the period 1600–1750. This distribution of chronological coverage (in part based on source-material availability) can be misleading. The American general public, nourished on Hollywood's portrayals, has the mistaken notion that "Indian wars" were most important after the Civil War; in fact, they were then (relative to America's native-settler ratio) least important in terms of constituting a threat to the established settler society. For two excellent overviews of the warfare between natives and settlers, see Robert M. Utley and Wilcomb E. Washburn, *The American Heritage History of the Indian Wars* (New York: American Heritage, 1977), and from the Indians' viewpoint, Alvin M. Josephy Jr., *The Patriot Chiefs: A Chronicle of American Indian Resistance* (1961; repr., New York: Penguin Books, 1994). The cruelties practiced by both sides in what he calls "the American-Indian War of 1622–1890" are examined in William M. Osborn's meticulously comprehensive catalog of incidents, *The Wild Frontier: Atrocities during the American-Indian War from Jamestown Colony to Wounded Knee* (New York: Random House, 2001).

Among the best of recent academic writings are Ian K. Steele, *Warpaths: Invasions of North America, 1513–1765* (New York: Oxford University Press, 1994); Armstrong Starkey, *European and Native American Warfare, 1675–1815* (Norman: University of Oklahoma Press, 1998); Alfred A. Cave, *The Pequot War* (Amherst: University of Massachusetts Press, 1996); Russell Bourne, *The Red King's Rebellion: Racial Politics in New England, 1675–1678*

(New York: Atheneum, 1990); Jill Lepore's 1999 Bancroft Prize–winning study, *The Name of War: King Philip's War and the Origins of American Identity* (New York: Random House, 1998); Patrick M. Malone, *The Skulking Way of War: Technology and Tactics among the New England Indians* (New York: Madison Books, 1991); Wiley Sword, *President Washington's Indian War: The Struggle for the Old Northwest, 1790–1795* (Norman: University of Oklahoma Press, 1985); Bil Gilbert, *God Gave Us This Country: Tekanthi and the First American Civil War* (New York: Atheneum, 1989); Remini, *Jackson and His Indian Wars;* Roger L. Nichols, *Black Hawk and the Warrior's Path* (Arlington Heights, Ill.: Harlan Davidson, 1992); Robert M. Utley, *The Indian Frontier of the American West, 1846–1890* (Albuquerque: University of New Mexico Press, 1984); and Robert Wooster, *The Military and United States Indian Policy, 1865–1903* (Lincoln: University of Nebraska Press, 1995).

60. Respectively, a massacre of Cheyennes by Colorado militiamen and in Wyoming a massacre by Lakota Sioux warriors of U.S. cavalrymen led by Lt. William Fetterman. See Bruce Cutler, *The Massacre at Sand Creek: Narrative Voices* (Norman: University of Oklahoma Press, 1995); and Dee Brown, *The Fetterman Massacre* (Lincoln: University of Nebraska Press, 1984; first published as *Fort Phil Kearny: An American Saga* [New York: Putnam, 1962]). In a bit of grisly quantitative history, John D. Unruh Jr. calculated that, over the period from 1840 to 1860, in both clashes and individual incidents, Indians killed a total of 362 settlers ("emigrants"), while the settlers killed 426 Indians. The Indians, he argues, were more often victims than aggressors, the settlers frequently shooting with little or no provocation. See Unruh's landmark work, *The Plains Across: The Overland Emigrants and the Trans–Mississippi West, 1840–1860* (Urbana: University of Illinois Press, 1979), pp. 156–200, especially table 4, p. 185.

61. A victim of savagery (the nineteenth-century-settler's viewpoint) or a martyr to Euroamerican guilt over continental conquest (many scholars and citizens today)? See, for example, that now thirty-year-old call to arms, Vine Deloria Jr.'s *Custer Died for Your Sins: An Indian Manifesto* (1969; repr., Norman: University of Oklahoma Press, 1988). Or is the Custer story just overblown propaganda—a case of a military detachment simply in the wrong spot at the wrong time? To most Americans, like him or not, "Custer" is one of those instantly recognizable names in American history. In August, 2002, an OCLC WorldCat online search for "George Armstrong Custer, 1839–1876" revealed a total of 1,166 books published about him, 277 of them since 1990; a descriptor search for "Little Bighorn, Battle of the, Mont., 1876" uncovered some 1,015 books published, 161 of them since 1990.

"Custer and the Little Bighorn" remains an inseparable mythology with many purposes and audiences. For children's stories, see Conrad Stein, *The Story of Little Bighorn* (Chicago: Children's Press, 1983); for Indian rebuttals, see Richard Hardorff, *Lakota Recollections of the Custer Fight* (Spokane, Wash.: Arthur H. Clark, 1991); for archaeological digs, see Richard Allan Fox, *Archaeology, History, and Custer's Last Battle* (Norman: University of Oklahoma Press, 1993), and Douglas D. Scott, P. Willey, and Melissa A. Connor, *They Died with Custer: Soldiers' Bones from the Battle of the Little Bighorn* (Norman: University of Okalahoma Press, 2002), as well as time-and-motion military studies such as John S. Gray, *Custer's Last Campaign: Mitch Boyer and the Little Bighorn Reconstructed* (Lincoln: University of Nebraska Press, 1991). In recent years the American public has been treated to the discovery of a long-lost eyewitness account; see William O. Taylor, *With Custer on the Little Bighorn*, ed. Greg Martin (New York: Viking Penguin, 1996); also see a novelist's best-selling biography and movie, Evan S. Connell, *Son of the Morning Star:*

Custer and the Little Bighorn (San Francisco: North Point Press, 1982), reprinted by a half-dozen presses including the History Book Club in 2001, winner of a 1985 *Los Angeles Times* book prize, and produced as a 1991 made-for-TV movie), and an all-you-ever-wanted-to-know-about-Custer compendium by "an advertising producer for whom Custer is a great hobby"—Thom Hatch's *Custer and the Battle of the Little Bighorn: An Encyclopedia of the People, Places, Events, Indian Culture and Customs, Information Sources, Art, and Films* (Jefferson, N.C.: McFarland, 2000).

The academics are not far behind. Robert M. Utley was the first to investigate *Custer and the Great Controversy: The Origin and Development of a Legend* (1962; repr., with an introduction by Brian W. Dippie, Lincoln: University of Nebraska Press, 1988). For recent academic assessments of Custer and the Little Bighorn, see Brian W. Dippie, *Custer's Last Stand: The Anatomy of an American Myth* (Lincoln: University of Nebraska Press, 1994), and Charles E. Rankin, ed., *Legacy: New Perspectives on the Battle of the Little Bighorn* (Helena: Montana Historical Society Press, 1996). Refreshing in its view of Sioux aggressiveness as well as Custer's arrogance is a recent study by James Welch (a Blackfoot Indian) and Paul Stekler, *Killing Custer: The Battle of the Little Bighorn and the Fate of the Plains Indians* (New York: W. W. Norton, 1994). The standard biography remains Robert M. Utley's *Cavalier in Buckskin: George Armstrong Custer and the Western Military Frontier* (Norman: University of Oklahoma Press, 1988). Two excellent recent studies that emphasize, respectively, the man's life and his myth, are Jeffrey D. Wert, *Custer: The Controversial Life of George Armstrong Custer* (New York: Simon and Schuster, 1996), and Louise Barnett, *Touched by Fire: The Life, Death, and Mythic Afterlife of George Armstrong Custer* (New York: Henry Holt, 1996).

62. Richard White, "When Frederick Jackson Turner and Buffalo Bill Cody Both Played Chicago in 1893," in *Frontier Experience*, p. 53. If Custer's death was a sacrifice to manifest destiny, his martyrdom was also a perfect fit for the 1870s—a decade when the United States was celebrating the centennial of its independence and busy with post–Civil War nation building. Not least in importance, the East Coast newspaper business was booming, stories about the West sold, and Custer's widow, Libby, was tireless in her promotion. By contrast, the earlier and far deadlier Indian victory at the Maumee River (1791) received little contemporary notoriety and, indeed, even now remains obscure and forgotten except by a handful of historians.

63. "The colonists avenged the death of their comrades by giving poisoned wine to 200 Indians, by ambushing another fifty in 1623, and by killing 800 in battle in July 1624." Peter C. Mancall, "Native Americans and Europeans in English America, 1500–1700," in *Origins*, p. 338.

64. Paul S. Boyer, Clifford E. Clark Jr., et al., *The Enduring Vision*, 1st ed., vol. 1, p. 26 ("greatest"); and Henry Dobyns, "Andean Epidemic History," p. 514, quoted in Alfred W. Crosby Jr., *The Columbian Exchange: Biological and Cultural Consequences of 1492* (Westport, Conn.: Greenwood Press, 1972), p. 39 ("most severe"). Dobyns was referring to the pandemic that swept through the Greater Antilles and Mexico, Central America, and Peru beginning in 1519. On disease, see Crosby's pioneer article, "Virgin Soil Epidemics as a Factor in Aboriginal Depopulation in America," *William and Mary Quarterly*, 3d ser., 33 (1976): 289–99; John W. Verano and Douglas Ubelaker, eds., *Disease and Demography in the Americas* (Washington, D.C.: Smithsonian Institution Press, 1994); Stephen J. Kunitz, *Disease and Diversity: European Contact and the Health of Indigenous Peoples of North*

America and Oceania (New York: Oxford University Press, 1994); and Clark S. Larsen and George R. Milner, eds., *In the Wake of Contact: Biological Responses to Conquest* (New York: John Wiley and Sons, 1994).

65. Contemporary quotations in Crosby, *Columbian Exchange*, pp. 36, 37, 58, and "oozing horror" (Crosby's words) on p. 56.

66. Roanoke and Massachusetts quotations in ibid., pp. 40–41, 42; William Bradford quoted in Nobles, *American Frontiers*, p. 42.

67. Nash, *Red, White, and Black*, 4th ed., p. 318.

68. Bruce G. Trigger, *The Children of Aataentsic: A History of the Huron People to 1660*, vol. 2 (Montreal: McGill-Queen's University Press, 1976), pp. 588–602, and Alfred W. Crosby, *Ecological Imperialism: The Biological Expansion of Europe, 900–1900* (Cambridge: Cambridge University Press, 1986), pp. 202 ("Omahas," "Mandans"), 203 (Vancouver quoted).

69. See Albert L. Hurtado, *Indian Survival on the California Frontier* (New Haven, Conn.: Yale University Press, 1988), a landmark study of the 1850s that won him the 1989 Billington Prize of the Organization of American Historians. See also Van H. Garner, *The Broken Ring: The Destruction of the California Indians* (Tucson: Westernlore Press, 1982), and Sherburne F. Cook, *The Population of the California Indians, 1769–1970* (Berkeley: University of California Press, 1976). Two collections of primary accounts (1847–1865), often chilling, are Robert F. Heizer, ed., *The Destruction of California Indians* (Santa Barbara, Calif.: Peregrine Smith, 1974), and Clifford E. Trafzer and Joel R. Hyer, eds., *"Exterminate Them!" Written Accounts of the Murder, Rape, and Enslavement of Native Americans during the California Gold Rush* (East Lansing: Michigan State University Press, 1999).

70. President Jackson's State of the Union address, Dec. 6, 1830, quoted in Perdue and Green, eds., *Cherokee Removal*, p. 120. For Jackson's speeches expressing his views on Indians, including the full text of the Indian Removal Act of 1830, see the website "Tracking Westward Expansion and the Trail of Tears," www.synaptic.bc.ca/ejournal/jackson.htm. "Widowed": Francis Jennings, *The Invasion of America: Indians, Colonialism, and the Cant of Conquest* (New York: W. W. Norton, 1976), chap. 2, "Widowed Land."

71. Henry F. Dobyns, *Native American Historical Demography: A Critical Bibliography* (Bloomington: Indiana University Press, 1976), pp. 12–14, 54, 56; Mancall, "Native Americans and Europeans," in *Origins*, p. 331. The standard works are Henry F. Dobyns, *Their Number Become Thinned: Native American Population Dynamics in Eastern North America* (Knoxville: University of Tennessee Press, 1983), and Russell Thornton, *American Indian Holocaust and Survival: A Population History since 1492* (Norman: University of Oklahoma Press, 1987).

72. Adam Smith (1723–1790), *The Wealth of Nations*, vol. 2 (1776; repr., London: Methuen, 1904), p. 66, quoted in Webb, *Great Frontier*, p. 343.

73. See David Cressy, *Coming Over: Migration and Communication between England and New England in the Seventeenth Century* (New York: Cambridge University Press, 1987); Marianne S. Wokeck, *Trade in Strangers: The Beginnings of Mass Migration to North America* (University Park: Pennsylvania State University Press, 1999), a superb study that examines linkages between migrants and merchants in the emerging eighteenth-century business of moving Europeans across the Atlantic; and Allan Kulikoff, *From British Peasants to Colonial Farmers* (Chapel Hill: University of North Carolina Press, 2000). See also David Dobson, *Scottish Emigration to Colonial America, 1607–1785* (Athens: University of

Georgia Press, 1994); and Aaron S. Fogleman, *Hopeful Journeys: German Immigration, Settlement, and Political Culture in Colonial America, 1717–1775* (Philadelphia: University of Pennsylvania Press, 1996). On eighteenth-century Irish immigration, see Miller, *Emigrants,* chaps. 4 and 5, and Kenny, *American Irish,* chap. 1; see also the sources in notes 28, 40, and 74.

74. A recent transatlantic study that traces the evolution of Ulster's Scots into America's Scotch-Irish is Ron Chepesiuk's *The Scotch-Irish: From the North of Ireland to the Making of America* (Jefferson, N.C.: McFarland, 2000). See also Charles Knowles Bolton's still useful *Scotch Irish Pioneers in Ulster and America* (1910; repr., Baltimore: Genealogical Publ. Co., 1998); James Leyburn's *The Scotch-Irish in America: A Social History* (Chapel Hill: University of North Carolina, Press, 1962), which discusses the emerging American term "Scotch-Irish" on pp. 327–34; Carlton Jackson, *A Social History of the Scotch-Irish* (Lanham, Md.: Madison Books, 1993); and Blethen and Wood, eds., *Ulster and North America* (1997), passim. On their early concentration in Pennsylvania, see Griffin, *People with No Name,* passim, and James T. Lemon, *The Best Poor Man's Country: A Geographical Study of Early Southeastern Pennsylvania* (Baltimore: Johns Hopkins Press, 1972). A broader context is furnished in David Hackett Fischer's *Albion's Seed: Four British Folkways in America* (New York: Oxford University Press, 1989). Scots-Irish were active and prominent in the fight in the 1770s against the English government; see David Noel Doyle, *Ireland, Irishmen, and Revolutionary America, 1760–1820* (Dublin: Mercier Press, 1981), and Ronnie Hanna, *Land of the Free: Ulster and the American Revolution* (Lurgan, Armagh, Ireland: Ulster Society, 1992).

75. This "army" of seven million Euroamerican "emigrants" was spreading across land occupied by no more than 300,000 Indians. See Robert H. Jones, "Industrial Society and the Opening of the West: The American Indian in the Trans–Mississippi West and the Impact of the American Civil War," in *American Indian Experience,* p. 121.

76. Down to our own times, the volume of immigration to the United States has of course remained large. Over the subsequent seventy-year period, 1890–1960, the United States drew in 26.4 million (official) immigrants, and since 1960, another 16 million. However, there have been big changes: Europe no longer exports its people to the United States. As late as the period from 1951 to 1960, 53 percent of immigrants were European; four decades later, fewer than 10 percent are. Since 1970, four-fifths of immigrants (divided roughly equally) have come from Latin America and Asia. Overall, in the past 180 years (from 1820 to 2000), it is estimated that nearly 60 million people have legally entered the United States as immigrants, about three-fifths of them from Europe. See David M. Reimers, *Still the Golden Door: The Third World Comes to America,* 2d ed. (1985; New York: Columbia University Press, 1992); and Elliott R. Barkan, *And Still They Come: Immigrants and American Society, 1920 to the 1990s* (Wheeling, Ill.: Harlan Davidson, 1996).

77. Older surveys of immigration that are still valuable are George M. Stephenson, *A History of American Immigration, 1820–1924* (1926; repr., New York: Russell and Russell, 1964); Oscar Handlin, *The Uprooted: The Epic Story of the Great Migrations That Made the American People* (New York: Grosset and Dunlap, 1951); and Maldwyn A. Jones, *American Immigration,* 2d ed. (1960; Chicago: University of Chicago Press, 1992). The standard survey by Leonard Dinnerstein and David A. Reimers, *Ethnic Americans: A History of Immigration,* 4th ed. (1977; New York: Columbia University Press, 1999) is now supplemented by Roger Daniels's excellent *Coming to America: A History of Immigration and Ethnicity in*

American Life (New York: Harper Trade, 1990). Two recommended popular histories are Philip A. M. Taylor, *The Distant Magnet: European Emigration to the U.S.A.* (New York: Harper and Row, 1971), and Terry Coleman, *Going to America* (1972; repr., Baltimore: Genealogical Publ. Co., 1998). For a collection of essays by immigration specialists covering different countries of origin, see Rudolph J. Vecoli and Suzanne M. Sinke, eds., *A Century of European Migrations, 1830–1930* (Urbana: University of Illinois Press, 1991). On nineteenth-century British immigration, see Charlotte Erickson, *Invisible Immigrants: The Adaptation of English and Scottish Immigrants in Nineteenth-Century America* (1972; repr., Ithaca, N.Y.: Cornell University Press, 1990), and her recent work, *Leaving England: Essays on British Emigration in the Nineteenth Century* (Ithaca, N.Y.: Cornell University Press, 1994). See also William Van Vugt's excellent study of migration in the context of an Anglo-American transatlantic culture, *Britain to America: Mid-Nineteenth-Century Immigrants to the United States* (Urbana: University of Illinois Press, 1999). For sources on Irish emigration, see notes 28, 40, and 74.

78. Pres. Andrew Jackson's State of the Union address, Dec. 6, 1830, quoted in Perdue and Green, eds., *Cherokee Removal*, p. 120.

79. See Peter S. Onuf, *Statehood and Union: A History of the Northwest Ordinance* (Bloomington: University of Indiana Press, 1987).

80. California's estimated population in 1845 was 1,000 Anglo-Americans, 7,000 Mexicans, and 70,000 Indians.

81. Webb, *Great Frontier*, p. 5 ("locusts").

82. Calculated from population data (1790–1986) in tables in Nash, Jeffrey, et al., *American People,* 2d ed. (1990), vol. 1, appendix, pp. A-28, A-30. In the 2000 census (see http://www.census.gov/), 16 percent of those reporting said they were of German ancestry, 14 percent Irish or Scotch-Irish (altogether, 38 million people), and 12 percent English/Welsh/Scottish; rising fast, of course, was the Hispanic share, 12 percent (see also notes 1 and 76). See the 2000 census at "C2SS Supplementary Survey," "ancestry data."

83. See graph in Nash, Jeffrey, et al., *American People,* vol. 1, appendix, p. A-28.

84. Reginald Horsman, *Race and Manifest Destiny: The Origins of American Racial Anglo-Saxonism* (Cambridge: Harvard University Press, 1981), p. 199.

85. George W. Knepper, "Breaching the Ohio Boundary: The Western Tribes in Retreat," in *American Indian Experience,* p. 94; and Clay quoted in Horsman, *Race and Manifest Destiny,* p. 198.

86. O'Gorman to O'Brien, Jan. 1, 1859, quoted in Kerby Miller and Paul Wagner, *Out of Ireland: The Story of Irish Emigration to America* (Dublin: Roberts, Rinehart, 1997), p. 61, emphasis added. The fifty-five-year-old O'Brien declined the offer. Pardoned after serving six years' penal servitude (1848–1854) in Australia, O'Brien had returned to Ireland in 1856. He spent his last years living quietly on his Limerick estate and traveling on the Continent. He died in Wales in 1864. In New York, Richard O'Gorman (1821–1895) became wealthy, important, and corrupt. In the thick of the Boss Tweed crowd at Tammany Hall, O'Gorman developed a sharp but shady reputation as he prospered in service, successively, as city attorney, judge, and justice on the New York Superior Court. The words in his 1859 letter to William Smith O'Brien were prescient: "The honest fellow I left behind me in Ireland is now owner of a corner grocery in New York and covets the post of alderman and scents plunder from afar."

87. From the speech of Tecumseh to Gen. Sir Isaac Brock, Aug. 14, 1812, quoted in Glenn

Tucker, *Tecumseh: Vision of Glory* (1956; repr., New York: Russell and Russell, 1973), p. 265. Fourteen months later Tecumseh was killed at the Battle of the Thames, his body mutilated by the Americans, then buried; see John Sugden, *Tecumseh's Last Stand* (Norman: University of Oklahoma Press, 1985), the title a clever play on Custer's. Sugden has also written an excellent recent biography, *Tecumseh: A Life* (New York: Henry Holt, 1998). For the broader problems facing four Indian leaders, including Tecumseh, see Gregory E. Dowd, *A Spirited Resistance: The North American Indian Struggle for Unity, 1745–1815* (Baltimore: Johns Hopkins University Press, 1993).

88. For a general introduction, see Leonard M. Thompson, *A History of South Africa*, 3d ed. (1990; New Haven: Yale University Press, 2001); T. R. H. Davenport and Christopher C. Saunders, *South Africa: A Modern History*, 5th ed. (1977; New York: St. Martin's Press, 2000); and Christopher C. Saunders , Nicholas Southey, and Mary-Lynn Suttie, *Historical Dictionary of South Africa*, 2d ed. (1983; Lanham, Md.: Scarecrow Press, 2000). Two engrossing popular histories by fifth- and eighth-generation South Africans, English and Afrikaner, respectively, are Allister Sparks, *The Mind of South Africa* (London: Heinemann, 1990), and Marq de Villiers, *White Tribe Dreaming* (New York: Viking, 1987). Not recommended, though useful for flashes of insight as well as anger, is the crude Marxist overview by Hosea Jaffe, *European Colonial Despotism: A History of Oppression and Resistance in South Africa* (London: Karnak House, 1994). A radical academic since the 1940s, Jaffe is a native South African who fled apartheid and has lived in Europe since the 1960s (see Saunders, *Making of the South African Past*, pp. 135–36). Another emigrant, South African–born Canadian journalist Noel Mostert, has produced a sprawling (1,355 pages), lyrical, and insightful behemoth, *Frontiers: The Epic of South Africa's Creation and the Tragedy of the Xhosa People* (New York: Knopf, 1992).

89. On the provocative if not persuasive "fragment theory" of colonial development, see Louis Hartz, *The Founding of New Societies: Studies in the History of the United States, Latin America, South Africa, Canada, and Australia* (New York: Harcourt, Brace, and World, 1964), pp. 3–65.

90. A. J. Boeseken, "The Settlement under the Van Der Stels," in C. F. J. Muller, ed., *Five Hundred Years: A History of South Africa* (Pretoria and Cape Town: Academica, 1969), p. 33; and Gerrit Schutte, "Company and Colonists at the Cape, 1652–1795," in *The Shaping of South African Society, 1652–1840*, rev. ed., ed. Richard Elphick and Hermann Giliomee (Middletown, Conn.: Wesleyan University Press, 1988), p. 298 ("lower strata").

91. McNeill, *Great Frontier*, p. 41 ("anarchic"), and Eric A. Walker, *The Great Trek*, 5th ed. (1934; London: Adam and Charles Black, 1965), p. 8 ("central event"). The centrality of the Great Trek in Afrikaner history can be seen in the fact that Prime Minister Frederik Willem de Klerk titled his autobiography "The Last Trek," and a writer on the current white emigration from South Africa has titled his book "The New Great Trek" (see notes 127 and 141). On the effect of "Great Trek Virus" (GTV) on the teaching of history in South Africa, see the comments of historian Charles van Onselen (University of Pretoria) in Sasha Polakow-Suransky, "Reviving South African History: Academics Debate How to Represent and Teach the Nation's Past," *Chronicle of Higher Education* (June 14, 2002): A37. My thanks to colleague Richard Francaviglia for this reference.

92. M. D. Nash, "The 1820 Settlers," in Cameron and Spies, eds., *Illustrated History of South Africa*, p. 94 ("first"). See Guy Butler, ed., *The 1820 Settlers: An Illustrated Commentary* (Cape Town: Human and Rousseau, 1974); Harold E. Hockley, *The Story of the British*

Settlers of 1820 in South Africa (Cape Town: Juta, 1957); and Graham B. Dickason, *Irish Settlers to the Cape: History of the Clanwilliam 1820 Settlers from Cork Harbour* (Cape Town: A. A. Balkema, 1973).

93. J. B. Peires, "The British and the Cape, 1814–1834," in Elphick and Giliomee, eds., *The Shaping of South African Society,* pp. 474–75 ("urban"). On immigration statistics, which he describes as "frustratingly sketchy" (p. 73n1), see Donald Harman Akenson, *Occasional Papers on the Irish in South Africa* (Grahamstown, South Africa: Institute of Social and Economic Research, Rhodes University, 1991), table 1, p. 54; on Irish immigration, see note 97. Much important work remains to be done on the subject of European immigration. A recent focused study is Cecillie Swaisland's *Servants and Gentlewomen to the Golden Land: The Emigration of Single Women from Britain to Southern Africa, 1820–1939* (Pietermaritzburg, South Africa: University of Natal Press, 1993).

94. As time is critical for the power of capital to compound, so too for populations. Thus, for any population group the *time of arrival* is critically important and indeed possibly more important than the *volume* of immigration. The earlier an ethnic group arrives, the more time for geometric increases to perform the wonders of compounding ($2 \times 2 = 4, 4 \times 4 = 16$, etc.). Thus, points out Donald H. Akenson, contrary to popular belief, more of the United States' Irish Americans are of Protestant ancestry (55 percent) than Catholic (44 percent), simply because the multiplier effect of the earlier (mostly Protestant) eighteenth-century immigration trumps the greater volume of the later (mostly Catholic) nineteenth-century immigration. *Irish in South Africa,* pp. 19–20.

95. White Australia grew rapidly. Founded as a penal colony as late as 1788, Australia soon escaped its convict origins and attracted an overwhelmingly British settler population that, by 1850, totaled more than 400,000. Ongoing immigration tripled Australia's population to more than 1 million English-speaking settlers by 1860.

96. C. F. J. Muller, "Conclusion: Factors Which Shaped the History of South Africa," in *Five Hundred Years,* p. 422. Modern-day writings on the subject tell the tale, too. A July, 2002, OCLC WorldCat online search for books in the subject area of "emigration and immigration" for the three countries yielded these results: United States, 2,565 book titles; Ireland, 297; and South Africa, 222. The South African number is high because of the commingling of immigration and emigration. Immigration studies on South Africa tend to focus either on the past influx of Asian (Indian, Chinese) workers or on the contemporary African migrant labor problem (see note 142)—but not on historical European immigration. Because of its rarity, an almost humorous instance of the latter is Eero Kuparinen's *African Alternative: Nordic Migration to South Africa, 1815–1914* (Helsinki: Finnish Historical Society, 1991).

97. Of all of the nations in the Irish diaspora, argues Donald Akenson, "South Africa received the best of the Irish emigrants, if one uses their economic background in Ireland as the criterion" (*Irish in South Africa,* p. 41). According to UK emigration statistics for 1912 and 1913, only 2.2 percent of Irish immigrants to South Africa were "unskilled laborers," compared to 48.2 percent of all Irish immigrants to the United States and 44.5 percent of those going to Canada. Nearly half (48.7 percent) of the Irish immigrants to South Africa (in 1912 and 1913) indicated they were in "commerce/finance/professions," compared to only 8.3 percent of Irish immigrants to the United States and 17.3 percent of those going to Canada (ibid., p. 80). Other striking differences emerge. America's intake of the Irish dated to the seventeenth century, South Africa's only from the 1880s. America's

mostly unskilled Irish immigrants tended to come from the western half of Ireland; South Africa's mostly skilled ones, from eastern Ireland. America's nineteenth-century Irish immigrants were overwhelmingly Catholic; South Africa's newly arrived Irish population was 55 percent Protestant (1926 census). In Akenson's words, South Africa's Irish immigrants were "privileged" and America's "ghettoized" (ibid., p. 94).

If South Africa's Irish immigrants were more educated, skilled, and well off, they were also very few in number. Sketchy data (1877–1936) suggest a few dozen to a few hundred immigrants from Ireland coming to South Africa each year before 1895, then only several hundred to a few thousand a year up to 1910, and falling off thereafter (see also note 101). One quickly gets a sense of the trickle of Irish emigration to South Africa by glancing at comparative decennial tables for Irish emigration worldwide, c. 1820–1920. The United Kingdom Emigration Commission maintained figures in four categories, one of them titled "Other Overseas" (to many nations, including South Africa). The tables show that in the six decades before 1901, Irish "other overseas" emigrants ranged from 4,000 to 11,000 *per decade*. Even in the peak decade of 1901–1910, when 16,343 people left Ireland for "other overseas" destinations, Australia and New Zealand attracted 11,885 Irish emigrants; Canada, 38,238; and the United States, a teeming 418,995 (86.3 percent of the decade's total of 485,461).

The Irish who came to live in South Africa were always a tiny part of the small settler population (see Donal P. McCracken's *Irish in Southern Africa, 1795–1910* [Durban: Ireland and Southern Africa Project, 1992]). In the Cape Colony in 1891 and later in the Union of South Africa in 1926, people of Irish descent formed about 4 percent of the white population and 11 percent of the population of United Kingdom ancestry (Akenson, *Irish in South Africa*, pp. 66, 68). Of all of the UK immigrants coming to South Africa in the early twentieth century, Akenson reports that the Irish tended to be as skilled and educated as the English and more so than the Scottish. (Given the Ulster home rule crisis of c. 1912–1921, one wonders whether these "privileged" and often Protestant Irish were fleeing "native" unrest in Ireland.) Once settled in, Irish immigrants had a good chance of "getting on" in South African society, where issues tended to be framed in terms of white-black (settler-native), not English-Irish or Protestant-Catholic.

Sources. Perhaps because there was so little of it, British authorities in South Africa in the nineteenth century kept only haphazard records on immigration. For UK statistics of Irish emigration (from both Irish ports and all British Isles ports) to South Africa in each year from 1877 to 1936, see Akenson, ibid., table 2, pp. 56–57. In their record keeping of all overseas emigration from Ireland, the United Kingdom Emigration Commissioners distinguished four destinations: the United States, British North America (Canada), Australasia (Australia and New Zealand), and "other overseas" (principally South Africa but also Mexico and Latin America; note that this category does not specify countries). Decennial tables of Irish emigration by these areas of destination, arranged with slightly different ranges of dates, are available in Miller, *Emigrants,* appendix, table 1, p. 569, distinguishing nine time periods from 1851 to 1921, and in Akenson, *Small Differences,* table, appendix 1, p. 183, distinguishing ten time periods from 1825 to 1920, and the data dramatically presented in his graph on p. 46.

98. Thus, as late as 1953, officials at the General Register Office of the United Kingdom could report the following: "As South Africa has a high proportion of native population, it has no need to introduce white labourers, with the result that British [Isles] emigrants

travelling there are of a higher class *than those to any other country.*" Overall, in the period from 1918 to 1950, nearly 19 percent of all UK emigrants to South Africa belonged to these "higher classes" engaged in "commercial, professional, or skilled occupations"; from the Irish Free State after 1921 (Protestants fleeing native Catholic rule?), as many as 80 percent of all emigrants were in such occupations. See Akenson, *Irish in South Africa,* pp. 79–80, emphasis added.

99. See Thomas Pakenham, *The Boer War* (New York: Random House, 1979); Bill Nasson, *The South African War, 1899–1902* (London: Arnold, 1999); and Keith M. Wilson, ed., *The International Impact of the Boer War* (New York: Palgrave, 2001). Several hundred Irish Catholic nationalists headed to South Africa to help David fight Goliath. See Donal P. McCracken, *MacBride's Brigade: Irish Commandos in the Anglo-Boer War* (Dublin: Four Courts Press, 1999).

100. But see Peter D. Warwick, *Black People and the South African War, 1899–1902* (Cambridge: Cambridge University Press, 1983), and Bill Nasson, *Abraham Esau's War: A Black South African War in the Cape, 1899–1902* (Cambridge: Cambridge University Press, 1991).

101. Milner to Sir Percy Fitzpatrick, Nov. 28, 1899, quoted in Leonard M. Thompson, *The Unification of South Africa 1902–1910* (Oxford: Clarendon Press, 1960), p. 6, emphasis in original. A self-admitted "British Race Patriot," Milner continued (unsuccessfully) to push for heightened British immigration in order to make English speakers the majority of South Africa's "European" population. See S. B. Spies, "Reconstruction and Unification, 1902–1910," in *Five Hundred Years,* pp. 320–23; and Thompson, *Unification,* especially chap. 1. See also Bernard M. Magubane's sharp-edged study, *The Making of a Racist State: British Imperialism and the Union of South Africa, 1875–1910* (Trenton, N.J.: Africa World Press, 1996).

102. See the map of population distribution in Colin McEvedy, *The Penguin Atlas of African History* (Harmondsworth, Middlesex: Penguin Books, 1980), pp. 80–81. Starting points for the history of South Africa's native peoples are the pioneering work by Sol T. Plaatje (1876–1932), *Native Life in South Africa,* introduction by Brian Willan (1916; repr., Athens: Ohio University Press, 1991); the brief survey by Martin West and Jean Morris, *Abantu: An Introduction to the Black People of South Africa* (Cape Town: C. Struik, 1979); Leonard Thompson's edited work, *African Societies in Southern Africa* (New York: Praeger, 1969); the solid academic study by Paul Maylam, *A History of the African People of South Africa: From the Early Iron Age to the 1970s* (Cape Town: David Philip, 1986); and J. B. Peires's elegant piece of detective work, *The House of Phalo: A History of the Xhosa People in the Days of Their Independence* (Johannesburg: Ravan Press, 1981).

103. "Bushmen" is self-explanatory. The origin of "Hottentot" is uncertain, dating from the Cape Dutch, c. 1670–1680. According to a leading scholar, the word may derive from settlers hearing a Khoikhoi dance chant, *hau-ti-tau,* in the natives' click-filled Khoisan language. (See Richard Elphick, *Kraal and Castle: Khoikhoi and the Founding of White South Africa* [New Haven: Yale University Press, 1977], pp. xv–xvi, 4, 23–24.) Others report that the early settlers described the strange "click" language they heard as "consisting of nothing more than the sounds *hot* and *tot*" (www.worldlanguage.com/Languages/Hottentot.htm). *The Oxford English Dictionary,* citing a 1670 source, says the word came into Cape Dutch to describe a "stammerer" or "stutterer," suggested by the Khoikhoi speech patterns. On the debate, see also Richard Elphick and V. C. Malherbe, "The

Khoisan to 1828," in Elphick and Giliomee, eds., *The Shaping of South African Society,* pp. 3–7; and Monica Wilson, "The Hunters and Herders," in Monica Wilson and Leonard Thompson, eds., *A History of South Africa to 1870* (Cape Town: David Philip, 1982, and Boulder, Colo.: Westview Press, 1983), p. 41n2 (this book is a slightly amended reprinting of vol. 1 of *The Oxford History of South Africa,* 2 vols. [New York: Oxford University Press, 1969–1971]). As used by the settlers, "Hottentot" quickly became a pejorative term, one moreover that evolved into a synonym not only in South Africa but throughout eighteenth-century Europe for a person of extreme primitiveness. The people so targeted never called themselves "Hottentots" but rather Khoikhoi (or Kwekwena), meaning "men of men" (compare to note 51).

104. Thompson, *History of South Africa,* pp. 38–39, 46, 49; Elphick, *Kraal and Castle,* pp. 110–16, 126–34, 229–36.

105. Portuguese quoted in T. R. H. Davenport, *South Africa: A Modern History,* 3d ed. (Toronto: University of Toronto Press, 1987), p. 11; Dutchman quoted in Thompson, *History of South Africa,* p. 21.

106. "Bantu" was a term coined in 1862 by W. H. Bleek, a linguistic scholar, to identify the language group of many native peoples throughout equatorial and southern Africa. Native Africans, like African Americans, have been called many things. "Kaffir" is probably the worst. Originating with Arab traders from the Middle East, the term (also spelled "caffre") came to be commonly used by European settlers to refer to any Bantu-speaking African native of the eastern half of South Africa. More than any specific meaning, the word in the twentieth century long functioned as a generalized and severe pejorative. Listen to Mark Mathabane: "The word *Kaffir* is of Arabic origin. It means 'infidel.' In South Africa it is used disparagingly by most whites to refer to blacks. It is the equivalent of the term *nigger*. I was called a 'Kaffir' many times" (*Kaffir Boy: The True Story of a Black Youth's Coming of Age in Apartheid South Africa* [New York: New American Library, 1986], p. xiii).

In the 1960s, the term "Bantu" replaced "Kaffir" among more educated South African whites until, in time, the government's policies on "Bantu education" and "Bantu affairs," as well as its administration of bantustans (a word, created in 1949, to designate independent tribal "homelands"), came to discredit the word. So "blacks" (as in America, a term that does not accurately describe a person's color) briefly displaced "Bantu." Finally, in the postapartheid 1990s, there emerged the simple term "Africans," which is now commonly used to describe "the mixed farming peoples who spoke Bantu languages and whose descendants are the vast majority of the inhabitants of modern Southern Africa" (Thompson, *History of South Africa,* p. 306n18). But this word choice has its own problems, for now the (native) Khoisan people, who are Africans, are not "Africans."

We are left to wonder what words may emerge in the future to denominate South Africa's other population groups—Cape Colored, Indians, whites. If, as we have seen, North America's demographically dominant settlers (who displaced the natives) could come to call themselves "Americans," can the day be far off when all South Africans, native and settler, are simply called "Africans"?

107. However, for twentieth-century African "malnutrition" in the context of "European" policies of paternalism and scientism, see Diana Wylie, *Starving on a Full Stomach: Hunger and the Triumph of Cultural Racism in Modern South Africa* (Charlottesville: University Press of Virginia, 2001).

108. Donald Denoon and Balam Nyeko, *Southern Africa since 1800,* rev. ed. (1972; repr.,

London: Longman, 1984), pp. 5 ("decisive"), 78 ("seasonal"); and Robert Ross, "Capitalism, Expansion, and Incorporation on the Southern African Frontier," in Lamar and Thompson, eds., *Frontier in History*, p. 211 ("cattle").

109. See J. B. Peires, *The Dead Will Arise: Nongqawuse and the Great Xhosa Cattle-killing Movement of 1856–1857* (Johannesburg: Ravan Press, 1989), and "Contagious Bovine Pleuropneumonia in Southern Africa: Conceptualizing the Xhosa Cattle-killing Episode of 1856–1857," http://www.fao.org/DOCREP/004/Y3428E/y3428e03.htm, bulletin of the Emergency Prevention System (EMPRES) for Transboundary Animal and Plant Pests and Diseases, a division of the Food and Agriculture Organization (FAO) of the United Nations. (The FAO website has abundant information on cattle diseases.) South Africa's Xhosa cattle killing was not a unique phenomenon. In America, the "Ghost Dance" of the Sioux in the 1890s represents a similar, if far paler, example of natives turning to cultural revitalization in a last, desperate effort to ward off final defeat. A prophecy of the Paiute mystic Wovoka, the Ghost Dance preached self-denial and promised that regular ritualistic dancing would raise Sioux warriors from the dead, make the whites disappear, and return the land to its rightful inhabitants. Nevertheless, between the Xhosa and Sioux millenarian events there were some key differences. The Sioux were not victims of self-inflicted starvation (the whites' killing of the buffalo had accomplished that). And the Sioux, unlike the Xhosa, were simply shot down by white firepower. At Wounded Knee Creek, South Dakota, in 1890, panicky U.S. 7th Cavalry soldiers opened fire on hundreds of Ghost Dance men, women, and children. The killing was one-sided: 250 Indians dead but only 25 soldiers. See Robert M. Utley's classic, *The Last Days of the Sioux Nation* (New Haven, Conn.: Yale University Press, 1963); James Mooney, *The Ghost-dance Religion and the Sioux Outbreak of 1890* (Chicago: University of Chicago Press, 1965); and Michael Hittman, *Wovoka and the Ghost Dance* (Lincoln: University of Nebraska Press, 1997). Dee Brown used the U.S. military's suppression of the Ghost Dance as a coda to the whites' continental conquest in his trailblazing bestseller, *Bury My Heart at Wounded Knee: An Indian History of the American West* (New York: Holt, Rinehart, and Winston, 1971), pp. 389–418; the book has been in print ever since (New York: Henry Holt, 2001).

110. See Richard Elphick and Rodney Davenport, eds., *Christianity in South Africa: A Political, Social, and Cultural History* (Berkeley and Los Angeles: University of California Press, 1997).

111. Thompson, *History of South Africa*, p. 87. But see the two maps and discussion of "the myth of the empty highveld" in Davenport, *South Africa*, 3d ed., pp. 14–15.

112. Christopher Saunders, "Political Processes in the Southern African Frontier Zones," in Lamar and Thompson, eds., *Frontier in History*, p. 150.

113. In Afrikaner history, December 16 (in 1838, a Sunday), the date of the battle at Blood River (as the whites renamed the Ncome), would become an important day of remembrance and thanksgiving. Celebrated originally as Dingane's Day, in the era of Afrikaner nationalism the event was renamed (1952) the Day of the Covenant and then (in 1980) the Day of the Vow. During the apartheid era (1948–1994), December 16 was observed as a state holiday. See Leonard Thompson, *The Political Mythology of Apartheid* (New Haven, Conn.: Yale University Press, 1985), pp. 144–88, 270n1.

114. C. F. J. Muller, "The Period of the Great Trek, 1834–1854," in *Five Hundred Years*, pp. 138–41; Leonard Thompson, "Co-Operation and Conflict: The Zulu Kingdom and Natal," in *South Africa to 1870*, pp. 147–65.

115. British-protected Basutoland (1868) later became part of the Cape Colony (1871–1884), but continuing Sotho resistance persuaded the British to create the separate Crown Colony of Basutoland (1884). This landlocked, autonomous African kingdom became the independent nation of Lesotho in 1966. See Leonard Thompson, *Survival in Two Worlds: Moshoeshoe of Lesotho, 1786–1868* (Oxford: Clarendon Press, 1975); Peter Sanders, *Moshoeshoe, Chief of the Sotho* (London: Heinemann, 1975); and Elizabeth A. Eldredge, *A South African Kingdom: The Pursuit of Security in Nineteenth-Century Lesotho* (Cambridge: Cambridge University Press, 1993).

116. On the Pedi, see Peter Delius, *The Land Belongs to Us: The Pedi Polity, the Boers, and the British in Nineteenth-century Transvaal* (Berkeley: University of California Press, 1984).

117. Saunders, "Political Processes," in *Frontier in History*, p. 165.

118. "Terror": Sir John Cradock to Lord Liverpool, Mar. 7, 1812, quoted in Ben Maclennan, *A Proper Degree of Terror: John Graham and the Cape's Eastern Frontier* (Johannesburg: Ravan Press, 1986), p. ix; and Peires, *The Dead Will Arise*, pp. 9–30. The best recent study of this pivotal region is by Clifton C. Crais, *White Supremacy and Black Resistance in Pre-industrial South Africa: The Making of the Colonial Order in the Eastern Cape, 1770–1865* (Cambridge: Cambridge University Press, 1992); see also Les Switzer, *Power and Resistance in an African Society: The Ciskei Xhosa and the Making of South Africa* (Madison: University of Wisconsin Press, 1993). An overview of the wars is in Kevin Shillington, *A History of Southern Africa* (London: Longman, 1987), pp. 29–30, 57–59, 78–80, 97–98.

119. The Xhosa homeland would become a native reserve in the Union of South Africa and, in the republic in the 1960s, one of the government's bantustans. Perhaps the most famous living Xhosa today is Nelson Mandela, descended from chiefs of the Thembu, a tribe that is part of the Xhosa nation. See Mandela's autobiography, *Long Walk to Freedom* (Boston: Little, Brown, 1994), pp. 3–31.

120. As in America with Custer and the Sioux, the writing on South Africa's most warlike native people has been voluminous. Donald R. Morris, *The Washing of the Spears: A History of the Rise of the Zulu Nation under Shaka and Its Fall in the Zulu War of 1879* (New York: Simon and Schuster, 1965) remains the standard history, though it is unannotated and in places now seems a bit dated. A recent perceptive study, published in South Africa in 1995 as *Rope of Sand*, is John Laband's *Rise and Fall of the Zulu Nation* (London: Arms and Armour Press, 1997). Other recommended studies are Jeff Guy, *The Destruction of the Zulu Kingdom: The Civil War in Zululand, 1879–1884* (London: Longman, 1979); John Laband and Paul Thompson, eds., *Kingdom and Colony at War: 16 Studies on the Anglo-Zulu War of 1879* (Pietermaritzburg, South Africa: University of Natal Press, 1990); John P. Laband, *Kingdom in Crisis: The Zulu Response to the British Invasion of 1879* (Manchester, UK: Manchester University Press, 1992); and Richard Cope, *The Ploughshare of War: The Origins of the Anglo-Zulu War of 1879* (Pietermaritzburg, South Africa: University of Natal Press, 1999). For comparisons to North America, see James O. Gump, *The Dust Rose Like Smoke: The Subjugation of the Zulu and the Sioux* (Lincoln: University of Nebraska Press, 1994).

121. After Chief Bhambatha's killing, for purposes of identification, his head was cut off. South Africa's frontier thus closed as America's had opened—with the hunting down, killing, and decapitation of the Indian sachem Wingina at Roanoke, Virginia, in 1586. S. B. Spies, "Reconstruction and Unification, 1902–1910," in *An Illustrated History of South Africa*, p. 226; and Karen Ordahl Kupperman, *Roanoke: The Abandoned Colony* (Totowa,

N.J.: Rowman and Littlefield, 1984), chap. 5. On the 1906 rebellion, see the economic interpretation by Shula Marks, *Reluctant Rebellion: The 1906–1908 Disturbances in Natal* (Oxford: Clarendon Press, 1970), and the recent cultural analysis by Benedict Carton, *Blood from Your Children: The Colonial Origins of Generational Conflict* (Charlottesville: University Press of Virginia, 2000).

122. Respectively, Dennis Edwards, *The Gold Fields of South Africa* (1890), p. 39, and K. F. Bellairs, *The Witwatersrand Goldfields: A Trip to Johannesburg and Back* (London, 1889), pp. 33–34, both quoted in *Source Material on the South African Economy, 1860–1970*, vol. 1, ed. D. Hobart Houghton and Jenifer Dagut (Cape Town: Oxford University Press, 1972), pp. 302–304.

123. H. Hamilton Fyfe, *South Africa Today* (London, 1911), 39, quoted in *Source Material*, vol. 2, p. 152. On the transition to a highly regulated native workforce, see Shula Marks and Richard Rathbone, eds., *Industrialisation and Social Change in South Africa: African Class Formation, Culture, and Consciousness, 1870–1930* (New York: Longman, 1982); Alan Jeeves, *Migrant Labour in South Africa's Mining Economy: The Struggle for the Gold Mines' Labour Supply, 1890–1920* (Montreal: McGill-Queen's University Press, 1985); and Alan Jeeves and Jonathan Crush, eds., *White Farms, Black Labour: Agrarian Transition in Southern Africa, 1910–1950* (London: Heinemann, 1995). An important recent book that lets us hear from the African workers themselves is Keletso E. Atkins's *The Moon Is Dead! Give Us Our Money!: The Cultural Origins of an African Work Ethic, Natal, South Africa, 1843–1900* (London: Heinemann, 1994). The associated hardening of segregation patterns is examined in John Cell, *The Highest Stage of White Supremacy: The Origins of Segregation in South Africa and the American South* (Cambridge: Cambridge University Press, 1982), chaps. 2, 3, 8; and Saul Dubow, *Racial Segregation and the Origins of Apartheid in South Africa, 1919–1936* (New York: St. Martin's Press, 1989).

124. The apt description is that of Elias L. Ntloedibe, *Here Is a Tree: The Political Biography of Robert Mangaliso Sobukwe* (Mogoditshane, Botswana: Century-Turn Publ., 1995), p. 37. Sobukwe (1925–1978) broke from the African National Congress (ANC) to become a founding member (1959) and first president of the Pan–Africanist Congress (PAC).

125. After the wartime defeat in 1902, concepts of *helpmekaar* and *volkskapitalisme*—mutual aid and people's capitalism—became core parts of Afrikaners' yearnings for *hereniging* (reunion) and *volksredding* (rescuing of the people). The Second Language Movement (promotion of Afrikaans) was part of the resistance to Anglicization and the inroads of "a foreign culture which claims for itself the right to overrun and conquer the world" (*Die Huisgenoot,* July, 1919, quoted in Isabel Hofmeyr, "Building a Nation from Words: Afrikaans Language, Literature, and Ethnic Identity, 1902–1924," in *The Politics of Race, Class, and Nationalism in Twentieth-Century South Africa,* ed. Shula Marks and Stanley Trapido [New York: Longman, 1987], p. 110). For the Afrikaners' field of vision, see three books (of course, first published in Afrikaans) by F. A. Van Jaarsveld: *The Awakening of Afrikaner Nationalism, 1868–1881* (Cape Town: Human and Rousseau, 1961), *The Afrikaner's Interpretation of South African History* (Cape Town: Simondium, 1964), and *From Van Riebeeck to Vorster, 1652–1974: An Introduction to the History of the Republic of South Africa* (Johannesburg: Perskor, 1975).

Several books trace the development and activities of the secretive pressure group that sought to promote Afrikaner self-identity and access to and later control of political power. See T. R. H. Davenport, *The Afrikaner Bond: The History of a South African Politi-*

cal Party, 1880–1911 (Cape Town: Oxford University Press, 1966); J. H. P. Serfontien, *Brotherhood of Power: An Exposé of the Secret Afrikaner Broederbond* (Bloomington: Indiana University Press, 1978); Ivor Wilkins and Hans Strydom, *The Super-Afrikaners* (Johannesburg: Jonathan Ball, 1978), which was published abroad as *The Broederbond* (New York: Paddington Press, 1979); and Charles Bloomberg (d. 1985), ed. Saul Dubow, *Christian Nationalism and the Rise of the Afrikaner Broederbond in South Africa, 1918–1948* (Bloomington: Indiana University Press, 1989). For the cultural and economic context, see Heribert Adam and Hermann Giliomee, *Ethnic Power Mobilized: Can South Africa Change?* (New Haven, Conn.: Yale University Press, 1979); Dan O'Meara, *Volkskapitalisme: Class, Capital, and Ideology in the Development of Afrikaner Nationalism, 1934–1948* (New York: Cambridge University Press, 1983); T. Dunbar Moodie, *The Rise of Afrikanerdom: Power, Apartheid, and the Afrikaner Civil Religion* (Berkeley: University of California Press, 1975); and Thompson, *Political Mythology,* chaps. 2, 3, 5, 6. On the executive's wide use of power from 1948 to 1990, see Robert A. Schrire and Laurence Boulle, eds., *Malan to de Klerk: Leadership in the Apartheid State* (Cape Town: Oxford University Press, 1994).

For bold yet often strained comparisons, see Donald Harman Akenson, *God's Peoples: Covenant and Land in South Africa, Israel, and Ulster* (Ithaca, N.Y.: Cornell University Press, 1992); and Mark Suzman, *Ethnic Nationalism and State Power: The Rise of Irish Nationalism, Afrikaner Nationalism, and Zionism* (New York: St. Martin's Press, 1999).

126. See Andre Odendaal, *Vukani Bantu!: The Beginning of Black Protest Politics in South Africa to 1912* (Cape Town: David Philip, 1984); Thomas Karis, Gwendolen Carter, and Gail Gerhart, eds., *From Protest to Challenge: A Documentary History of African Politics in South Africa, 1882–1990,* 5 vols. (vols. 1–4: Stanford, Calif.: Hoover Institution Press, 1972–1977; vol. 5: Bloomington: University of Indiana Press, 1997); and Sheridan Johns and R. H. Davis Jr., eds., *Mandela, Tambo, and the African National Congress: The Struggle against Apartheid* (New York: Oxford University Press, 1991). On the government's reaction, see Paul B. Rich, *State Power and Black Politics in South Africa, 1912–1951* (New York: St. Martin's Press, 1996); Heribert Adam, *Modernizing Racial Domination: South Africa's Political Dynamics* (Berkeley: University of California Press, 1971); Robert M. Price, *The Apartheid State in Crisis: Political Transformation of South Africa, 1975–1990* (New York: Oxford University Press, 1991); and Heribert Adam and Kogila A. Moodley, *South Africa without Apartheid: Dismantling Racial Domination* (Berkeley: University of California Press, 1986).

127. On the "negotiated revolution" (1985–1994) that would create a "New South Africa," transferring power from Afrikaner to African, de Klerk to Mandela, see Adrian Guelke, *South Africa in Transition: The Misunderstood Miracle* (London: I. B. Tauris, 1998), and two outstanding works: Allister Sparks, *Tomorrow Is Another Country: The Inside Story of South Africa's Road to Change* (Sandton, South Africa: Struik, 1995; New York: Hill and Wang, 1995), and Patti Waldmeir, *Anatomy of a Miracle: The End of Apartheid and the Birth of a New South Africa* (New York: W. W. Norton, 1999). De Klerk's autobiography reveals that his relations with Mandela were not as cordial as they appeared to the outside world; see *The Last Trek—A New Beginning: The Autobiography* (London: Macmillan, 1998). Riveting reactions to the coming transfer of power are in June Goodwin and Ben Schiff, *Heart of Whiteness: Afrikaners Face Black Rule in the New South Africa* (New York: Simon and Schuster, 1995), based on 125 interviews in 1992. The watershed event is covered in R. W. Johnson and Lawrence Schlemmer, eds., *Launching Democracy in South Africa:*

The First Open Election, April, 1994 (New Haven, Conn.: Yale University Press, 1996). On choices and challenges, see Heribert Adam and Kogila A. Moodley, *The Opening of the Apartheid Mind: Options for the New South Africa* (Berkeley: University of California Press, 1993); and Heribert Adam, F. Van Zyl Slabbert, and Kogila Moodley, *Comrades in Business: Post-liberation Politics in South Africa* (Cape Town: Tafelberg, 1997).

128. William King, *The State of the Protestants of Ireland under the Late King James's Government* (Dublin, 1691), p. 292, quoted in Bartlett, Curtin, et al., eds., *Irish Studies*, p. 48.

129. An English cartographer in Ireland actually referred to the events of 1641–1652 as a "Game or Match," the winner obtaining the spoils, or, in his words, "a Gamester's Right at least to their Estates." Sir William Petty, *The Political Anatomy of Ireland* (written in 1672 and published in London, 1691; repr., Shannon: Irish University Press, 1970), p. 24. Petty was physician general with Cromwell's army in Ireland and later coordinated the "Down survey" (1654), the first scientific mapping of the recently conquered island.

130. Richard White, "Frederick Jackson Turner and Buffalo Bill Cody," in *Frontier Experience*, p. 47.

131. Webb, *Great Frontier*, p. 3n3.

132. Webb called his classic only an "introductory" study that brought "familiar things into different focus. . . . In the study of the Great Frontier there is room for all sorts of investigation." Ibid., pp. 409, 410, 412. Tragically, Webb died in a car accident in 1963 at age seventy-four.

133. For the moment, city names remain unchanged, but local urban councils have been renamed. The council representing Pretoria is now known as Tshwane Metropolitan Council, and Port Elizabeth's has been renamed Nelson Mandela Council. "It's the business of reinventing a new national identity," pronounced a professor at the University of the Witwatersrand. "Why don't they focus on building houses and creating jobs?" protested a white taxi driver in Port Elizabeth. See Rachel L. Swarns, "Bidding Farewell to the Names That Evoke Apartheid," *New York Times* (Nov. 5, 2000), p. A-6.

134. See Carter Meyer and Diana Royer, eds., *Selling the Indian: Commercializing and Appropriating American Indian Cultures* (Tucson: University of Arizona Press, 2001).

135. Cease-fires by Protestant and Catholic paramilitaries were followed by the historic agreement in April, 1998, to abandon direct rule by London in exchange for the restoration of democratic representative institutions (a power-sharing Northern Ireland assembly), creation of interregional British-Irish and north-south governmental councils, human rights pledges, arms decommissioning, and reforms in policing and the judicial system. Protestant perceptions of Sinn Fein/IRA misbehavior and foot-dragging on destroying weapons caches led to the restoration of direct rule. The referendum on the 1998 agreement turned out 81 percent of Northern Ireland's electorate; 71 percent voted "yes" on the question of approval (an estimated 96 percent of Catholics and 52 percent of Protestants). See "Good Friday agreement" and "referendum," respectively, at the CAIN (Conflict Archive on the Internet) website, http://cain.ulst.ac.uk/faq/faq2.htm#why. Based at the University of Ulster–Magee campus, CAIN (an intended allusion to the biblical brothers) is an outstanding source for a wide variety of information on Northern Ireland from 1968 to the present. Among the best of the recent books on "the troubles" are Marc Mulholland, *The Longest War: Northern Ireland's Troubled History* (Oxford: Oxford University Press, 2002); Jack Holland, *Hope against History: The Course of Conflict in Northern Ireland*

(New York: Henry Holt, 1999); and John McGarry and Brendan O'Leary, *Explaining Northern Ireland* (Oxford: Blackwell, 1995). For a look at the negotiation process and the tentative transition to peacemaking and power sharing, see Mike Morrissey and Marie Smyth, *Northern Ireland after the Good Friday Agreement: Victims, Grievance, and Blame* (London: Pluto Press, 2002); and Michael Cox, Adrian Guelke, and Fiona Stephen, eds., *A Farewell to Arms?: From Long War to Long Peace in Northern Ireland* (Manchester: Manchester University Press, 2000).

136. By the late 1990s (before the high-tech "wreck" in global stock markets), Ireland's "Celtic tiger" economy was growing in the range of 7–9 percent per year. The Irish Republic's GDP (gross domestic product) per capita, which, in 1987, was just 63 percent of Britain's, by 1996 had overtaken Britain in world rankings, Ireland being twentieth and Britain twenty-second ("Ireland Shines" and "Europe's Tiger Economy: Green Is Good," *Economist* [May 17, 1997]: 16, 21–24). See Peadar Kirby, Luke Gibbons, and Michael Cronin, eds., *Reinventing Ireland: Culture, Society, and the Global Economy* (London: Pluto Press, 2002); and Richard B. Finnegan and Edward T. McCarron, *Ireland: Historical Echoes, Contemporary Politics* (Oxford, UK, and Boulder, Colo.: Westview Press, 2000), chaps. 4–7.

137. The Catholic share is growing in a small and essentially stable population: Northern Ireland's population was 1.69 million in 2001 and by 2021 is projected to be no more than 1.72 million. "Size of Catholic Population in Northern Ireland—Census Returns and Estimates, 1961, 1971, 1981, 1991" and "Population Projections for Northern Ireland, 1997–2026," CAIN website, http://cain.ulst.ac.uk/ni/popul.htm#6.

138. As part of the republic's referendum on the 1998 Good Friday agreement, voters were asked to vote "yes" or "no" on the repeal of the clause in the 1937 constitution that claimed Northern Ireland as sovereign territory of the Irish Republic. Voter turnout was low "given the position that partition and the north played in modern Irish history. Yet the evidence that the north did not have primacy of place on the agenda of politics in the Republic had long been clear" (Finnegan and McCarron, *Ireland*, p. 359). Only 56 percent of the south's electorate bothered to vote; of those voting, 94 percent voted "yes" to repeal this clause that had long been a symbolic cornerstone of nationalist, "antipartition" political orthodoxy. On the referendum, see http://cain.ulst.ac.uk/issues/politics/election/ref1998.htm.

139. De Klerk quoted in interview with Arnaud de Borchgrave, "The Mandate for a 'New Society,' " *Insight on the News* (South African periodical) (July 2, 1990). A central aim of President Mandela's government was "to come to terms with [the injustices of] their past on a morally accepted basis and to advance the cause of reconciliation." For the 2,800-page report of the commission that heard evidence from 21,000 victims and perpetrators, white and black, in the years from 1960 to 1994, see *Report of the Truth and Reconciliation Commission of South Africa*, 5 vols. (Cape Town, London, and New York: Macmillan Reference, 1998–1999); for reactions to the commission, see Charles Villa-Vicencio and Wilhelm Verwoerd, eds., *Looking Back, Reaching Forward* (Cape Town: University of Cape Town Press, 2000); Karin Chubb and Lutz Van Dijk, *Between Anger and Hope: South Africa's Youth and the Truth and Reconciliation Commission* (Johannesburg: Witwatersrand University Press, 2001); and Jonathan D. Tepperman, "Truth and Consequences," *Foreign Affairs* 81(2) (Mar./Apr., 2002): 128–45.

140. "U.S. May Get Cool Greeting at Environment Summit," *USA Today* (Aug. 30, 2002), p. 11A. The announced aims of the Johannesburg "earth summit" (Aug. 26–Sept. 4,

2002) were halving global poverty by 2015, improving health access and care, and promoting environmental advances such as cleaner water and nonpolluting energy resources (see http://www.un.org/events/wssd). On the Durban-hosted "World Conference against Racism, Racial Discrimination, Xenophobia, and Related Intolerance" (Aug. 31–Sept. 7, 2001), see the UN's human rights conference website (www.un.org/WCAR).

141. The white flight is to more developed—or, as Adam Smith might observe, "native-less"—English-speaking countries: the United Kingdom, United States, Canada, Australia, and New Zealand. A Paris-based study by the Institute for Development Research has reported that, between 1987 and 1997, around 234,000 people (41,000 of them "professionals") had emigrated from South Africa to these five countries. Some say that over the past forty years, in both the apartheid era and its aftermath, nearly 2 million people, white and black, may have left to live abroad. According to official South African statistics, 10,000 people emigrated in 2000; since many people simply leave without making an official declaration, some estimates put the real volume of annual emigration at three times the number in the government figures. One must keep in mind that even if the recent annual outflow is about 30,000 people, this exodus accounts annually for a loss of only 0.5 percent of the nation's white population of 6 million (in a country of 43 million people).

The subject of emigration frequently comes up among white South Africans and has even become the subject of humor. "'It is essential for South Africans caught up in the chaos and turmoil of the transitional process to take a long view of the social, political, and economic situation,' advises a top South African clinical psychologist in a reverse-charges telephone call from Toronto" (quotation from Gus Silber's book of nervous humor, *Braaivleis of the Vanities: How to Stay Sane in South Africa* [London: Penguin Books, 1992], pp. 4–5). Clearly, the long-term emigration problem is threefold: the *proportion* of those going who are skilled, highly educated professionals; the cumulative factor, a decade's *total number* of emigrants; and the *generational* factor represented by a youth exodus (many white families have children now scattered to Sydney, Toronto, or Dallas). In the long term, unless the hemorrhaging is stopped, the exodus of nearly a quarter of a million people between 1987 and 1997 represents the loss of not just 4 percent of the white population but of the society's skills and its near-term future. Recent studies cite the reasons given by skilled professionals for their departure: high crime (Silber's book *Braaivleis* has sections on "how to hijackproof your vehicle" and "how to barricade your suburb"), low salaries, a deteriorating health-care system, and limited prospects for career advancement (as Africans, not "Europeans," benefit from new hiring and promotion preferences). Not surprisingly, South Africa's President Mbeki has chided those leaving as being unpatriotic; to humorist Silber, they are "outwardly mobile ex-patriots" (p. 134). Afrikaners used to deride English South Africans for leaving the country in the 1970s and 1980s; now ANC politicians deride Afrikaners and English alike for doing the "chicken run." See "The Brain Drain—Africa's Achilles Heel," World Markets Research Centre: World Markets in Focus 2002, http://www.worldmarketsanalysis.com/In Focus2002/articles/africa_braindrain.html; Jonathan S. Crush, David A. McDonald, et al., *Losing Our Minds: Skills Migration and the South African Brain Drain* (Cape Town: IDASA, 2000); and Johann Van Rooyen, *The New Great Trek: The Story of South Africa's White Exodus* (Pretoria: UNISA Press, 2000). Emigration guides are themselves revealing: For the apartheid era, see Vincent Leroux, *Leaving South Africa: A Guide to Emigrating to English-speaking Countries* (Cape Town: Anubis Press, 1985); for the postapartheid, Andrew Neville, *Emigrating from South Africa: To Aus-*

tralia, Canada, New Zealand, United Kingdom, and United States, 3d ed. (Cape Town: Glendale, 1996).

Finally, I must stress that South Africa's current emigration dilemma is a pale reflection of even more serious problems in literacy, education, and skills throughout the continent. For example, according to studies by the Geneva-based International Organization for Migration and the UN's Economic Commission for Africa, the entire continent has a total of only 20,000 scientists and engineers (4 percent of the world's scientific population). They serve a population of 600 million. More Nigerian doctors (21,000) practice in the United States than in Nigeria. A few years ago Zambia (2000 pop., 10 million) had 1,600 doctors (not many), but now it has only 400; they have gone to Europe, the United States, and neighboring Botswana. Africa's problems—and the solutions—go deeper than just racial issues.

142. A factual summary is in Thompson, *History of South Africa,* 3d ed., pp. 284, 293–94. On the crime problem (e.g., Johannesburg has the highest murder rate of all of the world's cities), see Lorraine Glanz and M. G. T. Cloete, eds., *Managing Crime in the New South Africa* (Pretoria: HSRC Publ., 1993); Tony Emmett and Alexander Butchart, eds., *Behind the Mask: Getting to Grips with Crime and Violence in South Africa* (Pretoria: HSRC Publ., 2000); and Mark Shaw, *Crime and Policing in Post-apartheid South Africa* (London: Hurst, 2002). On poverty, see Robert A. Schrire, ed., *Wealth or Poverty?: Critical Choices for South Africa* (Cape Town: Oxford University Press, 1992); Julian May, *Poverty and Inequality in South Africa: Meeting the Challenge* (Cape Town: David Philip, 2000); and *The State of South Africa's Population Report: Population, Poverty, and Vulnerability,* 2000 (Pretoria: National Population Unit, Dept. of Social Development, 2000). On the influx of African migrant labor, see David A. McDonald, ed., *On Borders: Perspectives on International Migration in Southern Africa* (New York: St. Martin's Press, 2000); Jim Whitman, ed., *Migrants, Citizens, and the State in Southern Africa* (New York: St. Martin's Press, 2000); and Jonathan S. Crush, ed., *Beyond Control: Immigration and Human Rights in a Democratic South Africa* (Cape Town: IDASA, 1998). In 1997, economists estimated that 12 percent of South Africa's population were undocumented immigrants, many of them contributing to the increase in crime.

143. Probably not. Zimbabwe is a smaller, much poorer, and far more fragile country than South Africa. It offers no match to the latter's wealth and economic infrastructure. Settled late (1890) by Cecil Rhodes's British South Africa Company, the land north of the Limpopo River became the British colony of Rhodesia (1923) and later a self-declared white-ruled nation (1965) before African-majority rule, independence, and renaming (Zimbabwe) came in 1980. The settler population has always been tiny. From a peak of 280,000 in 1970 (4 percent of population), it is now down to about 70,000 whites, who constitute less than 1 percent of Zimbabwe's population of 12 million (2002). Thus it may be observed that, statistically, Zimbabwe's settlers are nowadays as demographically irrelevant as America's Indians.

Yet, of course, economically for the past century the handful of white settlers has owned huge chunks of the region's arable land (70 percent in 1980). Zimbabwe's seventy-eight-year-old Pres. Robert Mugabe, reelected in a much-manipulated national election, accelerated in 2002 his government's scheme of land redistribution to landless Africans, who were "victims of British colonialism." In August of that year, President Mugabe insisted on the final confiscation of 2,900 of the remaining 4,500 white farmlands, two-thirds of the land seizures to come without compensation. Like his reelection, Mugabe's land plan has involved the use of intimidation and hooliganism. Some scenes are reminiscent of Cromwellian behavior in seventeenth-century Ireland. Zimbabwean law courts have been ignored, opposition leaders arrested, and newspapers banned, even as white landowners—many of them fleeing to Mozambique and South Africa—have finally agreed to relinquish ownership so long as there is an organized plan and some compensation. The stench and stridency in the whole business have worsened as news reports have filtered in of relatives, friends, and cronies of Mugabe awarding themselves land parcels. Worst of all, prolonged drought in the region has exacerbated Zimbabwe's political turmoil and dislocated economy. Church and relief societies reported in 2002 that 6 million people (half of Zimbabwe's population) were facing famine and that some families had "resorted to eating grass seed to avoid starvation" (Tearfund Christian Relief Agency, June 26, 2002, "Southern Africa Humanitarian Crisis," accessed at http://www.reliefweb.int). See "Zimbabwe's Mugabe Says White Farmers Must Clear Out," Reuters, Aug. 12, 2002, www.nytimes.com; "Zimbabwe Gets Tough with Whites," *Arlington Star-Telegram* (Aug. 17, 2002), p. 11A; "Land Seizure Aids Mugabe's Friends, Family," *Arlington Star-Telegram* (Aug. 27, 2002), pp. 1A, 7A; and "African Acquiescence," *Arlington Star-Telegram* (Sept. 6, 2002), p. 10B.

144. "AIDS May Drop Life Span to 30 in Parts of Africa," *Arlington Star-Telegram* (July 11, 2000), p. 8A; "In Africa, a Scourge beyond Imagining," *US News and World Report* (Dec. 18, 2000), pp. 34–37; "AIDS: South Africa's Trial and Tragedy," *World Press Review* (June 2001), pp. 6–9; "S. Africa Must Offer Pregnant Women AIDS Drugs," *Arlington Star-Telegram* (Dec. 15, 2001), p. 23A; "CIA—The World Factbook—South Africa," accessed Sept. 4, 2002, www.cia.gov/cia/publications/factbook/geos/sf.html; and Helen Epstein's important articles, "The Mystery of AIDS in South Africa" (July 20, 2000) and "The Hidden Cause of AIDS" (May 9, 2002), in the *New York Review of Books* (see www.nybooks.com). Also useful are the following websites: www.unaids.org; www.aids.org.za; and http://www.iasociety .org. Until recently, the government's mishandling of the crisis has exacerbated the death toll through unspent financial allocations and denial of medical treatment (the drug AZT was even caricatured as "part of a conspiracy to kill Africans"). President Mbeki's skepticism that HIV causes AIDS—which he announced, most embarrassingly, in July, 2000, when Durban was hosting the Thirteenth International World AIDS Conference—only added insult to injury by making the postapartheid government seem a laughingstock on this lethal issue. At length, in December, 2001, AIDS activists won a victory when the Pretoria high court ruled that the government must make key drugs available to HIV-positive pregnant women (a ruling that may save fifty thousand newborn lives a year). Recently, the government has stepped up and better coordinated its efforts to respond medically to the huge challenge of the HIV and AIDS crisis. On the Durban conference, see the eight-hundred-page published proceedings, *XIII International AIDS Conference, Durban, South Africa, 2000* (Bologna: Monduzzi Editore, 2000). Two websites provide medical reports and conference papers (www.aidslaw.ca/durban2000/e-durban2000.htm and www.cdc .gov/nchstp/od/Durban/default.htm), while another (by the advocacy group "Act Up") gets into the politics of AIDS (www.actupny.org/reports/durban.html).

The literature, like the disease, is growing. For an introduction, see Patrick O'Sullivan, *HIV/AIDS in Sub–Saharan Africa: A Development Issue for Irish Aid* (Dublin: Irish Aid Advisory Committee, 2000); Lorenzo S. Togni, *AIDS in South Africa and on the African Con-

tinent (Pretoria: Kagiso Publ., 1997); and Mary Crewe, *AIDS in South Africa: The Myth and the Reality* (London: Penguin Books, 1992). Recommended longer works are Zia Jaffrey, *AIDS in South Africa: The New Apartheid* (London: Verso, 2001); Alan Whiteside and Clem Sunter, *AIDS: The Challenge for South Africa* (Cape Town: Human and Rousseau, 2000); Philip Setel, Milton Lewis, and Marginez Lyons, eds., *Histories of Sexually Transmitted Diseases and HIV/AIDS in Sub–Saharan Africa* (Westport, Conn.: Greenwood Press, 1999); and I. O. Orubuloye, ed., *Sexual Networking and AIDS in Sub–Saharan Africa: Behavioural Research and the Social Context* (Canberra: Health Transition Centre, Australian National University, 1994). Studies that focus on AIDS and the abuse of women include Lisa Vetten, *Violence, Vengeance, and Gender: A Preliminary Investigation into the Links between Violence against Women and HIV/AIDS in South Africa* (Braamfontein, Johannesburg: Centre for the Study of Violence and Reconciliation, 2001), and Inonge M. Kamungoma-Dada, *AIDS and the Disadvantaged Sex: Women in Sub–Saharan Africa* (Devon, UK: University of Exeter, 1990). A study that places AIDS in the broader context of women's health is Christopher Paul Howson, Polly F. Harrison, and Maureen Law, eds., *In Her Lifetime: Female Morbidity and Mortality in Sub–Saharan Africa* (Washington, D.C.: National Academy Press for the [U.S.] Institute of Medicine, 1996). For Internet sites that maintain historical and current information, as well as future projections, see the AIDS websites of the United Nations (www.unaids.org) and the AIDS Foundation of South Africa (www.aids .org.za); a new site, launched on World AIDS Day, Dec. 1, 2002, is that of the American International AIDS Foundation (www.aids.com).

145. Roy Anderson of Oxford University, quoted in *Arlington Star-Telegram* (July 11, 2000), p. 8-A.

146. "If we can get Coca-Cola and cold beer to every remote corner of Africa, it should not be impossible to do the same with drugs." From the speech of Joep Lange, president of the International AIDS Society, Fourteenth International AIDS Conference, Barcelona, Spain (quoted in *Arlington Star-Telegram* [July 14, 2002], p. 18A; see also http://www .iasociety.org).

147. In a nation of 249 million, the 1990 census counted 1.79 million Indians, who composed 0.074 percent of the total U.S. population. Because in the 2000 census people for the first time could report more than one race (2.4 percent did), the racial data for the two censuses are not directly comparable. In the 2000 census, 2.07 million people identified themselves as single-race Indians, and 3.44 million people checked off "Indian" plus a second race. The discrepancy does not matter much: In the year 2000, Indians thus accounted for between 0.07 percent and 1.2 percent of the total U.S. population of 281 million. The 2000 census identified other groups: "white people, not of Hispanic/Latino origin," 69.1 percent; Hispanic and Latino people, 12.5 percent; and African American people, 12.3 percent. The University of Louisville Libraries have a useful website for recent Indian demography: http://www.louisville.edu/government/subjects/indians/indcensus .html.

Their contemporary demographic insignificance should not detract from the importance of studying America's twentieth-century Indians. Indeed, they have been much studied: A July, 2002, online OCLC WorldCat search discovered a total of 226 books on the subject "Indians of North America: Government Relations, 1934–Present." See Vine Deloria and Clifford M. Lytle, *The Nations Within: The Past and Future of American Indian*

Sovereignty (1984; repr., Austin: University of Texas Press, 1998); Stephen E. Cornell, *The Return of the Native: American Indian Political Resurgence* (New York: Oxford University Press, 1988); Kenneth R. Philp, ed., *Indian Self-rule: First-hand Accounts of Indian-White Relations from Roosevelt to Reagan* (1985; repr., Logan: Utah State University Press, 1995), which is a 340-page report of the proceedings of a 1983 conference, where 31 of 49 participants were Indians, and Philp's *Termination Revisited: American Indians on the Trail to Self-Determination, 1933–1953* (Lincoln: University of Nebraska Press, 1999). Also of interest is that rambling, angry, and effective work, *Where White Men Fear to Tread: The Autobiography of Russell Means* (Indian activist, written with the assistance of historian Marvin Wolf; New York: St. Martin's Press, 1995), a street punk-turned-accountant who became a leader of AIM (the American Indian Movement). AIM's activities included the 1972 takeover of the U.S. Bureau of Indian Affairs (BIA), which was briefly renamed the "Native American Embassy," as well as the symbolic two-month Indian occupation (2 dead, 300 later indicted) at Wounded Knee, South Dakota, in 1973. For a review of the Indian Rights movement of 1969–1973, see Paul Chaat Smith (activist) and Robert Warrior (Stanford historian), *Like a Hurricane: The Indian Movement from Alcatraz to Wounded Knee* (New York: New Press, 1996).

148. Since 1970, two-fifths or more of all legal U.S. immigrants have arrived from Asia. In the past thirty years they have been outnumbered only by Spanish-speaking newcomers entering the United States from myriad points of origin between the Rio Grande River and Tierra del Fuego (statistics in Nash, Jeffrey, et al., *American People*, 2d ed., vol. 1, appendix, p. A-30; see also note 76.)

149. See George M. Frederickson's examination of race relations, *White Supremacy: A Comparative Study in American and South African History* (New York: Oxford University Press, 1981). The American Indians disappear from Frederickson's story about a sixth of the way through his three-hundred-page book. For a recent assessment that resulted from a symposium at University College, London, in 1996, see [University of London, auth.], *Beyond White Supremacy: Towards a New Agenda for the Comparative Histories of South Africa and the United States* (London: Institute of Commonwealth Studies, 1997).

150. Conquered as early as 1282 and 1283, Wales in the Tudor era was joined to the English Crown by acts of union in 1536 and 1543. The Scottish monarchy was subsumed in the English in 1603, when James VI of Scotland became James I of England; subsequently, the kingdom of Scotland was annexed by England in the 1707 act of union, creating Great Britain. British state and cultural formation has attracted much recent excellent work. See Linda Colley, *Britons: Forging the Nation, 1707–1837* (New Haven, Conn.: Yale University Press, 1992); Alexander Grant and Keith J. Stringer, eds., *Uniting the Kingdom? The Making of British History* (London: Routledge, 1995); Brendan Bradshaw and John Morrill, eds., *The British Problem, c. 1534–1707: State Formation in the Atlantic Archipelago* (New York: St. Martin's Press, 1996); and Colin Kidd, *British Identities before Nationalism: Ethnicity and Nationhood in the Atlantic World, 1600–1800* (Cambridge: Cambridge University Press, 1999).

151. For some discussion of failed policies and projects, as well as acts of omission, see Sir John Davies, *A Discovery of the True Causes of Why Ireland Was Never Entirely Subdued and Brought under Obedience of the Crown of England until the Beginning of His Majesty's Happy Reign* (1612; variously reprinted, most recently, Washington, D.C.: Catholic Uni-

versity of America Press, 1988); and Hans S. Pawlisch, *Sir John Davies and the Conquest of Ireland: A Study in Legal Imperialism* (New York: Cambridge University Press, 1985). See also Petty, *Political Anatomy of Ireland* (1691), and note 129.

152. But not unprecedented. In early frontier history, before lines of race and class hardened, socializing between "Europeans" and Khoikhoi on the Cape's far northern interior, around the Orange River, had produced by the late 1700s a people contemporaneously called the *Bastaards,* who later (at the urging of missionaries) renamed themselves the Griqua. See Monica Wilson, "The Hunters and Herders," in *South Africa to 1870,* pp. 68–70, and Martin Legassick, "The Northern Frontier to c. 1840: The Rise and Decline of the Griqua People," in *The Shaping of South African Society,* pp. 358–420. Thus, it is a matter of deep irony that, in modern-day South Africa, the northern hinterlands of the Cape Province have been mentioned by a few small extremist settler groups as a possible site for a secessionist, separate "white state."

SOURCE CITATIONS FOR FIGURE AND MAPS

Figure 1. From Sir Thomas Herbert (1606–1682), *Th: Herberts zee-en lant-reyse, na verscheyde deelen van Asia en Africa . . . ,* trans. Lambert van den Bos (Dordrecht: A. Andriessz, 1658), p. 8, the Dutch edition of Herbert's *A relation of some years travaile, begunne anno 1626, into Afrique and the greater Asia, especially the greater territories of the Persian monarchies, and some parts of the Oriental Indies . . .* (London: W. Stansby, 1634; subsequent English editions in 1638, 1665, and 1677). This untitled engraving of Europeans trading at the Cape of Good Hope appears only in the 1658 Dutch edition. A reproduction of this engraving appears in R. F. Kennedy, *Catalogue of Prints in the Africana Museum and in Books in the Strange Collection of Africana in the Johannesburg Public Library up to 1870,* 2 vols. (Johannesburg: Africana Museum, 1975), vol. 1, citation H111E. Drawings, prints, and museums are of course cultural artifacts. In 1994, in postapartheid South Africa, the Africana Museum (established in 1935) separated from the public library, relocated, and was renamed Museum Africa; its collections were reorganized and have been exhibited to reflect new political realities. The Harold Strange Library of African Studies (originally the Strange Collection, acquired in 1913) remains housed in the Johannesburg Public Library. See Charisse Levitz, "The Transformation of Museums in South Africa," *Cidoc Newsletter* 7 (Aug., 1996) at www.willpowerinfo.myby.co.uk/cidoc/arte031.htm; and Denver A. Webb, "Winds of Change," *Museums Journal* 4 (1994): 20–24.

MAPS

Map 1. Inset of Atlantic Ocean regions from the map titled Typus Orbis Terrarum (1587), by Abraham Ortelius (1527–1598), 1587 facsimile map, call no. 64/1 96–333, Map Room, Special Collections, University of Texas–Arlington Libraries.

Map 2. Drawn from data and maps readily available.

Map 3. Rainfall and elevation: "Eire," *World Book Encyclopedia,* vol. 3 (Chicago: Field Enterprises, 1953), pp. 2234ff. Rainfall: map of "annual precipitation in Europe," in *Climates of Northern and Western Europe,* vol. 5, ed. C. C. Wallen, *World Survey of Climatology* (Amsterdam: Elsevier, 1970), fig. 10, facing p. 16.

Map 4. County famine starvation rates: Kennedy, Ell, et al., *Mapping the Great Irish*

Famine, map 44, p. 108. County emigration rates, 1856–1910: Miller, *Emigrants and Exiles,* table, p. 578. Catholic emigration bar graph: calculated from data in Miller, *Emigrants,* pp. 137, 152–57, 169–70, 193, 291, 297, 346, 350, 569.

Map 5. Land, ownership patterns, and confiscations: Ruth Dudley Edwards, *An Atlas of Irish History,* 2d ed. (London: Methuen, 1981), pp. 171, 173, 176. Percentage of Protestants (1861) by county: Kennedy, Ell, et al., *Mapping,* map 37, p. 91. Protestant emigration bar graph: calculated from data in Miller, *Emigrants,* pp. 137, 152–57, 169–70, 193–94, 197–98, 297, 350, 370–71.

Map 6. Rainfall and elevation: "United States of America," in *World Book Encyclopedia,* vol. 17 (1953), pp. 8294ff. For rainfall, see also the map titled "Mean Annual Precipitation," *National Atlas of the United States of America* (Washington, D.C.: Dept. of Interior, U.S. Geological Survey, 1970), p. 97.

Map 7. Removals: Paul S. Boyer, Clifford Clark, et al., *Enduring Vision,* vol. 1, p. 283; and Jeanne Boydston, Nick Cullather, et al., *Making a Nation: The United States and Its People,* vol. 1 (Upper Saddle River, N.J.: Prentice Hall, 2002), p. 327. Dates of statehood: Boydston, Cullather, et al., *Making a Nation,* vol. 1, appendix, p. A-17.

Map 8. Westward settlement by date: Alan Brinkley, *American History: A Survey,* 11th ed., vol. 1 (Boston: McGraw Hill, 2003), p. 106 (proclamation line); Boydston, Cullather, et al., *Making a Nation,* vol. 1, p. 282; and Faragher, Buhle, et al., *Out of Many,* pp. 217, 259. City populations: James A. Henretta, W. Elliot Brownlee, et al., *America's History,* 3d ed., vol. 1 (New York: Worth, 1997), appendix, p. A-8. State populations: *The Statistical History of the United States from Colonial Times to the Present,* rev. ed. (Stamford, Conn.: Fairfield, 1965), pp. 12–13.

Map 9. Elevation: "Union of South Africa," *World Book Encyclopedia,* vol. 17 (1953), pp. 8256ff. Rainfall: For 20-inch rainfall areas, see Lamar and Thompson, eds., *Frontier in History,* p. 339; and Thompson, *History of South Africa,* p. 3. For a map identifying 15- and 30-inch rainfall regions, see Donald Denoon and Balam Nyeko, *Southern Africa since 1800,* rev. ed. (London: Longman, 1984), p. 2. For comprehensive rainfall maps, see the map of mean annual rainfall in South Africa, c. 1970, in *Climates of Africa,* vol. 10, *World Survey of Climatology,* ed. J. F. Griffiths (Amsterdam: Elsevier, 1972), fig. 9, p. 512, and "Map 2: Rainfall Distribution over South Africa," 1999 Dept. of Environmental Affairs and Tourism, Environmentek, CSIR, South Africa, at www.ngo.grida.no/soesa/nsoer/general/about .htm.

Map 10. Expansion of settlement: C. F. J. Muller, ed., *Five Hundred Years: A History of South Africa* (Pretoria: Academica, 1969), p. 27; Elphick, *Kraal and Castle,* pp. 93, 220; Lamar and Thompson, *Frontier in History,* p. 341; Cameron and Spies, eds., *Illustrated History of South Africa,* p. 67; and Elphick and Giliomee, eds., *Shaping of South African Society,* p. 68. Boundary changes: Muller, *Five Hundred Years,* p. 84; Basil A. Le Cordeur, *The Politics of Eastern Cape Separatism, 1820–1854* (Cape Town: Oxford University Press, 1981), pp. 28–29; Cameron and Spies, eds., *Illustrated History of South Africa,* p. 171; Shillington, *History of Southern Africa,* p. 58; Davenport, *South Africa,* pp. 99, 126; Elphick and Giliomee, *Shaping of South African Society,* pp. 23, 68, 481; and Thompson, *History of South Africa,* p. 34. 1820 settlers: Le Cordeur, *Politics,* p. 289; and Cameron and Spies, eds., *Illustrated History of South Africa,* p. 98. The Great Trek: Muller, *Five Hundred Years,* p. 123; Lamar and Thompson, *Frontier in History,* p. 343; Davenport, *South Africa,* p. 51; and Thompson, *History of South Africa,* p. 89. Diamond fields' cartographic shenanigans:

Cameron and Spies, eds., *Illustrated History of South Africa*, p. 166; and Shillington, *Southern Africa*, p. 86. Witwatersrand: Shillington, *Southern Africa*, p. 164.

Map 11. Historical tribal regions: Shillington, *Southern Africa*, p. 16; and Thompson, *History of South Africa*, p. 3. Eastern Cape frontier wars: Davenport, *South Africa*, p. 126; Cameron and Spies, eds., *Illustrated History of South Africa*, pp. 87, 171; Shillington, *Southern Africa*, p.79; and Elphick and Giliomee, *Shaping of South African Society*, p. 481. Difaqane, mfecane: Cameron and Spies, eds., *Illustrated History of South Africa*, p. 123; and Shillington, *Southern Africa*, pp. 36, 45; Elphick and Giliomee, *Shaping of South African Society*, p. 388; and Thompson, *History of South Africa*, p. 82. Xhosa cattle killing: J. B. Peires, *The Dead Will Arise*, pp. 65, 167, 320. Zulu wars: Davenport, *South Africa*, p. 166; and Shillington, *Southern Africa*, p. 100. Fort Hare: Shillington, *Southern Africa*, p. 160. Tribal "homelands," 1913 and 1936: Denoon and Nyeko, *Southern Africa*, p. 168; for maps of bantustans (at different dates) in the subsequent apartheid era, see Cameron and Spies, eds., *Illustrated History of South Africa*, p. 306; Davenport, *South Africa*, p. 414; Lamar and Thompson, *Frontier in History*, p. 346; Shillington, *Southern Africa*, p. 182; and Thompson, *History of South Africa*, p. 192.

Map 12. Atlantic-centered section of map of "The World. On Mercator's Projection," *Rand McNally and Co.'s Indexed Atlas of the World*, rev. ed., vol. 1 (Chicago: Rand, McNally, 1902), pp. 10–11. Call no. #AGC5390, Map Annex, Special Collections, University of Texas–Arlington Libraries.

ALUSINE JALLOH

In Search of America

THE NEW WEST AFRICAN DIASPORA

THIS CHAPTER EXAMINES the new diaspora of West Africans who moved to the United States from the 1960s to the 1990s, the postindependence period of West Africa.[1] This was a voluntary migration. In contrast, the old diaspora was a forced movement of Africans, mainly from West Africa, during the transatlantic slave trade that spanned the fifteenth through the nineteenth centuries. One scholar has characterized the two events as "the new diaspora of colonialism alongside the older diaspora of enslavement." He has further distinguished first- and second-generation West African immigrants in America from African Americans with the label "American Africans (or Americo-Africans)" for the former group.[2] Both migrations were part of a larger black diaspora in the United States that included black immigrants from other regions such as the Caribbean and Latin America. Together these black groups forged multiethnic and multinational communities of overlapping diasporas with shared and competing interests.[3]

Over the past three decades the study of the African diaspora, an ongoing dynamic process, in the United States and elsewhere, including Europe, Latin America, and the Caribbean, has become a growing multidisciplinary field of inquiry. In particular, historians, anthropologists, sociologists, economists, and political scientists have collectively produced several significant studies covering different aspects of the black experience outside of Africa. Themes such as involuntary and voluntary migration of black peoples, their settlement and adaptation to the complex political, social, economic, and cultural environments they encountered in their host countries, and their relationship with Africa as their ancestral homeland have dominated the literature. Nevertheless, more research is needed to expand our knowledge of these three key facets of the African migration. This chapter therefore seeks to contribute to our understanding of these themes from the perspective of the new West African diaspora in the United States.[4]

The chapter is divided into three sections. The first deals with the migration of West Africans to America, contrasting the different paths of migration from the fifteenth through the twentieth centuries. The second section examines the settlement of West African immigrants in different parts of the United States, including their multifaceted relationship with African Americans. The chapter concludes with a discussion of the political, cultural, and economic relationships West Africans in the United States maintained with their homeland.

WEST AFRICAN MIGRATION

The transnational exodus of West Africans to the United States in the postindependence period was built on two earlier streams of migration. The first, which began in the fifteenth century, was part of the forced movement of millions of enslaved West African ethnic groups such as the Yoruba, Fulani, Mende, Wolof, Mandinka, and Akan across the Atlantic to the Americas from the fifteenth through the nineteenth centuries. The vast majority of the enslaved Africans, who arrived at different times and in different numbers, were transported to plantations concentrated in states such as Virginia, Maryland, Georgia, and North and South Carolina. The slaves performed a variety of tasks, especially cultivating crops such as tobacco, rice, and cotton for both the American and overseas markets. Before the American Revolution of 1776, slavery was sanctioned in all thirteen British North American colonies.[5]

The importance of West Africa as a source of slaves for the United States is well documented in the historical literature.[6] In particular, it has been shown that the Gullah, a distinctive group of African Americans in South Carolina and Georgia, are directly descended from slaves from Sierra Leone and its environs. During the 1700s, the American colonists in South Carolina and Georgia discovered that rice would grow well in the moist, semitropical area bordering their coastline. However, the colonists had no experience with the cultivation of rice, and they needed African slaves who knew how to plant, harvest, and process this difficult crop. The white plantation owners purchased slaves from various areas of Africa, but they generally preferred those from what they called the "rice coast" or "windward coast"—the traditional rice-growing region of West Africa, which stretched from Senegal down to Sierra Leone and Liberia. The plantation owners were willing to pay higher prices for slaves from this area, and West Africans from the rice coast were almost certainly the largest group of slaves imported into South Carolina and Georgia during the eighteenth century.[7]

However, aside from the slaves, only a few West Africans left their home-land for America before the 1960s. This movement is the second West African transnational migration to the United States. It was a voluntary migration that occurred when West Africa was under European colonialism, particularly that of Britain and France. Those who migrated came predominantly from English-speaking countries such as Nigeria, Ghana, and Liberia mainly in pursuit of higher education in America. For French-speaking West Africans, however, their resettlement in America is a fairly recent phenomenon. Prior to the 1980s, many of these immigrants went to France for their education or in search of jobs because of the strong cultural ties they shared with the French. But, in the 1980s, France made major changes to its immigration policies, which used to favor immigrants from former French colonies. These adjustments made it more difficult for French-speaking West Africans to migrate there. Consequently, French-speaking West Africans, especially the Senegalese, migrated to the United States.[8]

The vast majority of the West African immigrants to the United States during the colonial period, unlike those of the postindependence period, returned to their homeland to pursue careers in diverse fields such as politics and business after completing their studies in the United States. Of those who went to America during the colonial period, perhaps the most prominent were Nnamdi Azikiwe, popularly known as "Zik of Nigeria," and Kwame Nkrumah of Ghana. In 1925, Zik left Nigeria, the most populous country in Africa, for the United States to continue his education. He first attended Storer College, a school famous for its distinguished black pedigree. By 1930, Zik had obtained degrees from Lincoln University, Howard University, and the University of Pennsylvania, as well as a certificate in journalism from Columbia University. From 1931 until he left America in 1934, Zik taught political science at Lincoln University. Throughout his stay in America, Zik was greatly influenced by the writings of W. E. B. DuBois, Marcus Garvey, Carter G. Woodson, and Frederick Douglass, and, in fact, his Pan-African politics were born while he was in the United States. On returning to West Africa in 1934, Zik first settled in Ghana, where he was editor of the *Morning Post*. In 1937, because of his Pan-African politics, he was forced out of the country by the British colonial administration. Zik then returned to Nigeria, where he continued his journalistic career. He soon started Nigeria's first press conglomerate, with the famous *West African Pilot* as its flagship. Zik's newspapers, including the *Daily Comet, Eastern Nigerian Guardian, Nigeria Spokesman,* and *Nigerian Monitor,* played an important role in African opposition to British colonial rule. In 1938, Zik published *Renascent Africa*, which synthesized the ideas of Dubois, Garvey, and Douglass as they related to Africa. In 1963, after a long political career and following Nigeria's independence from Britain in 1960, Zik became the first president of the Republic of Nigeria. Until his death in 1996, Zik was a successful journalist, publisher, entrepreneur, nationalist, and politician.[9]

Nkrumah left his Ghanaian homeland, then called the Gold Coast, for the United States in 1935 and stayed for ten years. Before that, in the early 1930s, Nkrumah, while in Accra, the capital of Ghana, was greatly influenced by Zik and his writings. Zik, who was living in Accra, helped to inspire Nkrumah to study overseas rather than devoting the rest of his life to being a Catholic schoolmaster. When Nkrumah failed to gain acceptance to the University of London, he borrowed money from his extended family and, following Zik's example, set out for America in search of an alternative education and enrolled at Lincoln University. As a student, Nkrumah studied politics and theology. Like Zik, Nkrumah was greatly influenced by Garvey's ideas. In 1945, Nkrumah left the United States for Britain, where he worked with blacks from the Caribbean, the United States, and Africa in promoting Pan-Africanism and opposing European colonialism in Africa.[10]

Returning to the Gold Coast from London in 1947, Nkrumah founded the Convention People's Party (CPP) and mobilized a cross-section of the population to successfully challenge British colonial rule. In ten years Nkrumah's CPP won three elections and achieved independence for the new state of Ghana. Nkrumah's London years greatly influenced the development of his political career. In 1960, Nkrumah was elected the first president of the re-public of Ghana. As president, Nkrumah embarked on a domestic program that emphasized industrialization, agriculture, and education. He also worked hard to free Africa from European rule. Until his death in 1972, Nkrumah was a champion of Pan-African unity and black identity.[11]

However, West African immigrants like Nkrumah who went to the United States during the colonial period were a minority compared to those who went to Europe during the same era. They often went to the European countries, especially their capital cities, that had colonized their homeland in the nineteenth and twentieth centuries. Evidence of higher education in metropolitan countries such as Britain and France often resulted in greater social prestige and better-paying jobs for West Africans in their colonial homeland. A greater number of West Africans migrated to Europe as opposed to America because of the perception that higher education in Europe was superior to that in the United States. A large part of the West African presence in Britain, for instance, was made up of the children of the West African coastal elite who used their business profits to sponsor their children's education in the metropole. In addition, some West African clergy, lawyers, traders, and doctors made regular visits to Britain to further their professional interests.

Also, a significant number of Africans who went to Britain during the colonial period were seamen or manual laborers.[12]

Four important factors provide the background of the postindependence West African immigration to America. The first is European colonial rule in West Africa. European colonization started well before the nineteenth century, but it proceeded at an accelerated pace during the 1880s, when Britain and France took control of much of Africa. The partition of the continent formed part of a renewed upsurge of European domination in the world. African territories could now be controlled directly from Europe. By 1900, European colonial rule was entering a period of consolidation. This was greatly aided when, in the early twentieth century, the steamship and telecommunications industries brought the European continent much "closer" to the African colonies. The Second World War was both a political and economic watershed in West Africa. By the late 1950s, European colonial rule had entered the decolonization phase, which led to the independence of most African territories in the 1960s.[13]

Although of relatively short duration, European colonial rule, with its emphasis on Western culture and education, created an environment that exposed West Africans, especially the youth, to the West, including the United States. As a result, a new class of Western-educated West Africans was created in colonial West African cities. In addition to the colonizers, European missionaries played an important role in the spread of Western education in West Africa. The missionaries used Western education to convert the indigenous population to Christianity and assimilate them to a Western lifestyle. Besides the missionaries, both the Africans and the colonizers benefited from Western education. For the Africans, it created employment opportunities and social status, while the colonizers needed educated Africans as workers in the colonial state. Ironically, the new African intellectual elite, which was a product of both the Western formal school system in the African colonies and overseas Western institutions of higher education, would challenge colonialism and eventually replace the colonial administrators as the new leaders of independent Africa.[14]

European colonial rule in West Africa created both benefits and problems for the indigenous population. On the positive side, colonial rule brought, among other things, a relatively stable political-legal order; an improvement in the economic environment through the introduction of rail, sea, and road transportation; European banking and a uniformly accepted portable currency in both notes and coin; and the termination of domestic slavery. On the negative side, colonial rule led to, among other things, the loss of African freedom; human rights abuses involving women and children; and the restriction of African businesses through trade licensing, credit restrictions, and the introduction of statutory marketing monopolies granted only to non-African traders. Arguably, the former colonial powers share a large part of the responsibility for the outbreak of many crises of nation building, poverty, and undemocratic rule in postindependence Africa.[15]

The second factor in the postindependence West African immigration to the United States was the Cold War. West Africa, like the rest of the African continent, was not spared the effects of the politics of the intense rivalry between the United States and the former Soviet Union, the Cold War's chief protagonists. From the end of World War II until late 1984, which marked the start of a process that led to the end of the struggle, U.S. policies toward Africa were fundamentally shaped by the enmity. America's interest in Africa was defined primarily in strategic geopolitical terms and fluctuated with changing estimates of the threat posed by real or imagined Soviet progress in Africa. During the late 1940s and 1950s, the Truman and Eisenhower administrations were concerned chiefly with ensuring that Western Europe would become a stable bulwark against Soviet expansion. This preoccupation caused them to abandon the traditional role of the United States as an outspoken critic of colonial rule, which compromised American policy toward Africa. U.S. officials were concerned that criticism of European colonial policies in Africa might weaken or alienate allies such as Britain and France.[16]

In the late 1950s, however, the United States began to reassess Africa's geopolitical significance. The independence of African countries such as Ghana (1957) signaled the beginning of the end of European colonialism on the African continent. During the Kennedy administration in the 1960s, America's interest in Africa peaked, although it was still centered on geopolitical concerns. Administration officials called for a new approach to Africa that led to the launching of an energetic diplomatic effort to woo African leaders such as Kwame Nkrumah of Ghana. Not only did the Kennedy administration send young and enthusiastic ambassadors to Africa, it also welcomed more than twenty African heads of state, including Nkrumah, in Washington, D.C., between 1961 and 1963. Between 1958 and 1962, the United States increased the flow of assistance to Africa from $110 million to $519 million. Over this brief period, American aid to Africa increased from roughly 2 percent of total U.S. overseas assistance to 8 percent.[17]

Nevertheless, from the mid-1970s through the mid-1980s, the United States was more active in Africa than at any other time in its history. By this time the Soviet Union had gained a foothold on the African continent. Despite widely varying ideological positions, all three U.S. administrations that governed during this period—Ford, Carter, and Reagan—defined their African priorities largely by geopolitical considerations. American policymakers were apprehensive that political conflicts in southern Africa and the Horn of Africa, unless dealt with quickly, would benefit the Soviet Union. With the outbreak of the Iranian revolution in 1979, African countries (e.g., Somalia and Kenya) became strategically important to the United States because they served as way stations for troops and supplies headed for the Persian Gulf.

In West Africa, the United States, in pursuit of its Cold War interests, provided both direct and indirect support for higher education in the subregion, including funds for research projects and scholarships for West Africans to study in America. In fact, educational aid was an effective propaganda tool used by both the United States and the Soviet Union in West Africa. Their goal was to influence the minds of young African intellectuals to appreciate certain models of development based on Western or socialist cultures. For the United States, both governmental and nongovernmental agencies were active in West Africa. For example, the U.S. Information Agency for International Development (USAID) and Michigan State University collaborated with Zik and fellow Nigerians in the founding of the University of Nigeria in Nsukka in 1960. Also, funding agencies such as the Ford Foundation, the Rockefeller Foundation, and the International Council for Educational Development sponsored several workshops and awarded grants for travel and research projects. As a consequence, many West African intellectuals, especially in the Anglophone countries, became fascinated with the American model of higher education.[18]

The Cold War ended in Africa in 1988, with the signing of a tripartite agreement paving the way for the independence of Namibia and the withdrawal of Cuban troops from Angola. The recognition by the United States and the Soviet Union that neither would gain from further competition in Africa facilitated this agreement. With the end of the Cold War, the United States also abandoned its tendency to intervene in African conflicts. This was evident in Liberia, a major recipient of American military aid in the early 1980s, when the Bush administration refused to get involved in a horrific civil war that led to the ouster of Pres. Samuel Doe in 1990.

Throughout the Cold War, U.S. policy toward Africa was fundamentally at odds with the expressed commitment of the United States to democracy and development. American policymakers often overlooked and excused repression, injustice, corruption, and economic mismanagement in African countries such as the Democratic Republic of Congo (formerly Zaire) that were willing to oppose the Soviet Union. They repeatedly opposed popular nationalist movements in southern Africa such as the African National Congress (ANC), which they perceived to be on the wrong side of the East-West ideological divide. They also turned a blind eye to human suffering in countries like Niger that seemed to them to have no strategic value.[19]

Changes in U.S. immigration laws were the third factor influencing West African migration to America. In particular, these were the 1965 Immigration Act, the 1980 changes in laws relating to refugees, the 1986 Immigration Reform and Control Act (IRCA), and the 1990 Immigration Act. Collectively, these laws facilitated the immigration of thousands of West Africans to the United States. The 1965 act made it possible for children of nonimmigrants born in the United States to file visa petitions for their parents to be legally admitted into the country. The act also introduced the labor certificate and occupational preference and nonpreference provisions under which people (regardless of which hemisphere they were from) with skills that the U.S. Department of Labor considered desirable could be issued immigrant visas.

In the Refugee Act of 1980, the United States changed its definition of a refugee to conform to the UN's protocol of refugees. Previously, the United States had defined a refugee in narrow terms as someone fleeing from a country with a communist government or from the Middle East. West Africans benefited from the reconfiguration of U.S. policies on refugees, most of whom came from countries such as Liberia and Ghana. The immigration reforms of 1986 made it possible for undocumented West Africans then living in the United States to become permanent residents. It provided legal status through an amnesty offered to illegal aliens and workers without proper work permits. The 1990 Immigration Act contained two major provisions that had a significant impact on West African immigration to the United States. First, it made it possible to increase the total number of immigrants admitted on the basis of skills for employment in the United States. Second, to promote diversity among the immigrants admitted, a program was launched to increase the entrance of immigrants from countries and regions of the world with a low representation of immigrants, such as Africa. In 1995 alone, about 37 percent of the visas under the diversity initiative program were allotted to Africa.[20]

The final aspect of the background of the postindependence West African immigration to America was the economic crisis West Africa has been experiencing since the 1980s. This predicament has been marked by currency devaluation, high inflation, a decline in the production of export crops, rising interest rates, and the increased intervention of the International Monetary Fund (IMF) and World Bank in the West African economy. The World Bank, for example, called for the rationalization of the universities, which involved a reduction in the number of students and teachers as well as a diversion of funds to secondary education. West African universities have also suffered because of the weakened economies, leading to the migration of many West African academics and students to other regions of Africa, particularly South Africa, and the West, especially the United States.[21]

The evidence suggests that, instead of improving economic conditions in West Africa, the IMF's structural-adjustment programs exacerbated the crisis there and deepened poverty in the subregion. During the 1980s, poverty expanded markedly, and living standards deteriorated for the vast majority of West Africans. All segments of West African society experienced hardships because of the declining availability and quality of basic services such as health and education. In rural areas peasants were squeezed by low producer prices, rising inflation, and tattered infrastructure. For urban wage earners, too, inflation steadily eroded incomes. Consequently, many of them were pushed into the informal economy or back to rural areas. In countries such as Sierra Leone, Nigeria, Liberia, and Ghana, fixed salaries, when paid at all, depreciated rapidly. Because of budget problems and mismanagement, many West African governments, which were the largest employers, were delinquent in paying wages to their employees. As fiscal pressures mounted, these governments embarked on austerity measures involving cutbacks that removed many employees from the public sector payroll completely. In the private sector, decreasing profits and a growing tide of business failures put many employees out of work as well.

With the failure of formal economies in much of West Africa, many of the indigenous population resorted to informal activities or parallel markets for survival. In the cities this often meant a turn to petty trading and questionable activities such as smuggling and parallel currency markets, which characterized the "second economy." In the rural areas, many people shifted to subsistence activities, localized commerce, or cross-border trade. These coping mechanisms, however, had negative consequences for government revenues, national savings, investments, and the institutions of the formal economy. By the 1990s, a significant number of West Africans were dependent on the second or parallel economies for their livelihood.[22]

The rise of parallel economies in West Africa was interconnected with another important feature of the region's crisis: the decline of the state. As public resources waned and fiscal pressures grew, many governments were unable to sustain basic functions or services. They were also unable to raise additional internal revenues from their dwindling economies, and they could not adequately compensate for fiscal shortfalls through external borrowing or aid. Consequently, spending on basics such as infrastructure, administration, and social services declined noticeably. The failure of public institutions aggravated the course of economic decline and undermined the legitimacy of several regimes. In countries like Sierra Leone and Liberia, these conditions contributed to long and bloody civil wars.[23]

The transnational exodus of West Africans to the United States in the postindependence period was a multifaceted, difficult process and was characterized by multiple stages of migration. While many West African immigrants followed a direct migratory pattern to America, some embarked on a chain, or multistage, transnational path, usually leaving West Africa to work in other countries for a while, saving enough money to show proof of financial security at a U.S. consulate, and then undertaking the journey to America. For many West Africans in the United States, the migratory process began with intra-African or rural-urban migration.[24]

Four main factors help to explain the reasons West Africans left their homeland to move to America during the postindependence period. The first was to pursue higher education, especially in historically black colleges and universities like Howard University. This was motivated by an educational tradition that dated back to the colonial period, as previously discussed. Furthermore, the Cold War provided opportunities for many West Africans to engage in advanced studies in America.

The second was to exploit economic opportunities, particularly in higher education and business.[25] The economic crisis in West Africa created conditions for a cross-section of the population, including academics, business people, students, and ordinary workers to leave for better-paying jobs in the United States. The third was to escape political persecution and civil wars in countries such as Liberia and Sierra Leone. The fourth was to reunite with family members who were concentrated mainly in America's major cities.

Of these reasons, perhaps the most important was the search for "the American dream": the opportunity for self-enrichment and economic independence and the transfer of assets to West Africa to start business enterprises or retire in comfort. In short, for most West Africans, the American dream was the hope of economic prosperity that would return with them to their home countries, where they were convinced their future lay. This vision united West Africans from very diverse careers, skilled and unskilled backgrounds, political ideologies, ethnicities, and nationalities. The vast majority of the immigrants were from Nigeria, the most populous country in Africa. They took up residence in all of the major American cities, including New York, Chicago, Atlanta, Los Angeles, Washington, D.C., Boston, and Houston. In the Dallas–Fort Worth metropolitan area alone were more than ten thousand Nigerians.[26] Nigerian migration to the United States was limited before Nigeria became independent from British colonial rule in 1960. Before that time, Nigerians who traveled overseas generally went to Britain. The few who came to America were students.

With independence, large numbers of Nigerians began traveling to the United States to study various disciplines, especially medicine and engineering. This migration was greatly aided by Nigerian oil income in the 1970s and 1980s. In addition, the Nigerian civil war in the late 1960s and early 1970s produced numerous refugees, particularly among the Igbos in the secessionist southeast region, many of whom made their way to the United States. However, Nigerians began to immigrate in far larger numbers at the end of the oil boom in the mid-1980s and continued as controversy over military governance as well as religious and ethnic confrontations over electoral politics occurred in the 1990s. These factors plus endemic corruption in government circles led many Nigerians who were studying in America to remain there. Other large West African immigrant groups included Ghanaians, Liberians, and Sierra Leoneans. In Chicago alone, which has one of the largest West African communities in the United States, it is estimated that there were more than thirty thousand Ghanaians by the mid-1990s.[27]

SETTLEMENT IN AMERICA

West Africans were concentrated in the major American cities. The single largest West African community was in New York City, where there are even now more than fifty thousand residents, mainly Nigerians, Ghanaians, and Senegalese. Here they for the most part lived and did business with, but existed separately from, African Americans. They were concentrated in the Morris Heights area in the Bronx, Bedford-Stuyvesant in Brooklyn, and Harlem. In fact, the area of 116th Street between Frederick Douglass Boulevard on the west and Adam Clayton Powell Boulevard on the east in Harlem was called "Little Africa." In these communities West Africans have developed and expanded networks, institutions, and resources to help in their adjustment in America and to maintain meaningful social, cultural, economic, and political links with their homeland.[28]

Once in the United States, West Africans were sometimes disunited and at other times harmonious in their intragroup relations. They experienced rivalries, tensions, and cooperation. Although they constituted one of the most educated of the immigrant groups, there was much broader income distribution among them, from the very wealthy to the extremely poor. Nonetheless, the American environment provided an opportunity for them to redefine their social identities, particularly through education. Some were even to able to overcome the social liabilities of birth. Often the class distinctions that they brought from their home countries were erased as the educated and the semieducated, the highborn and the lowborn rubbed shoulders while pursuing the American dream.[29]

The West African presence in America was significantly shaped by urban-based life, which provided an important social environment for survival and nurture. Of value were ethnic churches, which were predominantly Pentecostal in orientation, ethnic associations, and mosques. Religious activity was a very important part of daily life in West Africa, and this cultural tradition continued when the immigrants made their new homes in America, where their religious institutions also dispensed social services. Some of these included immigration counseling, English classes, and after-school programs. The ethnic churches also served as information networks for jobs and housing. They were thus a vital substitute for kinship and family networks, which had been essential aspects of social life in their homeland. Ethnic churches also afforded opportunities for social gatherings such as marriages, baptisms, and picnics, where immigrants of the same ethnicity or nationality could meet and discuss issues pertaining to their home countries. For many hard-working immigrants, Sunday was the only day of rest, so Sunday services took on a festive quality.[30]

When many West African immigrants chose a church, ethnicity or nationality often took precedence over denomination. Examples of ethnic churches included the African Evangelical Baptist Church in the Dallas–Fort Worth metroplex and the Mount Zion United African Church of Philadelphia. The religious practices in these institutions differed from those of traditional American churches in various ways. There was an effort to recreate an atmosphere reminiscent of the home country through music and singing; thus many worshipers dressed in traditional clothing. Language use also differentiated these churches. During the service, most congregations used one or more West African languages, for example, Bassa (Liberia), Krio (Sierra Leone), Twi (Ghana), and Yoruba (Nigeria). Sermon topics often addressed immigration issues or events in the home countries. Churches also provided solace, especially for West African refugees who had witnessed atrocities such as the killing of relatives in their homelands. Prayers were often said for family members who were still living in difficult circumstances in West Africa, for those in refugee camps outside their home countries, for the souls of those killed during civil wars, and for immigrants who were suffering discrimination, particularly in employment, because of their skin color or accent. Worship thus was much-needed therapy for the distress associated with settlement in America.[31]

West African ethnic associations were concentrated in Chicago, Houston, New York, Washington, D.C., Boston, Los Angeles, and Atlanta, where they functioned as cultural and benevolent entities. These organizations provided social networks and services, as did the ethnic churches, but in addition recreated West African culture in America. Often West African rites of passage were celebrated, and bereaved members found participation in these associations a particularly comforting experience.

For Ghanaians, the oldest ethnic association in the United States was founded in 1982. The kings, queen mothers, and wing chiefs of these groups were modeled on the traditional Asante political system in the Ghanaian homeland. Asante kings were installed in organizations in New York, Washington, D.C., Houston, Chicago, and Atlanta with the endorsement of the Asantehene (king of the Asante) in Ghana.[32] In the Dallas–Fort Worth metroplex, for example, most of the ethnic associations were Nigerian (e.g., the Igbo Community Association of Nigeria and the Eme Association).[33]

The West African presence in America was extensively shaped by relations with African Americans. The relationship between these two black groups was complex. It was marked by both cooperation and conflict. The black diaspora in the United States was characterized by not only race but also nationality and culture. The resulting unity *and* diversity have characterized the relationship between black Americans and West Africans. Both black communities are separated by culture, history, geography, prejudice, and ignorance yet united by a common ancestry.[34]

Black Americans and West Africans have cooperated in many ways: They have entered into transatlantic marriages,[35] formed political alliances,[36] set up joint businesses on both sides of the Atlantic,[37] and shared membership in religious institutions.[38] One of the best examples of political cooperation between African Americans and West Africans concerns the Amadou Diallo killing in New York City, home of the largest West African population in America. In February, 1999, Diallo, a twenty-two-year-old West African immigrant, was shot down in a barrage of forty-one bullets by four white police officers in plainclothes from New York's Street Crime Unit even though he was unarmed and had no criminal record. Diallo, a Muslim Fula, had moved to New York City from his homeland of Guinea, a French-speaking West African country. A street peddler, Diallo had worked in Manhattan and lived in the Bronx. He first sold his wares in an outdoor market in Harlem, then moved south to 14th Street, where he displayed socks, videotapes, gloves, and other goods. Diallo's Fula ethnic group has a long mercantile tradition in their West African homeland, where they have achieved transnational entrepreneurial success.[39]

In response to the killing, outraged African American leaders—including Rev. Jesse Jackson; Kwesi Mfume, president of the National Association for the Advancement of Colored People (NAACP); Rev. Al Sharpton; David Dinkins, former mayor of New York City; and well-known attorney Johnnie Cochran, alongside West African community leaders—came together to organize protests, file wrongful-death and class-action lawsuits, and accuse the police of brutality. In February, 1999, not only did thousands of African Americans and West Africans participate in a series of protests (including outside police headquarters in Manhattan), they also attended a memorial service for Diallo before his body was flown to his homeland for burial. In addition, African Americans and West Africans organized interfaith services that emphasized unity among their religious communities.[40]

On the other side of this relationship, conflict sometimes appeared as cultural clashes in marriages but was centered on economic opportunities. Many black Americans believed that West Africans were taking their jobs, especially in view of the high educational attainment of the latter. At the same time, many West Africans perceived black Americans as underachievers in a land of opportunity. However, many West African immigrants were not knowledgeable about African American history, which included slavery, racism, and legal segregation, all of which compromised their ability to succeed in the United States.

WEST AFRICANS AND THEIR HOMELAND

The vast majority of West Africans in the United States maintained strong economic, social, and political links with their homeland, thus making their lives and interests transnational. Based on a physical presence in the United States as well as a strong emotional attachment to the homeland, this dual life transcended the many divisions in their community brought about by differences in ethnicity and class. The dream of the West African immigrant community in America was to eventually return to economic prosperity in their home countries.

The maintenance of links between West Africans and their homeland has been facilitated by jet travel and the revolution in communications technology. In particular, the internet, primarily e-mail, has played the most important role in keeping West Africans in the United States connected with their home countries on a daily basis. Internet technology also enables West Africans to read daily newspapers of their home countries from the relative comfort of their offices or homes in America. Individuals, national groups such as the Organization of Nigerian Nationals, ethnic associations such as Yoruba International, and branches of West African political parties such as the Sierra Leone People's Party (SLPP) have created or accessed websites and e-mail networks to inform and facilitate communication with different constituencies in the United States and their home countries. As a consequence of the "information age," West Africans in twentieth-century America were able to forge a closer linkage with their homeland than in any previous period. This technological achievement has also facilitated the flow of savings from U.S.-based West Africans to their home countries.[41]

From a political perspective, the United States provided both an opportunity for West Africans to run for local political offices and a base from which to remain politically and ideologically connected to their home countries.

Moreover, it helped to promote democracy in West African countries. In the 1980s, West Africans such as Frank L. Borges from the Cape Verde Islands were elected to state offices. Borges came to the United States at age seven. He went on to become a naturalized citizen, corporate lawyer, and deputy mayor of Hartford, Connecticut, before being elected that state's treasurer in 1986.

In addition to this group, a small cadre of West Africans was actively working on both sides of the Atlantic to secure dual citizenship for West Africans living in the United States. However, the vast majority of them were not politically assimilated as citizens and therefore could not participate in the American political process as either voters or candidates for elective office. The political consensus among West Africans was to retain their home countries' citizenship and concentrate on politics in their homeland as candidates or sources of political funding for candidates and political parties.[42]

A notable example of a West African who contributed to democratization in his home country from his base in the United States was Nigerian Wole Soyinka, the first African to win the Nobel Prize for literature in 1986. Playwright, political activist, and critic, Soyinka took up temporary residence in the United States in the 1990s to escape the undemocratic rule of Pres. Sani Abacha, whose administration was marked by despotism and economic decline. Soyinka had a long history of political activism in Nigeria. In the 1960s, he moved from his homeland to Ghana to avoid political persecution. He later returned to Nigeria, where, from 1967 to 1969, he was imprisoned during the civil war, most of which he spent in solitary confinement. From this experience he published *The Man Died* and *Ake,* his childhood biography. Voicing his opposition to President Abacha, Soyinka made several speeches and lectures across the United States and in Africa and published a major work, *The Open Sore of a Continent: A Personal Narrative of the Nigerian Crisis.*[43]

Some of the West African immigrants who became American citizens, especially those in Washington, D.C., used this privilege both to benefit themselves and to lobby American politicians on causes relating to their home countries or West Africa as a region. A significant number of the educated elite founded and joined advocacy groups based mainly in Washington, D.C., such as Free Africa Foundation, Voices of Africa, and the International Africa Foundation. These organizations provided information on African issues in both the United States and West Africa, lobbied American politicians and policymakers, provided technical assistance to civic groups in West Africa, and worked with nongovernmental organizations in West Africa on various matters, including democracy, HIV, and AIDS. Prominent among these leaders were academics such as George B. N. Ayittey from Ghana and Sulayman Nyang from the Gambia.[44]

An important vehicle that enabled West Africans to participate in the politics of their home countries was membership in American branches of political parties registered in their homeland. The American-based members played key roles in fund-raising for the national parties as well as educating and lobbying American politicians with regard to the major problems facing their homeland. But West Africans in the United States and those in their home countries often disagreed on political, economic, and cultural issues affecting their shared homeland. A notable example of an American-based branch of a West African political party was the SLPP, which played an important role in the electoral victory of Pres. Ahmad Tejan Kabbah in 1996, following four years of military rule. The American SLPP branch raised thousands of dollars and provided in-kind support such as the staple food, rice, for the party in Sierra Leone.[45]

From an economic standpoint, West Africans in America created both local and transnational businesses ranging in size from petty trading partnerships to multinational companies. Examples include the Cameroon-American Corporation of Houston; Y & A Trading, Banque de l'Habitat du Senegal, Homeland Fabric and Fashion, and Ghana Homes, Inc., all of New York City; and Freetown Market, Greenway Communication Services, Tropical Hair Designs, Palm Branch Corporation, and Makola African Fashion Boutique, all of Philadelphia. Among the diverse West African businesses were restaurants, banks, car-service enterprises, drug stores, money-transmission agencies, shipping companies, artifacts, hair-braiding salons, trading companies that dealt with products such as African foodstuffs, import-export businesses specializing in African fabrics, travel agencies, boutiques, real estate companies, and energy (oil and gas production and distribution) enterprises. The urban-based West African business community was not homogeneous: It was made up of American-trained entrepreneurs and professionals, unskilled workers, and women.[46]

A widespread and highly profitable business was the transmission of remittances totaling hundreds of millions of dollars. This money from West Africans in the United States to their relatives in their home countries constituted a major source of foreign revenue for many West African countries including Ghana, Senegal, Liberia, and Nigeria. This led some West African governments, such as Ghana's, to devise development policies that incorporated the West African community in America. Remittances led to the transformation of both social relations and business activities in the home countries. The money was used, for example, to create small businesses, especially in the service sector; increase access to informal credit, particularly for women; and expand the real estate sector and its related construction business. In fact, Senegalese immigrants in New York City created their own financial institutions to facilitate the transfer of funds to Senegal. Menial jobs that West Africans would have declined in their homeland were eagerly sought in the United States as valuable foreign currencies translated into comfortable incomes in devalued West African currencies. For Ghana, it is estimated that remittances ranged between $250 million and $350 million annually in the 1990s. Because of this transfer of funds, the American-based Western Union significantly increased its business presence in West African countries. Arguably, remittances from West Africans in America brought wealth to their relatives in their home countries but did not produce widespread development.[47]

For many West Africans, the mark of success was buying or building a big house back home. The difficulty they faced, however, was in doing so from thousands of miles away without losing their hard-earned money to dishonest relatives or housing companies there. This problem created an opportunity for some West African entrepreneurs in America, who started property and construction companies with offices in both the United States and West Africa. One such businessperson was Ghanaian Kwasi Amoafo, who founded Ghana Homes, Inc., in the Bronx in 1999. Such businesses faced competition from property developers based in West Africa, such as Construction Pioneers, Ltd., in Ghana, who were also trying to access West African consumers in the United States.[48]

The West African business people in America drew on Western business practices and their own culture in the start-up, organization, and management of their local and transnational enterprises. Personal ties, especially kinship relations, were important. In particular, extended family networks were quite useful for importers of African foodstuffs for the West African immigrant community in America. Kinship and ethnicity were valuable in securing venture capital, credit, and transportation of merchandise and in finding customers and selling goods. A major form of enterprise was family business in which owners based in the United States worked in conjunction with extended family members back home.[49]

CONCLUSION

In the United States, the old diaspora of African Americans, whose ancestors came mainly from West Africa as slaves, was expanded and enriched by the new diaspora of voluntary West African immigration during the postindependence period from the 1960s to the 1990s. The relationship between the majority African Americans and the minority West Africans was characterized by both cooperation and conflict, which reflected not only their shared heritage but also differences in culture and nationality. Unlike African Americans, West African immigrants maintained greater political, economic, social, and cultural ties with their homeland. They were connected to West Africa in diverse ways that were not technologically possible before the twentieth century.

Despite the great diversity of the West African immigrant population, they were united by their pursuit of the American dream and the desire to eventually return to their homeland. In spite of challenges such as racial discrimination, culture shock, language barriers, and adverse weather, West Africans made substantive positive contributions to America's economic, political, and social life during this period. By the 1990s, West Africans had become more visible socially, politically, economically, and culturally in America as they constructed stronger local communities and transnational linkages with their ancestral homeland.

NOTES

1. The study of the new West African diaspora is part of an expanding interdisciplinary academic inquiry into new migrations involving diverse groups from Asia, Europe, Africa, and the Middle East. See, for example, Nicholas Van Hear, *New Diasporas: The Mass Exodus, Dispersal, and Regrouping of Migrant Communities* (Seattle: University of Washington Press, 1998); and Robin Cohen, *Global Diasporas: An Introduction* (Seattle: University of Washington Press, 1997).

2. See Ali A. Mazrui, "Africans and African Americans in Changing World Trends: Globalizing the Black Experience," inaugural lecture of The Africa Program, University of Texas–Arlington, Feb. 25, 1999.

3. See George Gmelch, *Double Passage: The Lives of Caribbean Migrants Abroad and Back Home* (Ann Arbor: University of Michigan Press, 1992).

4. See Alusine Jalloh and Toyin Falola, eds., *Black Business and Economic Power* (Rochester, N.Y.: Rochester University Press, 2002); Isidore Okpewho, Carole Boyce Davies, and Ali A. Mazrui, eds., *The African Diaspora: African Origins and New World Identities* (Bloomington: Indiana University Press, 2001); Alusine Jalloh and Stephen E. Maizlish, eds., *The African Diaspora* (College Station: Texas A&M University Press, 1996); Joseph E. Harris, ed., *Global Dimensions of the African Diaspora* (Washington, D.C.: Howard University Press, 1982); and Judith Byfield, ed., "Africa's Diaspora: A Special Issue," *African Studies Review* 43(1) (Apr., 2000).

5. See Herbert S. Klein, *The Atlantic Slave Trade* (Cambridge: Cambridge University Press, 1999); John Thornton, *Africa and Africans in the Making of the Atlantic World, 1400–1800* (Cambridge: Cambridge University Press, 1998); Vincent B. Thompson, *The Making of the African Diaspora in the Americas, 1441–1900* (New York: Longman, 1987); and Philip D. Curtin, *The Atlantic Slave Trade: A Census* (Madison: University of Wisconsin Press, 1969).

6. See, for example, Boubacar Barry, *Senegambia and the Atlantic Slave Trade* (Cambridge: Cambridge University Press, 1998); Michael A. Gomez, *Exchanging Our Country Marks: The Transformation of African Identities in the Colonial and Antebellum South*

(Chapel Hill: University of North Carolina Press, 1998); and Gwendolyn M. Hall, *Africans in Colonial Louisiana: The Development of Afro-Creole Culture in the Eighteenth Century* (Baton Rouge: Louisiana State University Press, 1992).

7. See Judith A. Carney, *Black Rice: The African Origins of Rice Cultivation in the Americas* (Cambridge: Harvard University Press, 2001); Daniel C. Littlefield, *Rice and Slaves: Ethnicity and the Slave Trade in Colonial South Carolina* (Urbana: University of Illinois Press, 1991); Joseph A. Opala, "The Gullah: Rice, Slavery, and the Sierra Leone-American Connection," pamphlet (Freetown, Sierra Leone: U.S. Information Service, 1993).

8. See Waziri Adio, "Senegal Makes Good in Manhattan," *BBC Focus on Africa* (London: BBC, Apr.–June, 1999); Cheikh Anta Babou, "Brotherhood Solidarity, Education, and Migration: The Role of the Dahiras among the Murid Muslim Community of New York," *African Affairs* 101 (Apr., 2002): 151–70.

9. See Toyin Falola, *Nationalism and African Intellectuals* (Rochester, N.Y.: University of Rochester Press, 2001); Aka Ikenga, *Nnamdi Azikiwe: Tributes to an African Legend* (Lagos, Nigeria: Minaj, 1996); and Toyin Falola, *The History of Nigeria* (Westport, Conn.: Greenwood Press, 1999).

10. See Marika Sherwood, *Kwame Nkrumah: The Years Abroad, 1935–1947* (Accra-Legon, Ghana: Freedom Publications, 1996).

11. See June Milne, *Kwame Nkrumah: A Biography* (London: Panaf, 2000); and David Birmingham, *Kwame Nkrumah: The Father of African Nationalism* (Athens: Ohio University Press, 1998).

12. See David Killingray, ed., *Africans in Britain* (London: Frank Cass, 1994); Hakim Adi, *West Africans in Britain, 1900–1960: Nationalism, Pan-Africanism, and Communism* (London: Lawrence and Wishart, 1998).

13. See H. L. Wesseling, *Divide and Rule: The Partition of Africa, 1880–1914*, trans. Arnold J. Pomerans (London: Praeger, 1996); Patrick Manning, *Francophone Sub-Saharan Africa, 1880–1995* (Cambridge: Cambridge University Press, 1998); and J. D. Hargreaves, *Decolonization in Africa* (London: Longman, 1990).

14. See Falola, *Nationalism and African Intellectuals;* Michael Crowder, *West Africa under Colonial Rule* (London: Hutchinson, 1981); Ali Mazrui and Michael Tidy, *Nationalism and New States in Africa* (Nairobi: Heinemann, 1984); and Basil Davidson, *The Black Man's Burden: Africa and the Curse of the Nation-State* (New York: Random House, 1992).

15. See A. Boahen, *African Perspectives on Colonialism* (Baltimore: Johns Hopkins University Press, 1987); Basil Davidson, *Modern Africa: A Social and Political History* (London: Longman, 1994); and Adam Hochschild, *King Leopold's Ghost: A Story of Greed, Terror, and Heroism in Colonial Africa* (New York: Houghton Mifflin, 1998).

16. See Ebere Nwaubani, *The United States and Decolonization in West Africa, 1950–1960* (Rochester, N.Y.: University of Rochester Press, 2001).

17. See Michael Clough, *U.S. Policy toward Africa and the End of the Cold War* (New York: Council on Foreign Relations Press, 1992), p. 7.

18. See Robert Legvold, *Soviet Policy in West Africa* (Cambridge: Harvard University Press, 1970); Trevor Coombe, *A Consultation on Higher Education in Africa: A Report to the Ford Foundation and the Rockefeller Foundation* (London: Institute of Education, University of London, 1991); and Helen Kitchen, *U.S. Interests in Africa* (New York: Praeger, 1983).

19. See Naomi Chazan, P. Lewis, R. A. Mortimer, D. Rothchild, and S. J. Stedman, *Politics and Society in Contemporary Africa* (Boulder, Colo.: Lynne Rienner, 1999); J. Gus

Liebenow, *African Politics: Crises and Challenges* (Bloomington: Indiana University Press, 1986); and John Stockwell, *In Search of Enemies: A CIA Story* (New York: W. W. Norton, 1978).

20. See John A. Arthur, *Invisible Sojourners: African Immigrant Diaspora in the United States* (London: Praeger, 2000); and April Gordon, "The New Diaspora: African Immigration to the United States," *Journal of Third World Studies* 15(1): 79–103.

21. Thandika Mkandawire and Charles C. Soludo, eds., *Our Continent, Our Future: African Perspectives on Structural Adjustment* (Dakar: CODESRIA, 1999); and World Bank, *Adjustment in Africa: Reforms, Results, and the Road Ahead* (New York: Oxford University Press for the World Bank, 1994).

22. See David E. Sahn, Stephen D. Younger, and Paul Dorosh, *Structural Adjustment Reconsidered: Economic Policy and Poverty in Africa* (Cambridge: Cambridge University Press, 1997); Peter Gibbon and Adebayo Olukoshi, eds., *Structural Adjustment and Socio-Economic Change in Sub-Saharan Africa* (Piscataway, N.J.: Transaction, 1996); and Janet MacGaffey, *The Second Economy of Zaire* (Philadelphia: University of Pennsylvania Press, 1991).

23. See Earl Conteh-Morgan and Mac Dixon-Fyle, *Sierra Leone at the End of the Twentieth Century* (New York: Peter Lang, 1999); William Reno, *Warlord Politics and African States* (Boulder, Colo.: Lynne Rienner, 1999); and Sahr J. Kpundeh, *Politics and Corruption in Africa: A Case Study of Sierra Leone* (Lanham, Md.: University Press of America, 1995).

24. See Arthur, *Invisible Sojourners.*

25. See Emmanuel Akyeampong, "Africans in the Diaspora: The Diaspora and Africa," *African Affairs* 99 (2000): 183–215.

26. See Terry Schulte, "Ethnic Group Exclusivity: The Emergence of Nigerian Parochial Organizations in the Metroplex," in *The New Dallas: Immigrants, Community Institutions, and Cultural Diversity,* ed. Dennis D. Cordell and Jane L. Elder (Dallas: William P. Clements Center for Southwest Studies, Southern Methodist University, 2000).

27. See Arthur, *Invisible Sojourners;* Akeyeampong, "Africans in the Diaspora"; and *African Immigrants Directory: A Guide to Community Resources in the Greater Philadelphia Area* (Philadelphia: Balch Institute for Ethnic Studies, 2000).

28. See Paul Stoller, *Money Has No Smell: The Africanization of New York City* (Chicago: University of Chicago Press, 2002); Paul Stoller, *Jaguar: A Story of Africans in America* (Chicago: University of Chicago Press, 1999); Sylviane Diouf-Kamara, *Senegalese in New York: A Model Minority?* trans. Richard Phicox (Bloomington: Indiana University Press, 1997); and Leslie Goffe, "Now Is the Time to Put Our Money Where Our Mouths Are," *New African* (Oct., 2001): 34–35.

29. See Dennis Onyango, "'I'm Like a Baby Again': African Refugees Lost in the American Dream," *New African* (Apr., 2000): 40–43.

30. See Schulte, "Ethnic Group Exclusivity"; Birgit Meyer, *Translating the Devil: Religion and Modernity among the Ewe in Ghana* (London: International African Institute, 1999); and Paul Gifford, *African Christianity: Its Public Role* (Bloomington: Indiana University Press, 1998).

31. See *Extended Lives: The African Immigrant Experience in Philadelphia* (Philadelphia: Balch Institute for Ethnic Studies, 2000).

32. See Agyemang Atta-Poku, "Asanteman Immigrant Ethnic Association: An Effective

Tool for Immigrant Survival and Adjustment Problem Solution in New York City," *Journal of Black Studies* 27 (1996): 56–76; and Pashington Obeng, "Re-membering through Oath: Installation of African Kings and Queens," *Journal of Black Studies* 28 (1998): 334–56.

33. See Chinwe Ajene, "Our Culture Is the Tie That Binds the Fabric Together: Igbo Migration and the Creation of Transnational Igbo Communities in the United States," honors thesis, Department of History, Dartmouth College, 1998; and *The African* (Dallas–Fort Worth), (Dec., 2001), p. 12.

34. See Philippe Wamba, *Kinship: A Family's Journey in Africa and America* (New York: Plume, 1999); Robert G. Weisbord, *Ebony Kinship: Africa, Africans, and Afro-Americans* (Westport, Conn.: Greenwood, 1973); Keith Richburg, *Out of America: A Black Man Confronts Africa* (New York: Basic Books, 1997); and Darryl Fears, "A Diverse—and Divided—Black Community," *Washington Post* (Feb. 24, 2002), p. A-01.

35. For more information on African American and West African marriages, see Marita Golden, *Migrations of the Heart* (New York: Doubleday, 1983); and Bernadette G. Kayode, "African-Afro-American Marriages: Do They Work?" *Essence* (July, 1979), p. 106.

36. See Penny M. Von Eschen, *Race against Empire: Black Americans and Anticolonialism, 1937–1957* (Ithaca, N.Y.: Cornell University Press, 1997); and Kenneth Noble, "U.S. Blacks and Africans Seek Stronger Ties," *New York Times* (May 27, 1993), p. A-10.

37. See Alusine Jalloh and Toyin Falola, eds., *Black Business and Economic Power* (Rochester, N.Y.: University of Rochester Press, 2002); and Juliet E. K. Walker, *The History of Black Business in America* (New York: Macmillan, 1998).

38. See Josiah U. Young III, *A Pan-African Theology: Providence and the Legacies of the Ancestors* (Trenton, N.J.: Africa World Press, 1992); Gayraud S. Wilmore, *Black Religion and Black Radicalism: An Interpretation of the Religious History of Afro-American People* (New York: Orbis, 1983).

39. For more information about Fula entrepreneurship in West Africa, see Alusine Jalloh, *African Entrepreneurship: Muslim Fula Merchants in Sierra Leone* (Athens: Ohio University Press, 1999).

40. See Leslie Goffe, "My Life Will Never Be the Same," *New African* (May, 2000): 32–33; Wamba, *Kinship.*

41. Some of the many internet links and websites included naijanews-normal@onelist.com (Nigeria), Leonenet@listproc.umbc.edu (Sierra Leone), www.allafrica.com, and www.newsafrica.com.

42. See Laura J. Pires-Hester, "The Emergence of Bilateral Diaspora Ethnicity among Cape Verdean-Americans," in *The African Diaspora,* ed. Isidore Okpewho, Carole Boyce Davies, and Ali A. Mazrui (Bloomington: Indiana University Press, 2001), pp. 485–503; and "Africans in America: Thousands of Immigrants Find Success in Their Adopted Homeland," *Ebony* (Dec., 1988), pp. 48–56.

43. See Wole Soyinka, *The Open Sore of a Continent: A Personal Narrative of the Nigerian Crisis* (New York: Oxford University Press, 1996); and Falola, *The History of Nigeria.*

44. See Almaz Zewde, "African Institutions and Community Resources in the Washington, D.C., Metropolitan Area," project report submitted to the African Studies program, Georgetown University, Sept. 10, 1997.

45. See "A Little Help from Abroad," *West Africa* (June 10–16, 2002): 17.

46. See Everest Ekong, "Lawal's Billion-Dollar Success," *Business in Africa* (Oct., 2002): 50–55.

47. See Akyeampong, "Africans in the Diaspora: The Diaspora and Africa"; Adio, "Senegal Makes Good in Manhattan."

48. See Leslie Goffe, "Dream House in Ghana," *New African* (Nov., 2002), pp. 60–61.

49. For a discussion of kinship networks in West African commercial enterprise, see Jalloh, *African Entrepreneurship*.